MW00966058

The Concise Guide
to Global Human Rights

The Concise Guide
to Global Human Rights

Daniel Fischlin, Martha Nandorfy

BLACK
ROSE
BOOKS Montreal/New York/London

Copyright © 2007 BLACK ROSE BOOKS

No part of this book may be reproduced or transmitted in any form, by any means electronic or mechanical including photocopying and recording, or by any information storage or retrieval system—without written permission from the publisher, or, in the case of photocopying or other reprographic copying, a license from the Canadian Reprography Collective, with the exception of brief passages quoted by a reviewer in a newspaper or magazine.

Black Rose Books No. JJ348

National Library of Canada Cataloguing in Publication Data
Fischlin, Daniel, 1957-
The concise guide to global human rights / Daniel Fischlin, Martha Nandorfy

Includes bibliographical references and index.
ISBN: 1-55164-295-6 (bound)   ISBN: 1-55164-294-8 (pbk.)
(alternative ISBNs 9781551642956 [bound]   9781551642949 [pbk.])

1. Human rights. I. Nandorfy, Martha, 1957- II. Title.
(I am waiting on the National Library for this information.)

JC571.F58 2006   323   C2006-902802-8

For their kind permission to reprint images, we gratefully acknowledge
Gene Fellner, Joe Sacco, Fantagraphic, World Health Organization (WHO),
Aragi Inc., Ellen Papciak-Rose, and Rob Schmidt.

Cover Photo by Daniel Fischlin
Children playing in La Marina barrio of Matanzas, Cuba.

C.P. 1258	2250 Military Road	99 Wallis Road
Succ. Place du Parc	Tonawanda, NY	London, E9 5LN
Montréal, H2X 4A7	14150	England
Canada	USA	UK

To order books:
In Canada: (phone) 1-800-565-9523 (fax) 1-800-221-9985
email: utpbooks@utpress.utoronto.ca

In United States: (phone) 1-800-283-3572 (fax) 1-651-917-6406

In the UK & Europe: (phone) 44 (0)20 8986-4854 (fax) 44 (0)20 8533-5821
email: order@centralbooks.com

Our Web Site address: http://www.blackrosebooks.net

A publication of the Institute of Policy Alternatives of Montréal (IPAM)
Printed in Canada

Table of Contents

List of Illustrations

Acknowledgments

This book benefited enormously from the research assistance of Ben Authers and Louisa Sorflaten, and the help of Amnesty International Toronto Office Co-ordinator Nancy Cameron and Amnesty International Canada Information Services Co-ordinator Samantha Burdett. We offer heartfelt thanks to the numerous people in both Cuba and Mexico who welcomed us to share stories. We thank David L. Clark, Raúl Gática, Ajay Heble, Michael Keefer, Tom King, Belinda Leach, and Lewis Melville for providing us with so many provocations to further research, Eduardo Galeano for his extraordinary example, and Roger Clark (former Secretary General of Amnesty International Canada) and Marilyn McKim, Director of AI's Urgent Action Network (Canada) for their astute commentaries. The staff at the Bookshelf (Guelph, Ontario) kept us supplied with an amazing array of resources, and the members of *Jiwani* provided us with a wonderful supportive network. We thank Gene Fellner, the World Health Organization, Aragi Inc., Ellen Papciak-Rose, Rob Schmidt, and Joe Sacco and his editor at Fantagraphics Books, Kim Thompson, for permission to republish images from their works. Finally, our appreciation to Richard Swift at *New Internationalist*, Linda Barton, Upendra Baxi, Dorothy Hadfield, Lenore Latta, Vandana Shiva, and numerous others who contributed to shaping the manuscript.

Prologue

Human rights are the right to be fully human, and we can be fully human only through our common humanity.

The Concise Guide to Global Human Rights is a timely and necessary contribution to the human aspiration to be free. It goes beyond state-focused violations of human rights to address the new threats and violations from globalization and corporate rule.

Globalization is robbing all humans of their humanity. The poor, the marginalized, the excluded are not just losing their humanity by being denied livelihood, jobs, security—they are losing the most fundamental right of all, the right to live. As every resource is commodified, plants and seeds are patented, water is privatized, the poor are robbed of their means to create livelihoods and sustain their lives. Corporate profits are no longer based on extraction of surplus value. They are based on extraction of people's very lives. Thousands of Indian peasants have been pushed to suicide as corporate monopolies on seeds lock them into a debt trap. Thousands are being denied their right to food and water as these most basic needs are also transformed from means of life support and sustenance into commodities that generate corporate super profits.

But even the 'winners' of globalization are losers. They have lost their humanity by elevating greed to being the organizing principle of life. They have lost their humanity because they have ceased to experience it as one common and universal bond. They have lost their humanity because they have reduced this amazing planet to a market place where nothing is sacred and everything for sale.

Human rights, as articulated in this guide, are inclusive. Being fully human implies that the other must be included in our humanity. No group, no country can call itself human if it denies others their humanity. But being human implies more than a commonality of human rights. Being human involves caring for the web of life of which we are part—it calls for compassion for all beings, not just human beings.

Human rights are therefore about being citizens of the earth, being part of an earth family. Human rights in my view are exercised to their fullness through participating in earth democracy—the democracy of all life. And as earthlings, our human duties to protect the earth and all her beings are the ground from which human rights emerge.

Rights rooted in responsibility, rights rising from compassion and care, are the most powerful force in our times—a quiet force, a peaceful force, but powerful nonetheless. I hope it is this power in peaceful form that this guide will help unleash.

Dr. Vandana Shiva
Research Foundation for Science, Technology and Ecology (RFSTE)

Introduction

All humanity is one undivided and indivisible family, and each one of us is responsible for the misdeeds of all the others. I cannot detach myself from the wickedest soul. —Mahatma Gandhi

Injustice anywhere is a threat to justice everywhere...Whatever affects one directly, affects all indirectly. —Martin Luther King, Jr.

I have often asked myself why human beings have any rights at all. I always come to the conclusion that human rights, human freedoms, and human dignity have their deepest roots somewhere outside the perceptible world. These values are as powerful as they are because, under certain circumstances, people accept them without compulsion and are willing to die for them. —Václav Havel

The assault on vulnerable, fragile sections of society is so complete, so cruel and so clever that its sheer audacity has eroded our definition of justice. It has forced us to lower our sights, and curtail our expectations. Even among the well-intentioned, the magnificent concept of justice is gradually being substituted with the reduced, far more fragile discourse of 'human rights.' —Arundhati Roy

Mahatma Gandhi and Martin Luther King, Jr. were two of the most visible and effective human rights activists of the twentieth century. Gandhi led a movement that culminated in the independence of India and the eventual creation of the world's largest democracy. King led and inspired the American civil rights movement, arguably the source of some of the most significant and radical ideas about human rights in the most powerful and influential democracy in the world. Both saw the need, as evidenced in the first two epigraphs to this chapter, to articulate the relatedness of all human life, however radically disparate the divide between good and the 'wickedest soul.' And both saw the impossibility of dissociating the injustice of one from the pursuit of justice for all. Their vision of shared human responsibility is intrinsically unitary, based on reciprocal respect for life in its diversity and its inter-connectedness.

Both Gandhi's and King's ideas inexorably link rights with community —with the relations that define and make meaningful human interaction, and with the fundamental questions posed to that community by injustice, evil, detachment, and alienation. At the core of any understanding of rights, then, lies the notion of what it means to participate in community: What kinds of community best allow for justice and equity? What kinds of community take precedence over these principles? For some, like English philosopher Jeremy Bentham (1748–1832), fundamental rights were dangerous nonsense: 'natural and imprescriptable rights' were the 'mortal enemies of law, the subverters of government and the assassins of security' (from Bentham's essay 'Anarchichal Fallacies,' cited in Arslan 197). And for conservative eighteenth-century Irish statesman and political thinker Edmund Burke, the rights of man led to 'inexpiable war with all establishments.' Burke further argued that the 'pretended rights of men' are 'metaphysical abstraction,' arguing that 'Against these their rights of men…let no government look for security in the length of its continuance or in the justice and lenity of its administration' (from *Reflections on the Revolution in France,* cited in Arslan 198). Where Bentham and Burke might see a threat to the foundations of legal and governmental institutions and metaphysical trumpery, Václav Havel, President of the Czech Republic, internationally renowned writer, political dissident, and one of the leading rights figures in contemporary Europe, suggests that rights 'have their deepest roots somewhere outside the perceptible world,' representing a transcendent force that people are prepared to die for.

This force, which Indian author Arundhati Roy links with a deeply rooted, historical sense of justice, is under attack as a concept and as a lived reality—this in spite of the enormous growth in rights instruments, organizations, and awareness over the last fifty years. We begin with this diverse opining on rights to show not only the distance that rights discourses have traversed in a very short while but also to demonstrate the fundamental fissures at work in any thinking about rights. In fact, however naturalized rights may seem to citizens of the twenty-first century, formidable pressures have aligned and continue to align against rights and their promulgation. Paradoxically, these pressures often reside in the sovereign and absolutist assumptions of state laws and conventions. Rights ideas that imagine communities beyond those shaped only by law or state challenge such conventions.

Furthermore, as can be seen from the epigraphs to this chapter, complex notions of human responsibility, agency, justice, vulnerability, self-criticism, and disempowerment come together under the concept of rights. We openly acknowledge that no short book can possibly do justice to the full range of the topic since rights apply to virtually all aspects of human activity across all geographies, ethnicities, cultural differences, and ideologies. Nonetheless, in this book we lay the groundwork for understanding key issues relating to global rights across a wide range of topics. To do so, we have necessarily had to focus on specific areas of concern within the framework of a concise guide. Hence, we have written chapters that overview 'big picture' ideas related to emergent trends that have characterized rights discourses in the last half-century.

The signing of the Universal Declaration of Human Rights (hereinafter the UDHR) in 1948 signaled, in part, a global response to the horrors of the Second World War and to the growing targeting of civilians in times of conflict, exemplified in the appalling genocide of European Jews in the Holocaust. That global response has led to the proliferation of rights instruments, agreements, and actions even as the proliferation of violations and abuses has escalated. Rather than covering all possible rights groups fighting for particular and important issues (such as the right to linguistic diversity, various forms of cultural survival, reproductive rights, prisoners' rights, and the like), we integrate these in more general discussions of major issues. These pertain to globalization, minority and majority world rights, the threat to rights as a function of terrorism post 9/11, issues around communicating rights, and the future of rights—all of which try to take into account the larger contexts for a host of subsidiary issues.

Our approach to rights is based on a number of key premises. First, rights depend in part on legal, constitutional covenants between states and individuals such that all peoples are guaranteed a viable means of addressing oppressive, inequitable, and unjust treatment measured against a global standard. All too often, focus on rights is reduced to focus on these covenants. And we acknowledge, with qualifications that we outline throughout this book, the significance of these instruments and covenants as one of the means for achieving widespread social justice. The importance of the UDHR, first drafted by Canadian (McGill University) law professor John Peters Humphrey, cannot be underestimated as a major shift in establishing the basis for change in how rights are conceived and enacted at a global level.

In addition to this legalistic view of rights contained in covenants, there is another view of rights as a process of education and of access to alternative forms of social (in)formation that are deeply embedded in all human cultures, but need to be activated at a level of basic human interaction from the ground up. Constitutional and legal recourses to rights tend to be reactive and occur belatedly in response to a problem that frequently cannot be resolved meaningfully via only legal means. Rights organizations are often limited to making recommendations that have no legal implication (that are not backed by force of law), further underscoring the problem of rights thought of only as legal or political structures.

At a deeper level then, rights imply an approach to human identity and agency grounded in principles that are applicable across national and cultural divides. Neither a secular religion nor an ideology that caters to selective, single-state sovereign self-interests, human rights cut across all possible human relations. Rights are based on reciprocal respect, the valuing of all life, the integrity and dignity of all human beings (regardless of, among others, religious belief, class status, ethnicity, sexual orientation), and the desire to extend those basic values into all areas of human activity. Chandra Muzaffar, Director of the Centre for Civilizational Dialogue at the Science University of Malaysia, argues that 'an integrated approach to human rights is in fact related to a holistic vision of the human being—a vision which lies at the root of philosophies of almost all the major religious and cultural traditions...' (6).

Not idealist or utopian, the human rights understanding we advocate in this book is intensely pragmatic. If true and meaningful social change is to occur it will have to do so at a deep human level across all national borders. Not via gunpoint. Not via cultures of fear and misunderstanding. Not via intensifying the indefinite consumption of limited resources. Not via outmoded concepts of progress (the infinite growth model) tied only to the economic bottom line for shareholders of multinational companies. Not via disregard for the environmental conditions without which human beings could not exist. Not via recourse to apocalyptic scenarios that derive from religious fundamentalisms. Not via civil structures of impunity and lack of accountability. Not via decreased civil liberties. Not via ignorance and disinformation. Not via economic structures based on historic inequalities and exploitation.

This partial listing of obstacles to global rights recognizes the pragmatics of the challenge. But the list is also based on recognition of critical change and a purposeful sense of human potential linked to transnational and transcultural values rooted in an all-encompassing respect for life. We hasten to point out that such a view already exists across multiple cultures worldwide, from indigenous cultures through to local, national, and transnational cultures in which social justice is a preeminent value.

The challenge posed by internalizing and activating meaningful rights and social justice values globally may well be the single most important guarantee of long-term human existence. That challenge will require a massive reallocation of resources away from, among others, military spending toward investment in education, access to potable water, clean air, non genetically modified and un-contaminated food, not to mention an ongoing critical awareness of the ways in which rights can be used both to promote and diminish social justice.

We take Indian writer and activist Arundhati Roy's cautionary distinction between 'human rights' and 'justice' seriously. Roy states that 'Almost uncon-sciously, we…think of justice for the rich and human rights for the poor. Justice for the corporate world, human rights for its victims. Justice for Americans, hu-man rights for Afghans and Iraqis…It is…clear that violating human rights is an inherent and necessary part of the process of implementing a coercive and un-just political and economic structure on the world…Many resistance move-ments in poor countries which are fighting huge injustice and questioning the underlying principles of what constitutes "liberation" and "development" view human rights non-governmental organizations as modern-day missionaries who have come to take the ugly edge off imperialism—to defuse political anger and to maintain the status quo' ('What We Call Peace').

Roy's words raise important questions: At what point does 'humanitarian intervention' begin to sound like what might once have been called 'a civilizing mission'? When is humanitarian intervention justified, and when does it inter-fere with the rights of national cultures to define their own laws and customs? On what basis are such judgments made? Adamantia Pollis and Peter Schwab, in an influential essay published in 1979, 'Human Rights: A Western Construct With Limited Applicability,' argue that 'cultural and ideological ethnocen-trism' lie at the heart of the UDHR and that 'there is no universal concurrence as to the meaning of human rights, human dignity, and human freedom (1). But even as states have issued restraints in the name of their sovereign self-interest, making rights a relative concept dependent on specific social, cultural, historical, and economic factors (and thus confirming in part Pollis's and Schwab's initial thesis), it is clear that other forces are at work in the striving toward global understandings of social justice and the equitable distribution of rights. Not the least of these forces are those ideas, some of them cited at the beginning of this chapter, that advocate thinking of rights in terms of global communities of inter-connection and reciprocal responsibilities.

In these global imaginings, the dynamic interplay between universalist ideas of social justice and the local contextual features that define their local application are evolving into what Pollis in a later essay has described as 're-constructed universalism' ('A New Universalism' 27). Movement towards international structures of justice that address genocide, war crimes (including crimes related to how wars are initiated), environmental disasters, and so forth represent important steps in the creation of a reconstructed universalist approach—or what the Indian activist lawyer and rights advocate Upendra Baxi might call a pluriversalist conception of global rights issues. Notwithstanding these positive developments at the level of theorizing rights, great care has to be exercised in critically appraising the uses and foundations of rights talk—even as constructive critique must be balanced against advancing and achieving meaningful, *lived* social justice outcomes.

As we argue throughout, human rights need to be reclaimed, rethought, embodied, and reactivated with even greater energy, intensity, commitment, and passion. This book, then, examines crucial rights issues in concise form and offers itself as part of a much larger, necessary, and difficult conversation that bears directly on the most important choices 'we' as humans must confront in defining and living our shared humanity.

We grappled with the use of terms designating geo-political regions and decided to use both conventional language reflective of existent mindsets, as well as visionary language that strives to free us from these mindsets. Hence in those instances where the old prejudices seem to rule in material terms we succumb to using such oppositions as 'First World/Third World,' 'developed/developing,' 'Western/non-Western' (when in fact the division is most often North/South or East/West). This said, we need to clarify up front that we do not think that 'developed' is a critically accurate term; while countries referred to this way do tend to enjoy more freedoms, rights, and prosperity, for many other reasons that we explore throughout, it is not always a positive label. If anything, we argue that words like 'developing' and its cognate 'development' must be regarded with some degree of critical suspicion and questioned as to what concept of 'progress' they invoke. In accordance with non-Western thinkers and activists, we prefer to conceive of global inequity in terms of the majority world versus the over-developed nations. This preference is based not only on population numbers, but also on the fact that the environmental impact of the over-developed countries on the rest of the world is murderous and suicidal, and clearly unsustainable.[1] The 'majority' in the grassroots sense is a very different kind of moral majority from the exclusionary right wing meaning that prevails, especially in the U.S. Argentine philosopher Enrique Dussel draws an important distinction between 'morality,' seen as a set of social conventions operative within specific cultural perimeters, and 'ethics,' which is rooted in the individual person's spirit but connects persons within and across both localized and diverse communities of shared concerns globally.[2] In this sense, the concept of the majority world invokes the asymmetrical relationship between the many impoverished and the affluent few (majority in numbers), while restoring the notion that the majority world has a key ethical (and not only moral) role to play in a global struggle for rights.

A final authorial note: we co-wrote this book from our positions as engaged literary critics who have been led to consider wider issues of rights informing emergent literatures and other compelling forms of artistic expression that address social justice issues. Our own grounding in literary and critical discourses and our direct experiences in various rights actions and communities, particularly in relation to Latin America and Africa, have inevitably played a major role in shaping this book.

Notes

1. For further discussion of the implications of these terms, see Chapter 3 'Globalization and Development,' especially the section on 'The Racist Foundations of Developmentalism.'
2. For Dussel's discussion of this distinction, see Chapter 10 'Relative Morality, Absolute Ethics' in *Ethics and Community*.

For the members of CIPO-RFM,
Consejo Indígena Popular de Oaxaca "Ricardo Flores Magón"

And in memoriam Peter Benenson, 1921-2005

It is time to move from the rhetoric of universal commitment to the reality of universal achievement. —*UN Human Development Report 2000: Human Rights and Human Development*, 112

Let us rejoice! Here, among friends,
Let there be embraces.
We live on the flowered earth.
Here, no one will bring to an end the flowers, the songs;
They endure in the house of the Giver of Life.
     —from a Nahua poem, *In the Language of Kings*, 84

Chapter 1

Human Rights In Theory And Practice

The single biggest problem facing human rights is the gap between their theory and practice. In this section we outline some of the associated issues that arise from how rights get defined, who determines why they matter, and how rights activists must press for concrete outcomes and not just unrealized ideals. Crucial to this discussion are the global distributions of power and how these effect the movement to define transnational rights.

What Is a Human Right?

Rights give expression to how all humans participate fully in civil society, defining the idealized norms against which a society may be measured. As expressions of the civic values that operate within any society, rights derive from the marriage of religious, philosophical, and legal principles that address social justice in the context of worldwide struggles to combat oppression and inequity. They do so out of an underlying, deep-rooted respect for human life, dignity, and diversity.

Rights cannot be thought of in isolation from each other. They are part of an integrated vision of what it means to participate in diverse human experiences. These run from the most basic interaction with the environment to the ways in which people live day-to-day to catastrophic events like war, genocide, or pandemics. Rights affect local and intimate human relationships and the global relations that govern the ways human capital and energy are exchanged, manipulated, and exploited.

Rights typically entail freedoms that make them seem individual-oriented. But they also address the duties and responsibilities that make these freedoms more than simplistic expressions of individual self-interest. Finding the appropriate balance between individual self-interest and broader civic, communitarian interests is the crucial problem at the heart of most rights debates. Rights operate across disparate cultures, which further make the values and beliefs they express cause for serious consideration. Any simplistic, one-size-fits-all attempt to define them needs careful evaluation, especially in relation to the balance between their universal application and the relative, local way in which they are activated in both diverse historical circumstances and varied cultural, economic, political, or social practices. What follows, then, are some guidelines for answering the question 'What is a human right?'

Human rights are frequently reduced to two opposing visions. The first posits a universal, absolute moral/ethical structure that underlies all forms of human culture and civil organization from which no one is exempt, and to which *no* exceptions are possible. In the universal view there is an unalterable, intrinsic quality of being human that confers unalterable, intrinsic rights on a person. These rights extend beyond the rights of states to impose legal codes that may contravene universal rights principles. Universality is based on the fundamental respect for differential forms of being human and is not to be confused with uniformity or plurality—all humans share universal rights based on respect for life, which entails respect for the diversity of life.

The second view posits a more relative, fluid conception of rights. It holds that the meaning of a right changes from context to context, and culture to culture. Similar outcomes are deemed important to achieve a just and equitable recognition of all humanity, but taking culturally relevant factors into account. Rights theorists tend to see these two views as opposed, binary opposites that are largely incompatible. This incompatibility is hugely troublesome in terms of how a right is defined and implemented.

The universalist view posits rights as inherent and innate to all human beings. The second view begs the question of inherent rights, suggesting instead that rights are a function of culturally specific contexts that determine their social use. The first view presents a no-loopholes view of rights, consistent across all cultural and historical situations. The relativist view nuances what it means to have rights and does so in response to complicated scenarios in which different rights come into conflict with each other. For example, the accrued rights of a local community developed over centuries of unquestioned cultural practice may be opposed to the rights of newcomers to that community who question precedent practices, as is the case with Female Genital Mutilation (FGM) in Africa and the Middle East or the use of *Shari'a* law (Islamic canonical law based on the *Qur'an*) by Muslim immigrant communities living in the West. In both cases, rights advances made in relation to women's universalized disempowerment have put the relative rights of community practice and interpretation to the test. We argue that these two views—the universalist and the relative—can be seen as related members in a family dispute where their very differences can lead to a more comprehensive notion of rights. Here, then, are some basic principles and criteria crucial to defining rights.

First, abstract principles that underlie any human rights instrument, legal document, or case study must address the actual lived experience of any and all individuals in quite different circumstances. Abstractions count for nothing if you're dying of hunger or are about to be tortured to death or are an innocent civilian caught in a war zone. One of the perhaps unintended effects of globalization has been to alter the way in which conceptions of the individual are morally tenable within much larger transnational contexts. We are becoming aware of how individual agency (the capacity to act within a given set of circumstances) radiates out and causes effects well beyond its immediate context, like the concentric circles of a pebble thrown in a pond. Hence, human rights occur at multiple levels of responsibility and inter-connectedness in relation to the actual lived experience of people on a day-to-day basis. The plain recognition of this fact contributes to defining what a right is. A right is not so much a definition as it is how the definition is applied in lived experience. And congruent with this principle of definition (one which takes as its starting point how people *actually* experience their rights) is the access people really have to instruments of law that meaningfully enact their rights.

A brief example is in order. Say a major chemical disaster involving a powerful multinational destroys a significant portion of the water supply in a large geographic area of a developing nation, poisoning the air, killing thousands of people, and leaving successive generations permanently at risk for chronic side effects that reduce life quality and expectancy. Here, clearly, a basic right to security of person has been massively infringed upon. Article 3 of the UDHR could not be more unequivocal: 'Everyone has the right to life, liberty and *security of person*.'

Moreover, in the situation we're describing, *the* crucial underlying right to all other rights (recognized in Article 3 of the UDHR) has also been violated —the right to *life*, a concept that has legal definition at an international level (in multiple treaties) and for which there is no legal restriction. Subsidiary rights that pertain to a sustainable environment, to the basic ethical responsibilities of communities and individuals to safeguard themselves, to an adequate standard of living (that gets destroyed when local environments are made toxic), to the right to the highest attainable standard of health, and a host of other rights are also at play in this scenario, which occurred in Bhopal, India, in 1984.

If how people in the afflicted region actually are forced to live as a result of such a chemical disaster violates their rights to 'security of person,' then the rights structures meant to protect them are degraded and emptied of meaning. If impunity overrides meaningful accountability, human rights are absent in practice even if they are still on the books. And the tension between their practical absence and theoretical presence is often a cause of ongoing abuses. When multiple constituencies are at stake (say multinational business, local community, state organisms at both the local and the national level and transnational non-governmental entities, kinship groups, specific disadvantaged groups like women and children, to name only a few), the situation quickly becomes more complicated. As Matthew Lippman observes in his study 'Multinational Corporations and Human Rights,' 'The lack of attention to the impact of the activities of multinational corporations on human rights in the Third World is reflected by the fact that liability for violation of individuals' human rights under all international human rights conventions is limited to "state parties" ' (392). How can a right be said to exist if the liability and responsibility for its violation or abuse cannot be enforced under such a circumstance?

In the case of the 1984 Bhopal disaster involving Union Carbide Corporation/Dow Chemical Company—in 2001 UCC became a fully owned subsidiary of Dow, the largest chemical company in the world—this is precisely what happened. Despite the presence of international human rights legislation and multiple rights definitions and covenants, the actual lived experience of those affected by the Bhopal disaster directly contravenes their theoretical rights. Responsibility has been shirked by a multinational (in tandem with a national government) using limited liability and the intricacies of international law to protect itself.

Can those who died or who are surviving this tragedy be said to have rights in any meaningful sense—especially by comparison with the ostensible rights of the corporate entity that killed or injured them? Emphatically not, especially when ongoing contamination deteriorates life expectancy and quality of life, and virtually nothing continues to be done to alleviate the problems arising from the contamination.

Twenty Years After the Bhopal Disaster: Some Facts as Reported by Amnesty International (in *Clouds of Injustice: Bhopal Disaster 20 Years On, 2004*)

A sampling of the rights (non)outcomes documented by AI in relation to the Bhopal disaster includes:

- Multiple attempts to restrict activists seeking adequate redress for the victims of Bhopal have occurred: in January 1985, 10 people were hospitalized after police beatings after the distribution of rations to victims was halted by the government; in June of the same year, 40 people were arrested after police raided a clinic set up by health professionals to provide services not available through government clinics—the following day 400 more were arrested at a rally protesting the closure; 'in September 1986, three activists were reportedly arrested and charged with violating the Official Secrets Act after recording a meeting discussing the medical condition of [Bhopal] survivors; in September 1986 another 2,000 people were arrested at another protest seeking adequate aid for survivors of the disaster; and as recently as 2002, another 70 people were arrested and some were beaten when they occupied the remnants of the factory, which to this day has not been properly decontaminated' (72-73). All these incidents highlight the rights abuses that have derived from the disaster and the failure to address its consequences justly and equitably.

- The AI report documents how 'according to the Sambhavna Trust Clinic, exposure to the toxins that leaked on the night of 2/3 December 1984 has resulted in chronic, debilitating illnesses for at least 120,000 people for whom treatment has proved largely ineffective' (12).

- AI estimates that between 7 and 10 thousand people died within three days of the gas leak: Union Carbide acknowledged that around '54,000 pounds (24,500 kg.) of unreacted MIC (methyl isocyanate) left tank 610 together with approximately 26,000 pounds (11,800 kg) of reaction products. Twenty years after the fatal leak, UCC has still not revealed the exact contents of the reaction products' (10).

- The catastrophe had multiple effects on workers and their families, including income reduction; inability to find adequate safe water; inability of women known to have been exposed to find marriage partners; and numerous health-related disorders ranging from anemia, breathlessness, weakness, and loss of vision, to vaginal secretions and changes in menstrual patterns and fertility.

- AI reports that there is 'overwhelming evidence' that Union Carbide was well aware of safety concerns at the Bhopal plant and did nothing to remedy them, largely as a function of cost-cutting measures that affected worker health and safety.

- AI has documented that after the disaster, Union Carbide produced a systematic response characterized by 'stonewall[ing]' of the legal process (49), refusal to pay interim relief, the withholding of crucial information, the discrediting of victims of the disaster (UCC lawyers actually argued, to their everlasting shame, that *'the plaintiffs are illiterate and do not understand the contents of the affidavits on which they have placed their thumbprints. Therefore…the complainants must be thrown out'* [51]), and by arguments that UCC was a U.S.-based enterprise with no affiliation with its Indian subsidiary, that MIC is not ultra-hazardous, and that UCC has no responsibility to clean up the mess left by the disaster much less compensate the victims adequately.

- against this backdrop of corporate and state evildoing, the 14th annual Goldman Environment Prize (considered by many as the Environmental Nobel Prize) was awarded in 2004 to two survivor-activists from Bhopal, Rasheeda Bi and Champadevi Shukla, who took their prize and set up both a trust for survivors and an award for activists pushing for corporate accountability.

The Bhopal catastrophe raises the specter of the following contradiction: never before have as many rights instruments existed as in the twentieth and twenty-first centuries.[1] And yet companies like UCC, directly implicated in significant rights violations and abuses, remain seemingly impervious to any action taken against them. The simple rule of 'polluter pays,' which should be operative in cases such as these, is undermined by legal constructs like limited liability, which diminish specific responsibilities for harm inflicted. What does such a situation reveal about the ways in which rights definitions work for the most disenfranchised and most disempowered?

A third factor in determining what a right means relates to the linked notions of inalienability, indivisibility, and sustainability. Rights cannot and should not be arbitrary designations, useful to some at a given moment, then forgotten about in the next, sustained when they support certain interests, then subverted when they no longer do so. Rights require consistent application across time (even as their application and practice may be thought of as evolving) and they need to address the truth that they are (and can be) arbitrarily applied. Standards must be set to articulate clearly principles that lamentably are all too often violated or abused.

Let's return to the Bhopal disaster and imagine a similar situation occurring in Fairfield County, Connecticut, one of the wealthiest and most affluent areas in the U.S.—an unlikely scenario given that the wealthiest people on the planet physically locate themselves away from the industrial corridors that pose extreme environmental threats. The bottom line is that class divisions limit access to costly legal mechanisms. Money, education, and networks of power are only truly accessible to those at the peak of the developed world, but not to most other human beings. The doublespeak we are pointing to here is brutally clear on one point: rights definitions may abound in theory, but global divisions of power dramatically subvert their meaningfulness.

A crucial aspect of meaningfully defining a right, then, has as much to do with the pre-existing access to rights instruments under the law as it has to do with implementing the right in a way that produces actual change. The Canadian Charter of Rights and Freedoms, lauded for good reason because it has made possible important advances in rights for different groups (including, most recently, rights relating to same-sex marriages in Canada), begins with the following guarantee: 'The Canadian Charter of Rights and Freedoms guarantees the rights and freedoms set out in it subject only to such reasonable limits prescribed by law as can be demonstrably justified in a free and democratic society.' But in section 24.1 of the document pertaining to enforcement is the following qualification, which echoes Article 8 of the UDHR: 'Anyone whose rights or freedoms, as guaranteed by this Charter, have been infringed or denied may apply to a court of competent jurisdiction to obtain such remedy as the court considers appropriate and just in the circumstances.'

How one applies to the court requires time, money, and education, all forms of active empowerment. The Canadian Charter makes access to legal instruments possible in theory (and in the context of a very wealthy country where relative access to the courts is in fact possible) but does not directly address the conditions and circumstances that lead to a court application for those most vulnerable and disadvantaged by reason of education, class status, or access to resources. This is a doctrine of rights based on passive denial: you have the right if you can actively pursue it or if your sphere of influence means access to power. Abuse of rights via omission, then, is a major concern. The lack of real access to rights instruments, government complicity with rights abuses, the legal, procedural dithering that slows down and complicates rights proceedings, and the lack of appropriate, timely process are all major hindrances to enacting rights.

If rights are most often violated in relation to the least powerful, then meaningful rights definitions have to address questions of what a right is in terms of how that right is accessed by the least advantaged. Moreover, such a definition must take into account how, once accessed, the right is enacted, supported, and made a living reality within civil society.

Rights definitions must articulate not just an abstract value but must face head-on the pre-conditions and after-conditions that relate to what a right actually means in a given circumstance (frequently of disempowerment or disadvantage). How just is it, for instance, that rights situations pitting massive corporations (with entire departments of legal counsel) against small, disempowered communities or individuals involve hugely differential, disproportionate access to meaningful rights instruments? Universal rights are meaningless without universal and equitable access to the legal means for enforcing these rights.

Impartiality of access and of application, then, is crucial to defining rights as lived events, and not just abstract ideals. The least vestige of privilege that permits differential treatment before the law weakens rights and threatens the structures of justice and equity on which they are based.

Rights definitions must be able to sustain critique from different worldviews in order to be meaningful. A good example of this is in the critique of the very term '*human* rights' for its undue focus on the *human* as opposed to the full environment, without which humanity would be unthinkable. It is impossible to conceive of human rights in any substantive way if rights do not meaningfully address the conditions in which humanity exists. From a variety of indigenous perspectives across the globe, the environment that produces and sustains humanity must be made an integral actor with real agency, legal and otherwise, before *human* rights can matter.

The critique we use here is not chosen randomly: it addresses how an oppressed and marginalized segment of aboriginal humanity offers a pertinent contribution to rights definitions. Significantly, in the UDHR, the explicit recognition of the environment as a fundamental pre-condition for the existence of meaningful rights is not acknowledged. The existence of such an obvious gap in a crucial document defining universal rights ignores the observation that 'the successful bio-regions of the future will mimic nature at every step' (Lasn): attention to the environment will ultimately determine the viability of human existence. Human rights and environmental rights are indivisible.

In fact, multiple clauses in the UDHR would come into conflict with such recognition, a major failure in that document's attempt to create a universal definition of rights. SUV owners' right to pollute, for example, under certain perverse interpretations could be defended using Article 22, which gives everyone 'the economic, social and cultural rights indispensable for the free development of his personality.' Similarly, the ongoing destruction of vast environmental heritage sites such as the Amazonian or Indonesian rain forests is allowable based on the local rights of farmers, corporations, and governments to economic development and on the absence of a clear statement on environmental rights. This major shortcoming of the UDHR ignores the environmental critique of how rights are defined coming from indigenous communities. In a later chapter we return to the significance of indigenous communities as a repository of a kind of cultural memory that underlies the most fundamental expressions of rights.

While human life depends on the natural environment, humans also create other highly mediated environments. The dense overlay of different information environments attests to this: from the Internet through to other forms of media, the mediascape has become a critical aspect in rights talk. Thus, Kalle Lasn and Tim Walker appeal for the creation of a new human right entitled the right to communicate. This right would guarantee access to the media thus empowering freedom of speech, especially where the mass media are recognized to be a highly limited forum in terms of access to dissenting opinions, critiques, and positions: 'The right to communicate is not an abstract demand. It's a remedy for distorted and misleading public discourse, the sort that allowed the U.S. to attack Iraq, that every day allows Palestinian suffering to go largely unnoticed, and that allows big business to keep global warming off the political agenda' ('Let's Fight for a New Human Right').

The call for such a right arose in response to the calculated refusal by the Canadian Broadcasting Corporation (remember, a national, *publicly* owned major broadcasting company) to air ads placed by *Adbusters* in the name of citizen-produced advocacy critiquing excess consumerism. And media access is important for all sorts of other reasons, including, general rights education; the pressures on public figures to act that can be triggered by media attention; and the articulation of alternative, informed, and critical viewpoints.

Media attention can be a double-edged sword. For example, in Laos, one of the poorest countries in the world and the third largest exporter of opium, a longstanding conflict between the ethnic Hmong (a word that means 'free' in the Tibeto-Burman languages spoken by this indigenous group) and the government has been protected from scrutiny. AI reported in 2004 on how, when two foreign journalists managed to visit a group of rebels and report on their conditions, not only was international attention on Laos heightened, it also resulted in a 'military crack-down, resulting in scores of reported civilian casualties' (AI *2004 Annual Report* 169). In this case, media attention clearly had a negative impact on human rights, while in others it enables people by informing them of injustices against which they should agitate. For example, in the UK, the media attention given to the enormous sales of arms and instruments of detention and torture, manufactured by UK-owned companies, led to heightened pressure to make these sales more open to scrutiny. That one of the supposed stalwart advocates of human rights was found to be trafficking to such a huge extent in arms and implements of torture (ranging from iron shackles through to electroshock batons, kinetic impact devices, chemical incapacitants, and more sophisticated weaponry) being sold to nations with extremely poor human rights records has been documented in detail by AI in two reports entitled *Made in Britain: How the UK Makes Torture and Death its Business* (1997) and *Undermining Global Security: The European Union's Arms Exports* (2004).

The dissemination of the first report's findings, based on initial investigative reports by Channel 4, has made it possible to articulate a crucial relationship. The arms trade and the business side of the massive military infrastructure that characterizes developed nations are directly linked to rights violations and abuses in developing nations.[2] That the UK in 1995 alone had in the order of 15,000 requests for defense export licenses indicates the extent of the trade, most of it done with no Parliamentary oversight.

Electroshock baton exports alone are significant because they are almost exclusively used for purposes of torture: 8,000 batons reportedly sold to Saudi Arabia; 10,000 electroshock shields and 5,000 electroshock batons arranged to be sold to Lebanon via Germany (AI *Made in Britain* 32) as documented by a Channel 4 team of reporters who impersonated an interested buyer. And these known cases represent the tip of the iceberg, pending proper disclosure of how the flow of these devices goes from the developed world to the developing world—revealing how profit is made from human rights violations and abuses. Such global struggles indicate that no proper definition of human rights can occur without truly democratic, accessible media, since being *human* and exercising one's rights depend on being informed.

A final word on rights definitions requires addressing the issue of freedom. Most conventional Western, Eurocentric definitions of rights begin with the concept of freedom. A right is a freedom; a freedom is a right—within certain limitations. The German philosopher Immanuel Kant's influential treatise on rights, *The Metaphysics of Morals*, for example, says the following under the heading 'There Is Only One Innate Right': '*Freedom* (independence from being constrained by another's choice), insofar as it can coexist with the freedom of every other in accordance with a universal law, is the only original right belonging to every man by virtue of his humanity' (63: 238). A widely circulated Internet definition of human rights is 'any basic right or freedom to which all human beings are entitled and in whose exercise a government may not interfere (including rights to life and liberty as well as freedom of thought and expression and equality before the law)' ('Wordnet').

Rights and freedoms are virtually interchangeable from this perspective, which sees freedom as an absolute embodied in the individual. This is an influential definition of a right, but we stress that it is *not* the only one. The concept of 'freedom' and how it is defined is, like the concept of rights, very much a matter of *who* is empowered to create the definition. Nor does it provide for resolving conflicting individual freedoms that arise from different interpretations of what freedom can mean.

Rights documents sensitive to the radically different material realities of diverse peoples recognize that freedom of the individual is a concept that requires careful balance and attention. Thus, AI's definition of human rights focuses on 'respect' for human life and on the intrinsic value of each human being (*Amnesty International Handbook* Ch. 2) as definitive of human rights, a definition that puts obvious limits on individual freedoms, where those conflict with respect for life. AI insists that we are all born free and equal in dignity and rights but its nuanced attention to how respect for life is a crucial pre-condition of that freedom is important. So, indeed, individual freedoms are one aspect of any meaningful definition of rights. But they are so within a sophisticated context of interlocking spheres of interest and influence, from the local to the global.

Individual freedom occurs within the context of communities of interest that require respect, reciprocity, and close attention to matters of difference. Article 13.1 of the UDHR, for instance, states that 'Everyone has the right to leave any country, including his own, and to return to his country.' But the actual individual freedoms of migrant workers, refugees, and even visitors from countries whose politics may offend can barely exercise this right, except at great risk or under huge constraints. Again, to return to Bhopal, how many of those affected could freely leave the region (let alone the country) to escape the toxic contamination that affects their basic rights to security of person and thus exercise their individual freedom to mobility? The supervening 'rights' of much more powerful entities override these people's rights in a way that empties Article 13.1 of its meaning for the victims of Bhopal, as it does for multiple majority world citizens hemmed in by poverty, lack of status, political disempowerment, prejudice, and restrictive legal instruments beyond their control.

Inequalities resulting from global dispositions of power and privilege that advantage the few over the many undermine the universal application of rights definitions. As Uruguayan author and activist Eduardo Galeano acerbically notes in his essay 'Ni Derechos, ni Humanos' ('Neither Rights, nor Human'), Article 30 of the UDHR proclaims that ' "no one can suppress any of these rights"…but there are those people who might comment: "Don't you see that *I* can?" Those people, which is to say, the global system of power, always accompanied by the fear that it spreads and the resignation that it imposes.' The radical challenge of defining rights must address the contradictions that separate the idealized, theorized definitions from the lived, practical experience of so many the world over. Multiple ways in which different stakeholders in the struggle for global rights are meeting this challenge will be evident in examples given throughout this book.

Human Rights Defenders Are Increasingly Targeted around the World

The collusion among governments aligned with narrow elite interests and military forces (official, paramilitary groups, and death squads) make prime targets of human rights organizations and those dedicated to speaking out on behalf of the persecuted. For governments and vested interests, rights activists are often unwelcome irritants. This ongoing persecution of rights defenders underlines the real importance of their work and the threat it poses to corrupt, state self-interest.

Increasingly, human rights advocates, including trade unionists, environmentalists, indigenous leaders, the relatives of victims of human rights abuses, human rights lawyers, journalists, and even judges, are harassed either by having spurious criminal charges filed against them, or receiving death threats; they have been arbitrarily detained, kidnapped, tortured and terrorized, and assassinated.

There are people hired to erase other people, to wipe out any trace that they ever existed. They are members of armies or of death squads associated with armies. Usually, they are financed by governments. They may travel in cars with tinted windows, without license plates and abduct their victims off the street in broad daylight. They may burst into private houses and drag the occupants to secret destinations. They may enter a village en masse and force the victims to march into the mountains or the jungles. In most cases the victims are never seen again and no bodies are ever found.

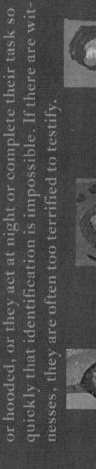

The abductors are hard to identify. They are often masked or hooded, or they act at night or complete their task so quickly that identification is impossible. If there are witnesses, they are often too terrified to testify.

Recently, Paul Foreman, the head of the Dutch branch of *Médecins sans frontières* (Doctors Without Borders), was arrested in Sudan for reporting hundreds of rapes in Darfur ('Sudan arrests aid worker'). And in Uzbekistan, dozens of activists opposing President Islam Karimov's authoritarian government were detained or forcibly kept from leaving their homes ('Uzbek police detain dozens of activists').

Tunisian human rights defenders face physical attacks, and are not permitted to call meetings or to book venues because they are denied the registration required for even such basic organizing, thereby violating their freedom of association and assembly. Publications that criticize the government are prevented from circulating, and websites carrying such information together with international news sites are made inaccessible to Internet users in Tunisia, showing that the 'worldwide' web does not include parts of the world where authorities have the power to control communication. In April 2005, authorities jailed lawyer and human rights defender Mohammed Abbou for three-and-a-half years largely for publishing critical articles on the Internet (AI 'Restrictions on Tunisian Human Rights Defenders' 1).

While the lamentable trend of violence against human rights defenders is apparent in every region of the world, Irene Khan, AI's Secretary General, identifies the Americas as the region where these abuses are reaching emergency proportions. And she explicitly names Canada and the U.S. as states where human rights abuses are increasing, especially in the contexts of peaceful assembly and public protest (AI 'Americas: Human Rights Defenders'). Further, a 2005 joint report prepared by the *International Federation of Human Rights* and the *World Organisation Against Torture* ('Human Rights Defenders on the Front Line') found that 'nations are using the fight against international terrorism as an excuse to trample on human rights...as they reported a doubling of repression against [rights] activists' ('Rights activists suffer in war on terror'). In 2004, the report documents how '1,154 human rights activists and more than 200 non-governmental organizations were targeted by "acts of repression" in 90 countries' (ibid.). The IFHR report also provides a useful summary of the dilemma faced by rights activists the world over:

> Defenders are up against a double difficulty: on the one hand, their task increases in importance with the rise of arbitrariness, social inequalities and violations concomitant with the 'security first' principle; on the other hand, the values they defend are undergoing

constant erosion, their freedom of expression is considerably curtailed and their message is ever more difficult to transmit. Whereas
their action is all the more necessary, they could well suffer the same
fate as the rights they defend.

Repression against human rights defenders continued in 2004,
and even gained in intensity in certain parts of the world, notably in
Asia and some Latin American countries. This repression is sometimes linked to a spurious use of the fight against terrorism. In certain countries, particularly in conflict-ridden areas (Colombia,
Nepal), defenders are considered as rebels or terrorists, and/or are
subjected to restrictive security legislation, like the Mapuche leaders
in Chile. (10)

Human rights advocates are stigmatized in the media, even in affluent nations
where the principle of freedom of the press is taken for granted. They are accused of everything from defending common criminals to being engaged in
criminal activities themselves, including anti-patriotic acts deemed to undermine state security. The U.S. Patriot Act enacted after 9/11 (and a legislative
tool we examine in greater depth in a later chapter) has had far-reaching, negative international consequences, with governments around the world emulat-
ing the rhetoric of counter-terrorism to shirk their international human rights
obligations (Deen).

Since August 2002, at least 15 human rights defenders and scores of trade
unionists have been killed in Colombia; in Honduras several environmentalists and one human rights lawyer died violent deaths between 2001 and 2003;
in Guatemala 18 human rights defenders were killed between 2000 and 2003.
The 1990 assassination of renowned Guatemalan anthropologist Myrna Mack
is a landmark case in convicting members of the military of murder, and in
achieving legal recognition and reparations. Mack was stabbed to death by
members of a military death squad, in retaliation for her anthropological research into the destruction of indigenous communities by the military during
the country's 36-year civil war.

In this particular case, the Guatemalan government and military did not
get away with their usual impunity. Mack's sister Helen Mack fought relent-
lessly to bring the guilty to justice, first managing to get a low-ranking security
officer convicted in 1993, but then climbing up the ladder of power to have two
colonels and a general indicted and brought to trial, with the aid of Human

Rights First which initiated an action before the Inter-American Commission on Human Rights of the Organization of American States. In 2002, Colonel Juan Valencia Osorio was convicted of the murder, but this conviction was overturned in appeals courts the following year and has been taken to Guatemala's Supreme Court.

Crucial in this process was the referral to the legally binding jurisdiction of the Inter-American Court of Human Rights. In its 240-page decision, this court unanimously found Guatemala in violation of right to life, humane treatment, judicial guarantees, and judicial protection of the American Convention on Human Rights. Among other penalties, the Court ordered Guatemala to pay damages to the Mack family (the highest amount ever awarded by this Court) and to prosecute all those involved in the killing and the cover-up, together with meaningful gestures to bring this kind of violence to public awareness: to publicly honor the memory of José Mérida Escobar, a police officer who was killed during his investigation of the Mack case, to establish and fund a scholarship in Myrna Mack's name and to name a street or plaza after her in the capital city ('Guatemala: State Publicly Acknowledges Responsibility for Mack Murder' 2). According to Human Rights First, 'These two parallel proceedings —the domestic criminal trial of the individuals responsible for the killing, and the international claim against Guatemala for breaching its responsibilities to uphold, protect and ensure human rights—are crucial in the pursuit of justice for the Mack family and in their contribution to Guatemala's progress towards a more democratic and rights-respecting society' ('Human Rights Defenders in Guatemala: The Case of Myrna Mack Chang' 2).

The high-profile case of Margaret Hassan, former head of Care International in Iraq, is perhaps more ambiguous. The identity of her killers is still unknown in a country where there are up to 20 insurgent groups, plus rival gangs of criminals seeking to extort money from hostage-taking (Fisk 'Margaret Hassan's Suspected Execution'). Regardless of who actually committed this killing, such acts create a climate of terror against people who work for and produce meaningful social change. But unlike the occupation of Iraq, the situation in the Americas is clear-cut: state agents and security forces commit the vast majority of violations. In the Americas, as reported by AI, those 'working to assess the relation between human rights and proposed free trade zones, investment and trade policies are increasingly facing attacks and intimidation' ('Americas: Human Rights Defenders'). Activities that are crucial for democratization and that should involve members of civil society are becoming the most risky endeavors, threatening both the rights defenders and democracy at large.

Mexico, a NAFTA member whose current conservative government led by Vicente Fox represents itself as a real democracy, is another site of routine threats, harassment, torture, and assassination of human rights workers. A recent, and much publicized, case involved the brutal killing of Mexico's best-known human rights lawyer Digna Ochoa. Those who discovered her body on Oct. 19, 2001, in a run-down building that housed the law office did not immediately call the police, because 'Digna Ochoa's colleagues are human rights lawyers and activists whose experiences with authority in Mexico have been bleak' (Diebel). Even so, it was the police that twice ruled homicide, 'but in 2003, Mexico City authorities in charge of the case flipped the verdict to "probably" suicide. The Fox government looked the other way and the leftist mayor of Mexico City, Andrés Manuel López Obrador, an early frontrunner' in the next presidential race 'supported the verdict' (Diebel). Disturbingly, Ochoa was not murdered out of the blue, but had been the victim of numerous death threats, two kidnappings, and an attempted murder, until she fled Mexico, clearly because there were no judicial guarantees or protection for even those professionals whose work puts them at great risk. She was killed after returning to Mexico City to resume her legal practice in human rights. International recognition, awards, admiration, and personal connections to Washington politicians and Hollywood actors did not protect Ochoa from those in power, who punished her for being 'involved in Mexico's most politically charged and controversial cases, cases that focused on allegations of torture, rape and murder by members of the army and other security forces' (Diebel).

Brazil has one of the worst records for extreme violence against rights defenders and environmentalists who for decades have been trying to defend indigenous groups and the Amazon rainforest from ranchers and developers. In February 2005 the point-blank shooting of Dominican nun Dorothy Stang, working on behalf of both the poor and the environment in the Boa Esperança settlement on the edge of the Amazon rain forest is a classic example. But there are many others who have fallen in the shadows beyond the glare of publicity, in the fight for equitable rights in Brazil. The media attention paid to the American-born Stang, while welcome and needed, highlights the lack of media attention paid to the hundreds who have died under similar circumstances in

Brazil. Rights defenders who denounce organized crime, corruption and impunity put themselves in the crosshairs. AI notes that Brazil was 'the first country in the region to develop a National Coordination Plan for the protection of human rights defenders which will facilitate the creation of commissions in those states where insecurity of human rights activists is greatest' ('Americas: Human Rights Defenders'). But if the State branches of the Human Rights Commissions in Mexico are any indication, these organizations are often established to simply placate international opinion. Mexican authorities have been quick to expel members of international NGOs' delegations investigating various human rights situations. This is routine in Cuba too where human rights groups are prohibited from conducting investigations, but is also prevalent in countries where rights bureaucracies have been set up to promote and protect human rights.

AI recommends that 'governmental' efforts for the protection of human rights defenders should integrate immediate protection measures with longer-term preventative measures. Priority must be given to thorough investigations of the violations and threats against human rights defenders and the bringing to justice of those responsible. Other preventative measures include education of security force agents on issues regarding human rights and social organizations, as well as public awareness campaigns' ('More protection, less persecution'). While these recommendations are eminently reasonable, they ignore the political reality of countries divided along class lines, with oligarchies having full support of the military to terrorize anyone who dares to agitate for basic rights and needs. How can education alleviate a situation in which the rich and powerful have no true interest in democratizing if that means sharing the wealth and power? An AI report on Brazil makes it clear that the police organization *Scuderie Detetive le Cocq* (SDLC), responsible for extra judicial executions, killings of human rights defenders, corruption and organized crime has significant links with powerful economic and political groups in the state, including members of the executive, legislative and judicial branches of power (AI 'Brazil: Espírito Santo state under siege').

Greed and injustice cannot always be remedied by knowledge, though public awareness campaigns must promote human rights to the public at large. How many more people among them will have the courage to face death to protect rights? It gets even messier when multinational corporations, international institutions, and first world governments do not support democratization and the defense of rights when they are in conflict with business interests. Given such global hypocrisy, further measures are desperately needed to provide accountability and global legal structures that have the power to enact that accountability.

Kofi Annan, UN Secretary General, has argued that 'a Special Rapporteur for Human Rights Defenders would play a pivotal role in protecting lawyers, journalists, students and activists who continue to be threatened, intimidated and even killed in their fight to protect human rights' (AI '2000 United Nations Commission'). And in August 2000 Hina Jilani, a prominent Pakistani lawyer, who started the first women's law firm in Pakistan in 1980, was appointed Special Representative of the Secretary General on Human Rights Defenders. Following on the heels of UN General Assembly resolution A/RES/53/144, which established the Declaration on Human Rights Defenders in March 1999, Jilani stated:

> The protection of [human rights] defenders is central to the promotion of human rights, the development and strengthening of democracy and the respect for the rule of law. The creation of the mandate of the Special Representative on human rights defenders is a measure on the one hand to monitor the situation of human rights defenders, and on the other to seek the implementation of the Declaration in a manner that eliminates the risks to which defenders are exposed. ('Hina Jilani')

Importantly, the UN Declaration on rights defenders is *not* a legally binding instrument, a measure of the degree to which generalized affirmations and specific enactments of rights instruments remain distinct. Such distinctions create highly problematic situations for rights defenders who rely on such quasi-legal declarations for protection in life-and-death situations. Important as such affirmations can be for taking first steps in the right direction, providing potential legal and rhetorical frameworks for rights articulations, their content is compromised, if not evacuated of meaning, by the lack of means to enact legally the principles they embrace.

Along with the UN initiatives described above, AI documents vigorous campaigning by human rights activists across the Americas together with significant recognition of their efforts to promote women's rights, sexual rights and HIV/AIDS prevention, and indigenous rights in relation to natural resources. Despite the dangers involved in human rights activism, rights defenders are increasingly vocal in their demands to hold governments and armed groups to their international and domestic human rights obligations (AI 'Americas: Human Rights Defenders' 4).

No discussion of rights, then, can fail to acknowledge the ways in which rights workers face significant obstacles and dangers in undertaking their work. And without this work, any notion of civil society is meaningless. These dangers come in many shapes, ranging from open repression to various shades of intimidation. A climate of pervasive anxiety and fear too often prevails. Even nebulous fear can be an effective means of limiting the energy of the wider human rights movement. Rights are ensured through their continual re-affirmation, establishment and renewal of spaces in which those rights are habitually exercised. The understanding of human rights at a global level must account for the often-perilous environment in which rights workers work and the real hazards that impede progress on multiple rights fronts.

Why Do Human Rights Matter? 'You Are, Therefore I Am'

Rights defenders and the peril they face show that people are courageously willing to fight almost impossible odds for a common good. Like no other issue, rights straddle national and cultural boundaries, ideological divides, and personal conviction to address what is the crux of human existence: How will we live? In what kind of a world will our children live? Who determines the basic structures of how we interact locally and globally? How can we live justly in every aspect of our lives? Rights touch upon everything from the food we eat to the waste we produce. Rights include the ways in which we express our love for each other and the ways in which we resolve our differences. They speak to how we can promote equality across diverse cultural formations. And they address the core question: what does it mean to be fully human?

Rights discourses worldwide have always existed across geographies of difference. This despite the distorted perception that somehow rights are solely the product of Western or Occidental, Eurocentric modes of thought, ethics, and political philosophy. But before rights ever got written down and made into law they existed in nascent, emergent, or full-blown form across multiple cultures, ethnicities, belief systems, and so forth. Despite the proliferation of rights covenants in the last century, the 'scale of abuses and effects [of those abuses] is far greater than ever before,' as Roger Clark, former Secretary General of Amnesty International Canada notes: 'We can see this [increase in abuses] in the large number of current civil wars, the number of collapsed governments, and the enormous effects of global economies, epidemics, and massive environmental destruction' ('Principles of Human Rights Monitoring').

Rights are social constructions that encode fundamental forms of social information. But, as Václav Havel eloquently puts it in a comment already examined earlier in this book, rights 'have their deepest roots somewhere outside the perceptible world.' As we have seen, some argue that rights are intrinsic to human consciousness and social organization, that they reveal in effect a form of human essence that is definitively, universally, a reflection of 'our' shared humanity. Others debate this, suggesting that, rather than being a human essence, rights are socially constructed. That is, rights are a matter of cultural forces growing out of deep historical and cultural processes necessary to the expression of shared human values that are constructed over time in specific places, languages, histories, and cultural differences. The cultural position can be (and has been) misused to deny the universality of rights and must be deployed with extreme care within the context of rights practices. Both positions are rooted in secular beliefs about the nature of human experience: rights either express a human, transcendent essence or they are essential to cultural constructions of what it means to be human.

Liberation theologian Enrique Dussel offers another perspective that circumvents the simplistic dualism of universality versus social relativism. In contrast to Havel's locating of ethics 'somewhere outside the perceptible world,' Dussel insists that the roots of ethics are in the flesh, which in the prophetic tradition of Christianity refers to the indivisible composite of body and soul or spirit that makes up the person. Dussel also insists on proximity and the need to behold the other face-to-face because 'the "flesh," the "flesh" of the other, his or her "face," is the only sacred thing in creation' (*Ethics and Community* 60). The carnal experience of pain or pleasure experienced in an individual person is irreducibly specific to that body but is simultaneously a universal and shared aspect of being human. Dussel anchors the materiality of the individual in the concreteness of community and rejects the abstractions of such European philosophers as Kant on the grounds that an 'absolute criterion of practical goodness cannot include any empirical, concrete content whatever...thus the way is open for a surreptitious elevation of the subject's (European or capitalistic) particularity to the status of universality (validity for every culture and system). With all the "good will" in the world, this subject can perform an objectively perverse action' (ibid. 76).

Dussel's insistence on not rejecting the body and not locating the source of justice in a metaphysical realm has profound implications for human rights thinking and practice. He searches for the root causes of suffering in localized, concrete situations, which nevertheless form a global web of injustice. According to the Western metaphysical tradition that severs body and mind or body and spirit, further associating the mind/spirit with the good, and the body with evil, the specificity of the other's suffering body can be dismissed as irrelevant. Statistics of tortured bodies, even photographic images of dead bodies become abstract in their numbing immensity and generality, a violation of the full corporeal integrity and personhood of each body tortured, maimed, or killed.[3] The spirit-centered view of the body as ephemeral (and thus of less value than the transcendent spirit) renders the most graphic images of wounded and decomposing flesh as ultimately meaningless. In the related and perverse view that only the soul has eternal worth, the body's suffering can be ignored, a perverse logic based on belief systems that disintegrate the integral, indissociable relation of body and spirit/mind as an aspect of embodied personhood, itself always placed in relation to embodied communities. 'Accordingly, nothing transpiring on this negative level—the realm of the body—is of any importance: daily manual labor, torture at the hands of a Latin American dictator or CIA trainee, and so on' (ibid. 62). This blindness Dussel calls the morality of domination, which he counters with the corporeal ethics of liberation—the recognition of the other as equal and free and possessing inalienable rights as an embodied person who is a member of a larger embodied community.

Dussel's concrete analysis of structural violence and resulting poverty locates the effects of injustice in the material sphere of the other's flesh and the cultural extensions of the flesh that are arbitrarily stunted by the dominators: 'Not only have the poor been deprived of their bread, their housing, their vesture—their consumer goods—they have been robbed of their productive goods as well, the tools they need to reproduce their life. They have no land of their own. They have no labor of their own initiative. They have only their suffering skin and their marketable labor...the lack of culture as instrumental totality, of technology as the extension of corporality, is likewise the cause of pain, suffering, and inequality' (ibid. 64). Likewise, the human response to the other's suffering must spring not from an imperceptible realm, but in face-to-face fleshy recognition: 'Praxis, then, is the actualization of proximity, of the experience of constructing the other as person, as end of my action and not as means. We are dealing with a relationship of infinite respect,' the Christian concept of *agape*, 'love for the other *as other*...love for the other in view of that other's own reality' (ibid. 10).

Paradoxically, this recognition of another's suffering rooted in the corporeal experience we all share is universal but not abstract. Even the privileged and protected know in their bodies the sensations produced by hunger and cold, however rarely they may experience them. In Dussel's vision, as long as we reject the ascetic moralities of domination (in which 'the body is of no value. That is, the body of the *other* is of no value' 62), and we recognize the other as a concrete wholeness, 'our neighbor's pain becomes a sign. Now this pain glows like a red light' (ibid. 63). While 'the pain of another becomes the very criterion of praxis' and that 'criterion is a "corporeal" one...the commitment it calls for, however, is "spiritual": it is the Spirit that moves me to the service of my neighbor' (ibid. 63). It must be remembered that the spirit invoked by Dussel is inseparable from the body. Dussel's work asks how to engage and activate a rights praxis that grounds itself in the material realities of shared corporeal life while retaining the spiritual empathy that allows for imagining and acting on the specific pain and suffering of the other.

We believe that given this fertile paradox of the flesh, these philosophical positions are far from mutually exclusive, but perhaps at this time only partially developed and confused by blind spots created by traditional blinkers shaped from within the dominant paradigm of *either* universalism *or* relativism. Rights are at once a statement of faith in a specific narrative of what it means to be most fully human but also, as we will show, a statement of embodied fact based on countless examples that cross cultural and geographic differences, historical differences, and lived practices.

The theory and practice of rights matter for many reasons. For too long, rights have been restricted to particular academic disciplines and professionals who get to determine *who* is 'certified' to talk about what is meant by human rights. Legal, political, juridical, philosophical discourses dominate, shaped largely by men with access to power and to the institutions that embody power, that is, courts, governments, and institutions of higher learning. Despite our belief that these organizations (reshaped by the peoples they are intended to serve) are ultimately necessary to a meaningful and accountable system of world rights, we oppose the restrictions and blinkers on these discussions.

Rights must be based on a simple rule of reciprocal inclusion, founded on a straightforward, core principle: for rights to truly matter they must begin by enacting a material improvement in the most basic living conditions of the poorest and the most oppressed, that is, people living in the so-called Third World —what we prefer to see as the majority world. For, as stated by the Salvadoran activist and Jesuit priest, Ignacio Ellacuría, brutally murdered in 1989 by the Salvadoran armed forces, 'The third world is the prophetic denunciation of how badly arranged are the things of this world. A society that makes possible the third world is an unjust society, an inhuman society, a society appallingly badly arranged' (Whitfield 41).

Ellacuría's vision of meaningful change for the disempowered and victimized serves as a baseline point of departure for rights practices. Or as Upendra Baxi succinctly puts it: 'communities in struggle against human violation are the primary authors of human rights' (89). The voices of the least empowered are the voices from which rights activists must take their cue: the oppressed have a great deal to teach their oppressors. The reciprocal relations that are the basis of all forms of human community, global or local, and of all forms of responsible rights thinking, require recognition of the Indian notion of *so-hum*: 'You are, therefore I am' (Shiva *Earth Democracy* 140). Abstract definitions of rights that corrupt this simple rule of thumb based on reciprocal, interdependent engagement, are simply academic constructs that serve the affiliations and networks linking rights discourses with imperial self-interest. Candid testimony before the U.S. House International Relations Committee on International Operations and Human Rights in 2001 by Stephen Rickard, Director of the Robert F. Kennedy Memorial Center for Human Rights, stated: '...the voice of the victims is still too often ignored in setting policy.' These are the voices that must now be heard.

Rights matter because they express transnational human solidarity in respect to achieving equitable living conditions for the most disadvantaged. And they do so by restoring the dignity, integrity, viability and value of all human beings regardless of what is in the interest of those who control the state. No doubt this view will enrage or perplex some because it attacks the privileges established among the wealthy few from whom, in this corrupt worldview, all that is good flows and guarantees the ongoing disempowerment of the majority who are always ostensibly on the 'take.' Rights matter because they address the disposition of power at local, national, and transnational levels and because they challenge the inequitable distribution of global wealth and resources.

Human rights are at the core of the most important 'clash of civilizations,' to borrow Samuel P. Huntington's hopelessly reductive and wrongheaded description of the clash between 'the West and the Rest.' Let it be said that both the 'West' and the 'Rest' are not homogenous entities but are made up of multiple constituencies. In our view, the real clash of civilizations occurs between competing transnational (and indeed trans-religious) worldviews over how the powerful relate to the disempowered. That is, between those who have rights and those who do not. The real clash of civilizations is a function of how plutocracies and oligarchies and other narrow circles of disproportionate power come into confrontation with those who challenge their priorities and prerogatives. This clash has resulted in what some have referred to as a 'rights revolution,' a meaningful rights movement to redefine what it means to be human in relation to power.

The Italian philosopher Giorgio Agamben has argued persuasively that the very structure of the nation-state as a dominant form of organizing power relations is predicated on 'birth.' That is, the rights of the nation to an individual via citizenship immediately supersede a person's own universal rights as soon as that person is born. The nation exercises its sovereignty (its right) over a person at birth by asserting state ownership through 'nationality.' This makes the individual simply an extension of the state's own power relations. The individual's rights are, in that sense, constituted from birth by the state, a relationship of power that is highly troubling if not outright fictional within the notion of universal human rights ('Beyond Human Rights' 20,1).

But rights need to transcend the nation-state. Too many states have put their own self-interest over larger rights principles: think the military dictatorships in Argentina, Chile, and Burma/Myanmar. Autocratic states' behavior overrides concerns with rights, which can lead to refugee problems and other forms of statelessness—say 'unlawful combatants' or the approximately '40 million children each year [who] are not registered at birth, depriving them of a nationality and a legal name' as reported by the UN High Commission on Refugees (UNHCR)—these factors threaten the fiction of the state to define human rights in terms of its supposed sovereign relation to its citizens.

Rights matter because they envision transnational global citizenship that lies beyond the conventional structures of power associated with the state.

Cuba: A Case Study of a Rights Enigma

Cuba presents a unique opportunity for examining the difficulty in achieving balance among different kinds of rights in a developing nation operating under severe economic and political constraints. Cuba's fraught relations with the U.S. are the result of a five-decade-long unilateral and unprecedented embargo, the longest in history in which medicine and food have been prohibited. Cuba has insisted on sustaining its political culture in opposition to that of the U.S., and refused to allow human rights observers from various NGOs (including United Nations observers) onto the island. The U.S. in the meantime has committed egregious human rights abuses at the U.S. naval station in Guantánamo on Cuban soil. Both its successes and its failures mean Cuba's situation merits close attention. In this section we briefly describe some of the paradoxes generated by the Cuban situation.

The split between basic rights to potable water, food, medical attention, access to education, security of person, and political rights such as freedom of expression, freedom of association, freedom of dissent and mobility vary dramatically in Cuba. During an extended stay in Cuba we experienced both: from arbitrary lengthy detentions of people plucked off the street with no charges laid (kept there for months and even years) to racial discrimination against black communities. We saw severe material shortages (sometimes deliberately created by the government to send a message) at the same time as school children were sent home daily carrying a loaf of bread. We saw an ambitious rationing system that was generally acknowledged to be inadequate, with monthly rations lasting no more than two to three weeks. We saw universal access at all levels to a developing educational system, a highly literate population, and access to a developed and caring medical community that, despite the lack of material resources, matched or exceeded care given in Canada. And we experienced a general security of person despite the obvious poverty that would be hard to match in relation to any other developing nation worldwide.

Some Facts about Cuba from the
United Nations' 2003 and 2005 *Human Development Reports*

- Cuba, despite its history of agrarianism and its status as a developing nation, is listed as having a high human development, ranking at number 5 out of 94 developing countries, above Singapore, Brazil, China, Ghana, India, and Mexico;

- Cuba's adult illiteracy rate is 0.3% (the best rate in the developing world and a crucial human indicator relating to producing an educated citizenry);

- Cuba's entire population has access to clean water sources, better than among others, Chile, Mexico, and Korea;

- Cuba has one of the lowest infant mortality rates in the developing world and has an infant mortality rate equivalent to the U.S. (7 per 1,000 live births), having reduced its rate from 34 mortalities per 1,000 in 1970, a major achievement given the economic restrictions it has faced and a major indicator of quality medical attention, itself a sign of access to rights (especially where material resources are as limited);

- Cuba spends a higher percentage of its GDP (as of 2000, 6.1%) on health than the U.S., the United Kingdom, Australia, and many other nations with a high level of human development; and Cuba's public expenditure on education as a percentage of GDP in 2000-02 was 9% as compared to 5.7% in the U.S., 5.2% in Canada, and 4.9% in Australia.

- Cuba has a significant percentage of seats in parliament held by women (36%) as opposed to 24.7% in Canada, 17.9% in the United Kingdom, and 14.8% in the U.S. The struggle to achieve gender equality in government is a crucial aspect of rights developments in terms of potential political change.

- In the 2005 UN Human Development Report, Cuba scored highest on a crucial indicator that shows the difference between a country's human development ranking and its ranking according to GDP per capita. The measure shows 'how effectively a country translates what it's [sic] "got" (in GDP terms) into actual well-being' (Stanford). Cuba ranked '52nd in the world by social progress—a full 40 places above its position in the GDP ranks. In the human development sweepstakes, therefore, little Cuba hits further above its economic weight than any other country in the world' (Stanford). A measure of this effectiveness occurred when the Category 5 hurricane Ivan struck Cuba in 2004 and approximately 2 million people were evacuated (along with animals) and not a single person died.

Based on a sampling of key rights indicators in the context of four decades of economic warfare, Cuba has achieved impressive gains that are meaningful in relation to an overall picture of human rights concerns. The sustained media attack on Cuba by Western media defies basic comparative honesty. Comparing the rights violations in a small developing nation under extraordinary external (let alone internal) pressures to the standards set for the developed world is highly questionable. Since Cuba shares more historical features with Latin America than with the U.S., comparisons with Bolivia or Guatemala would be more appropriate. There are no moral equivalencies between the harm done on a world scale by highly militarized developed nations (such as the U.S.) and a small developing nation. Comparative analyses of rights violations, however, can quickly degrade baseline, universal standards for acceptable rights conduct. Evaluation of context is crucial but must never detract from or dilute the objective assessment of a country's human rights record.

Cuba, then, challenges rights activists to rethink simple moral, absolutist stances in the context of specific rights environments. AI, in its 2002 *Annual Report,* explicitly notes that 'The four-decades-old embargo against Cuba by the USA continued to contribute to a climate in which fundamental rights were denied' (85) and José Miguel Vivanco, Executive Director of the Americas Division of the international NGO Human Rights Watch (hereinafter HRW), in 2002 called for an end to the embargo in order to 'improve human rights conditions in Cuba' ('Time to End the U.S. Embargo on Cuba'). Further, the AI report points out that in 2002 the UN Commission on Human Rights passed a resolution that 'stated for the first time that UN member states should take steps to improve the economic condition of the Cuban people.' But the condemnation of Cuba did *not* go hand-in-hand with the condemnation of the U.S. embargo. This hypocrisy typifies the contradictions that Cuba exemplifies: economic health is acknowledged to contribute to improved human rights conditions even as the deeper context for understanding economic health (that is, the decades-old U.S. embargo that has punished the island for sustaining its political autonomy by not adhering to American policy) is set aside.

An 18 March 2005 AI news release does make these connections: it calls for the immediate release of 71 prisoners of conscience from Cuban prisons while arguing that the embargo 'contributes to the undermining of key civil and political rights.' But at the same time AI 'also calls on the Cuban government to stop using the embargo as a pretext to violate the human rights of the Cuban people'

('Cuba: 71 prisoners of conscience'). AI's position neatly summarizes the problem of the universal versus relative rights positions, striving to adhere to universal standards while at the same time recognizing local realities.

In considering human rights it is important to evaluate context and to avoid absolutist judgments. Ultimately, all human rights, for better or worse, traverse the gauntlet of national self-interest. Political dissidence is being squelched in Cuba through imprisonment and harassment. In a recent case, three young men seeking to escape the island hijacked a ferry in Havana harbour in the hope of navigating it out into open waters. No one on board was harmed but the hijackers were executed within one week of their arrest. Such abuses of power need to be examined in relation to the political, economic, historic and cultural pressures that contribute to the complicated rights environment in Cuba. Here, a quick comparison with the U.S. is in order. President George W. Bush's abysmal record as Governor of Texas (a much larger political and geographic entity than Cuba), involved 152 people being 'texecuted' over eight years. This included the notorious incident involving Karla Faye Tucker whom Bush mockingly parodied in his famous 'Please don't kill me' interview. Cuba's actions, however despicable, stand in significant contrast to the scale of capital punishment in a developed country like the U.S., which until very recently (1 March 2005) permitted the execution of juveniles.

Media reports on the Cuban government's draconian response to the hijacking and to the imprisonment of approximately 75 dissidents during the same period ignored that there was heightened anxiety about a U.S.-led invasion. There was no mention of the morally relevant contexts that separate out the specificities of a Cuba from say a Texas. The lesson here is that we need to constantly reevaluate the ambiguous histories of validating and critiquing rights across multiple cultures. In non-capitalist states like Cuba where governments are attacked for human rights abuses, the tendency is to use concepts of human rights towards negative criticism that serves the propaganda interests of nations with differing political regimes.

There exists much documentation on the threat Cuba faces from a host of factors, such as terrorist actions on its own territory from American sources rooted in Miami: five Cubans, known as the 'Cuban Five,' were sent to Miami to infiltrate ultra-right organizations like Alpha 66, Omega 7, and Brothers to the Rescue who are funded by American sources and are charged with destabilizing Cuba through bombings, assassinations, and other forms of sabotage and terrorism. The five remain in jail in the U.S. after one of the longest trials in American history. The trial was held in Miami, contrary to defense concerns about due and fair process, and was virtually ignored by the American media. Other threats against Cuba include the open calls for the assassination of Castro in the U.S. (in contravention of U.S. law), a constant fear that any opening to American interests will immediately compromise the island's unique (and vulnerable) version of sovereign self-definition, and the possibility of an actual military invasion exacerbated by Guantánamo (or Gitmo). This massive American military base is implanted on Cuban sovereign territory where the U.S. violates human rights and the basic tenets of the Geneva Convention on the treatment of prisoners of war who are characterized by American officials as illegal combatants of the war on terrorism. As British journalist David Rose states: '…the [U.S.] administration was mounting attacks on two pillars of both the Enlightenment and the Constitution—on their retreat from torture, and on due process. They were only made possible by a third legal assault, against the separation of powers. Running through the entire documentary record of the war on terror is a single theme: The unlimited power of the American president to override treaties, conventions and laws in time of war' (149-50).

In the case of Guantánamo, Cuba has been placed in the humiliating and highly paradoxical situation of being condemned for its own local rights violations even as it became host to unprecedented violations of rights by the U.S. The area of Guantánamo is enormous, 116 square kilometers or approximately 45 square miles with some 7,000 troops permanently stationed and surrounded, until 1998, by the largest minefield in the Western hemisphere. Further, when Cuba attempted in April 2005 to have the UN Commission on Human Rights investigate the treatment of detainees in Guantánamo via an impartial, authorized fact-finding mission, the resolution was voted down 22-8 (China, South Africa, Guatemala and Mexico, among others, supported the resolution).

It is at least arguable that given these factors Cuba has maintained a justifiable state of high alert resulting in a predictably rigid, enclosed, and defensive posture with profound implications for the political rights of the Cuban people. As Tim Anderson notes, 'While an invasion of Cuba is uncertain, a similar "transition" plan [to that for Iraq] for the independent island was spelt out in the May 2004 report of the "Commission for Assistance to Free Cuba," headed by former Secretary of State Colin Powell. The report recommended increased U.S. funds for opposition groups, called for a "Truth Commission," and demanded a "market economy" for Cuba' (n.p.). Anderson notes how the United Nations' Commission on Human Rights' focus on Cuba's human rights violations with respect to dissidents (by comparison with what Anderson rightly calls 'monstrous' crimes elsewhere) 'tell[s] us quite a lot about imperial strategy in the current era, and the use of "human rights" as an instrument to leverage imperial "transition" ' (n.p.). While not excusing Cuba from its own rights violations, the scapegoating of Cuba as a rights violator is far in excess of its actions, especially when measured against those of Latin American democracies like Brazil, Colombia, Argentina, and even Mexico.

And in spite of the effects of the blockade, the military, political, and cultural powers arrayed against it, Cuba has made significant achievements in baseline human rights relating to education, medicine, women's rights, and so forth.

And yet Cuba remains a one-party state that still engages in capital punishment and is ruled by a dictator with dynastic pretensions, which does little to help the rights context—remember the old jokes about the difference between the former Soviet Union and the United States being only 'one party' (and let's not forget the dynastic forces at work in the U.S. relative to the Kennedy and Bush families). The fudging of community values with state values in Cuba—where the state stands for the community with the state leader, 'Fidel,' as grandfather—reinforces a paternalistic view of nation that imposes specific rights constraints.

Thus, paradoxes abound when thinking through rights issues in relation to Cuba. The lesson to be learned from this all-too-brief summary of a very complicated scenario is that simplistic judgments about complicated historical situations do little to advance the kinds of sophisticated understandings of rights issues that are needed to achieve the balanced, critical perspectives by virtue of which global rights standards and instruments can be articulated, improved, and enacted.

Transnational Rights and International Social Justice

There are countless examples of how rights continue to privilege the powerful over the powerless. But a worldwide movement to challenge these biases is gathering steam. The International Criminal Court (ICC), for instance—established in 1998, entered into force of law in 2002 and seated in The Hague in the Netherlands—establishes 'the first ever permanent, treaty based, international criminal court established to promote the rule of law and ensure that the gravest international crimes do not go unpunished.' The premise of the ICC is simple if not revolutionary: when national courts refuse to address grave violations of rights, human rights violators need to be held accountable. An international organ that litigates offences across all national boundaries is one way in which to achieve this outcome.

But HRW warns that manipulations of American law by Congress are working to create a system that privileges American national self-interest over that of the global community. The Nethercutt Amendment, 'part of an overall spending bill, mandates withholding antiterrorism funds and other aid from countries that refuse to grant immunity to U.S. citizens before the International Criminal Court' ('U.S.: Congress tries to Undermine War Crimes Court'). The effect of such intimidation tactics is simple: confirm the privilege of the most powerful as the most exemplary right, at the expense of majority global interests. At the time of this writing, 100 countries had ratified the Rome Statute that created the ICC and nearly 140 countries had signed the treaty. China, Pakistan, India, Indonesia, and Turkey rejected the treaty and Russia, Egypt, Israel, and Iran signed the treaty but failed to ratify it—all of these countries have significant domestic rights failures.

The ICC regrettably can investigate only those crimes against humanity committed after July 2002, and only those in countries that have signed up to the court, or in which cases are referred by the UN Security Council. In 2005 the ICC, led by Canadian Philippe Kirsch, was investigating suspects from four countries, *all* African: Uganda, Sudan (Darfur), Democratic Republic of Congo, and the Central African Republic. By contrast, 'The United States signed up under pressure, but withdrew support after President George W. Bush's election, claiming that it [the ICC] would become a "rogue court" bent on prosecuting American servicemen on overseas missions. The U.S. Congress went so far as to pass a law authorizing the use of force to rescue any Americans who might be hauled into the dock' (Ward, 'Canadian builds seat'). The exceptionalism of the U.S. approach to the ICC undermines, for the moment, the inexorable development of global notions of enactable social justice for crimes against humanity.[4] Rights and responsibilities exercised under internationally recognized and enacted agreements are crucial because they underlie 'a system of international justice to limit impunity for serious human rights crimes [that] has struck at outmoded notions of national sovereignty and the absolute prerogatives of states' (*HRW World Report* 2004 216). Even within such a context it must be remembered that the ICC, balanced so perilously between the strictures it faces and the potential it has to mete out some degree of justice for crimes against humanity, is reactive and not preventative. As such, it represents one direction for imagining the most productive avenue for addressing the root causes that lead to egregious rights abuses and violations.

The concentration of privilege in those countries most associated with producing rights talk is a major problem. Disproportionate wealth is equivalent to disproportionate power, which can in turn lead to disproportionate allocation of rights. In 2003, as reported by the *Human Development Report*, more than 1.2 billion people (1 in 5 people) survived on less than $1 a day (5); more than 1 billion people (1 in 5) in developing countries lacked access to potable water (9)—and as Eduardo Galeano stated in 2002, again based on UN reports, the ten wealthiest people on the planet possess more wealth than the aggregate wealth produced by 54 countries. And worse: since the signing of the UDHR in 1948, the gap between those who have and those who need has tripled ('Ni Derechos ni Humanos').

Unjust, disproportionate distribution of wealth is a global cancer metastasizing rapidly:

- when 'the richest ten percent of Americans alone (some 27 million people, not even one half of one percent of the world) has an income equivalent to that of the poorest forty-three percent of the world population' (George 21), and when wealth the world over is split along racialized lines (for example, in the U.S. in 2001 'the median net worth [assets minus debts] of black households was $10,700 compared to $106,400 for white households' [Yates 66]);

- when approximately 900 billion dollars a year ('Editorial: The 0.7-per-cent solution') is spent on military armaments and only 52 billion dollars a year in aid flows from rich to poor countries while these same rich countries 'provide roughly one billion dollars *every day* in agricultural subsidies and support, mostly to their own largest farmers' (George 21-22);[5]

- when the richest countries in the world abandon their own high principles in relation to foreign aid spending, or compromise those principles by using aid as a way of subsidizing their own multinational business interests—in the case of Canada, for instance, whose progressive Prime Minister Lester Pearson in the 1960s set 0.7% of gross domestic product as the target for developed nations, only a meager 0.28% of its GDP in 2004 went to foreign aid, a scandalously low amount;

- when on average some 6,500 people a day die in Africa from AIDS alone with approximately 11 million children orphaned by AIDS in Africa as well and when approximately 130,000 Africans, over half of them children, die *every week* as a result of preventable causes like contaminated drinking water, diseases like malaria and tuberculosis, childbirth-related causes, respiratory illnesses and so forth (Mitchell and Roter);

- when some 100,000 Africans own $825 billion while 300 million Africans live on less than $1 a day (and comparably well-off countries in Africa like Kenya have a staggeringly low average per capita yearly income of $458) (Hartley);

- when, as reported by UN High Commission on Refugees (UNHCR), approximately 'ten million children under the age of five die each year, the majority from preventable diseases and malnutrition' amounting to some 28,000 children under five *a day*...

Such appalling statistics point to the collective guilt of the 'haves' in robbing the 'have-nots' of the means to their own labour, and make it clear that massive structural changes are necessary to address the multiple violation of rights. Rights matter, then, because they seek to remedy the pathologies of indifference and imbalance that underlie these situations at a global level.

Frequently, anti-rights interests view rights law as interfering with the 'free' flow of market economies thus imposing collective values and limitations on individuals' freedoms—as if freedom were an absolute without relation to collective responsibilities that impose reasonable and balanced limits on human (inter)action. The frequent recourse to that absolute notion of freedom has given philosophical harbour to multiple excesses of despotic governance and corrupt business practices that have immeasurably increased suffering the world over. The failure to confront and rebut this argument decisively is a major shortcoming of rights theory generally. But as Indian author and UN official Shashi Tharoor states, 'the idea that human rights could be ensured merely by the State not interfering with individual freedom cannot survive confrontation with a billion hungry, deprived, illiterate and jobless human beings around the globe. Human rights, in one memorable phrase, start with breakfast' ('Are Human Rights Universal?').

Why Rights Matter

- Rights matter because they put the lie to structures that prioritize the minority rights of the wealthy few over the majority world, the lie to structures that perpetuate massive structural inequities that undermine the collective civil commons that is humanity. Rights matter because they make thinkable participatory, globalized rights that insist on, for instance, 'the collective right of peoples and communities to immunity from corrupt practices of governance' (Baxi 9).

- Rights matter because the scandalous state of affairs described above cannot help but offend any human being who seeks to live in an equitable and just community.

- Rights matter because they provide a transnational framework for imagining and achieving outcomes that address inequity and injustice.

- Rights matter because they offer the potential for transforming the ideals they imagine into concrete realities that affect the lived, material conditions of people globally.

- Rights matter because they articulate an emergent, sophisticated context for the needed, continuous dialogue and arbitration between collective and individual interests.

- And rights matter because they express the hope and potential for meaningful outcomes to situations of massive injustice at the local and global levels.

Notes

1. The proliferation of rights documents and covenants is a mixed blessing. On the one hand it marks how rights talk is increasingly infiltrating new jurisdictions with greater specificity. At the same time it shows how the UDHR, laudable as it may be, did not get it entirely right. And worryingly, the proliferation of documents can become a way of diluting the clarity of documents like the UDHR, effectively providing loopholes to specific covenants. For an example of this, see Fischlin and Heble, 34-35.

2. Developing nations like India and China cannot be excluded from the arms scenario and its impact on rights worldwide. The U.S. Congressional Research Service reported that from 1997 to 2004, India made 15.7 billion in arms purchases, approximately 10 percent of all such arms agreements. In 2004 'a total of $37bn in arms sales in both industrial and developing nations was concluded' with the U.S. taking 33.5% of the business (followed by Russia and Britain) ('India tops weapons purchase table'). The inter-relations between industrial and developing nations' economic and defense interests represents a serious challenge to the reallocation of resources in a manner that positively impacts human rights outcomes.

3. This numbing effect produces important rights outcomes, as, for instance, is the case in how the U.S. handled the issue of Iraqi war dead following the 1991 Gulf War. In that situation, Geneva Convention regarding collection of the dead, confirmation of death by medical examination, and identification of bodies, followed by honourable burial or cremation of the dead in identifiable graves were largely ignored—with still undetermined numbers of Iraqis entombed in the desert in mass graves. American military commanders, including General Norman Schwartzkopf, Rear Admiral John Stufflebeem, General Tommy Franks, and Defense Secretary Donald Rumsfeld have all indicated that the U.S. military does not 'do' body counts (see Conetta 27 and Fisk *The Great War* 692)—a direct violation of pertinent Geneva norms including Article 17 of the Third Geneva Convention and Articles 15, 16, and 17 of the First Geneva Convention. Robert Fisk details how the number of Iraqi dead was hidden from humanitarian workers (including members of the International Red Cross), a practice that continued into the 2003 war with Iraq (ibid. 692-93). The erasure of the particularity of each person killed, at even the most basic level of identifying the body and burying it properly, is part of a larger structure of disrespect for the life of the individual and the community that contravenes the most fundamental of human rights and natural justice norms. These comments should be kept in mind at later points in this book where conglomerate statistics are used (with these qualifications) to mark examples of exceptional global violence.

4. Exceptionalism with regard to the ICC must be understood within a larger framework of U.S. resistance to constructive and equitable development of international structures that address fundamental rights outcomes. Exemplary of this were the amendments tabled by U.S. Ambassador to the UN John Bolton who, on the eve of the September 2005 UN Summit to address UN reforms, tabled some 700 last-minute amendments that 'undercut commitments to end the worst world poverty within a decade, reject the obligation of nuclear weapons states to dismantle their arsenals, weaken measures to protect people under threat of massive human rights violations and limit a proposed peace-building commission's scope. "The U.S. proposals are more than just individual changes," [said] Phyllis Bennis of the Washington-based Institute for Policy Studies. 'They represent a full-scale declaration of war on the United Nations" ' (Ward, 'U.N. summit threatened').

5. The U.S. spends approximately 400 billion dollars a year on defense, a little bit more than the combined total of the 20 top-spending nations that follow after the U.S. (who spend approximately 396 billion). The correlation between those monies and human rights violations and abuses is clear, especially when mapped onto patterns of military intervention in U.S. history, with some 163 such interventions occurring since the early 19th century. As summarized by Nicholas Klassen: 'America is by no means the only party responsible for the glut of arms in the world. But as the number-one arms producer, it epitomizes the problem. It has almost continuously been in violation of the Nuclear Non-Proliferation Treaty—all the while trying to browbeat others into adhering to the treaty. Meanwhile, the U.S. accounts for almost half of global conventional weapons deals—with many of the goods destined for the third world' ('U.S. Foreign Military Interventions').

Chapter 2

Globalization And Development: Human And Sustainable Or Corporate And Cancerous?

Globalization refers to the current hyper-acceleration of communication and trade across geopolitical borders, though its roots can be traced back to European conquest and colonization on several continents. The two dominant forces that have shaped globalization are trade and war. Both have become increasingly intertwined since they depend on access to communication and media. The 'development' that invariably goes hand in hand with globalization can be an expression of genuine human progress or can mask the cynical profit seeking of governments, corporations, and their shareholders. The challenge for rights discourses is to promote sustainable development that is decided, directed, and controlled by the local community, whose long-term commitment to the region ensures responsible stewardship of the environment. Global sustainability is the guarantee for enduring human rights and genuine human development.

'Globalization' is usually used in exclusive reference to corporate business and international trade. The powerful decision makers who globalize from above are transnational corporations, elite financial institutions like the International Monetary Fund (IMF), the World Bank (WB), and the World Trade Organization (WTO), and governments, especially in their subordinate actions to the above institutions through negotiating, for instance, 'free' trade agreements. Globalization from below, however, is the grassroots networking of common people, NGOs, and civil society organizations (CSOs), all the various movers and shakers like labor groups, activists of many different stripes, women's groups, environmentalists, and so on; people primarily concerned with how corporate globalization is eroding not just their own human rights, but those of their sisters and brothers around the planet.

The mainstream media's use of the term 'globalization' erases the power dynamics associated with rich neo-colonial powers viewing the non-industrialized regions of the world as nothing more than natural resources and slave labor to be plundered and exploited. Obviously, this kind of relationship is based on inequality. The lack of a level playing field assures that maximum profits are always gained at the expense of the disadvantaged trading 'partner,' who in this inequitable arrangement is not so much a partner as an underdog who receives development aid together with orders on how to spend it (usually from the country where the aid originates).

Human rights are ignored and violated routinely when global trade decisions are based on getting the cheapest labor, slackest environmental and labor regulations, huge tax cuts for transnational corporations, and freedom from any kind of long-term commitment to the region in which these corporations operate. Poor countries are pitted against each other in self-destructive competition to attract foreign investment, even in the name of development. Such a scenario recalls terrible images of food being dropped from planes to desperate, starving people who push and beat each other trying to get their small share. How does the image of the global village fit into this scenario?

The Dream of Global Marketing: Confusing the Issues

The global village stresses our universal interconnectedness, especially through electronic technology that seemingly connects faraway places and reduces vast expanses to the intimate space of the village. This is particularly ironic given that villages everywhere in the world are being abandoned, as desperate people are forced to migrate to sprawling urban centers in search of menial labor, where they must again renounce many of their basic human rights in order to compete for the few jobs available. It is hard not to associate the idea of the global village with the IBM commercial that contributed to making it a common reference meant to trigger a warm and fuzzy feeling about we're not quite sure what: global solidarity? Our common humanity? The dream of progress that will liberate the First World from its colonial guilt?

The IBM image of half-naked tribal Africans surfing the web on their laptops speaks a thousand words while not addressing the realities of the Digital Divide (the gap between those with access to technology and those without).

The idea that communication is now open to all citizens of the planet across geo-political and less tangible borders is enticing, and appeals to a basic human desire to explore and to connect. But it also appeals to the desire of first world supremacists to see the Third World (the majority world, let us remember) aping them through activities that showcase technological development as the apex of human achievement. This deeply skewed vision is what drives developmentalism, the perversion of genuine human development. The representation of majority world people possessing expensive technology lays bare the crass one-sidedness and self-interested objectives of advertising and the mass media generally. The image of the tribal villagers actually disconnects human realities by suppressing the fact that these people are often denied access to basic human rights like land, food, clean drinking water, and the education that would be needed to create the literacy, not to mention technological literacy, required to use IBM's products.

Throughout history, trade among different regions and communities has been and continues to be essential for prosperity, and even basic survival. But a level playing field is a requisite for fair trade. Historically when geographical or climactic conditions disadvantaged certain communities, more prosperous ones often helped out the less fortunate, expecting the same just treatment in return: a kind of communitarian insurance policy based on mutual aid. In this sense, fair trade is really the only form of freedom, because it benefits vulnerable groups by allowing them to trade products whose value is not artificially deflated by arbitrary market forces. Addressed in the current context, the UN's *Human Development Report 2005* makes a similar recommendation, although the language of 'losers' versus 'winners' unthinkingly used even in this document perpetrates notions of supremacy and worthlessness: 'In order to maximize the welfare gains from trade, and to strengthen the political case for participation in trade, it is important that the winners compensate the losers. That compensation can take various forms, including transfers between countries and public policies within countries to create the conditions under which losers are protected and provided with opportunities' (124). Once again, we need to be reminded that poor countries do not necessarily need to be provided with opportunities, but rather that they should not be robbed of opportunities through policies devised by powerful countries in order to protect their own interests and corporations. Furthermore, the 'winners'/'losers' dichotomy suggests a static global structure without questioning the status quo or imagining social change that would make such a hierarchy obsolete.

One of the greatest challenges posed by a globalized market is that the rich Northern countries take their economic supremacy for granted instead of acknowledging how they acquired that supremacy through unjust trade policies based on colonialist and imperialist practices. To erase that past and suddenly declare all countries equal in world trade is a cynical move to continue exploiting the South under the guise of promoting development and offering aid. According to the UN's *Human Development Report 2005*: 'If Africa enjoyed the same share of world exports today as it did in 1980, its exports today would be some $119 billion higher (in constant 2000 dollars). That is equivalent to about five times aid flows and budget savings from debt service relief provided by high-income countries in 2002' (117).

The conflict between the global elites and the have-nots plays itself out in the power dynamics of the World Trade Organization. While the WTO is organized along democratic voting principles—one vote for each country regardless of status, the practical reality is cynically manipulated by the two most powerful players—the U.S. and the EU. On the other hand, 'What makes the WTO so powerful is that it has both the legislative and judicial authority to challenge laws, policies and programs of countries that do not conform to WTO rules and strike them down if they are seen to be too "trade restrictive." Cases are decided —in secret—by a panel of three trade bureaucrats. Once a WTO ruling is made, worldwide conformity is required. A country is obligated to harmonize its laws or face the prospect of perpetual trade sanctions or fines' (Barlow 3).

Commenting on the December 2005 round of WTO talks, such organizations as Oxfam, MakePovertyHistory, and the Trade Justice Movement, together with community media and the Inter Press Service News Agency all condemn the aggressive and inflexible position taken by rich countries and the consequently disappointing outcomes for poor countries. All small advances proposed primarily in agriculture were rendered insignificant in the face of the systemically unjust trade policies jealously protected by the wealthiest nations. These policies included the use of domestic subsidies, dumping products in poor countries, and restricting access by poorer countries to developed markets. Rich countries spend billions of dollars on agricultural subsidies, yet hypocritically preach and impose the open market and 'free' trade policies on the impoverished South. These double standards are only conducive to corporate development but detrimental to human development.

Walden Bello, Director of the Global South, bluntly sums up the WTO's performance: 'Ten years of the WTO has brought nothing but more poverty, more inequality, economic stagnation throughout many parts, throughout most of the developing world. This is not an institution that promotes development. This is an institution that promotes corporate trade, promotes corporate profit that promotes destruction of the environment. It is an anti-people organization' ('Protests Continue at WTO Conference' 1).

People who are impoverished and marginalized as a result of the U.S. and EU control of the WTO are well aware of the roots of their problems and join in mass protests to make their views known. Reporting on the 2005 talks held in Hong Kong, Anuradha Mittal gives a poignant account of peoples' desperation and determination: 'We have seen the Korean farmers jump into the harbor yesterday in the cold water just to be able to have their voice heard at the convention center. We have seen them being pepper-sprayed today in the streets of Hong Kong, just because they have tried to get close to the convention center' (ibid. 3-4), and even *China View* guardedly reports that during the violent demonstrations, 'around 114 were injured during the clashes between protesters and police'...and that 'around 900 protesters were arrested' ('188 anti-WTO protesters released').

Despite the shamelessly exploitative stance of the rich countries, we are finally seeing resistance not just at the street level of pepper-sprayed individuals, but in the will and planning of poor countries' governments that have decided to band together to counteract the U.S. and EU. In December of 2005 'five leaders of small alliances of developing countries met to form a larger bloc to lobby on key issues like agriculture and cotton. The groups are the G20, G33, Africa Group, the Least Developed Countries Group and the Africa, Caribbean and Pacific Group' (Mekay, 'WTO Special: Developing Nations Push Back' 1). These in turn are discussing the creation of an umbrella alliance of 110 of the WTO's 149 members. Such new alliances open the way to the possibility of fair trade, notwithstanding political motives for sharing the wealth as in the case of Venezuela's president Hugo Chavez, who has announced that his country guarantees petroleum and gas for South America for at least 200 years. Furthermore, South American governments are envisioning an umbrella oil company called Petroamerica 'under which Venezuela has agreed to sell fuel to other countries in the region under preferential terms and with low interest financing' ('Venezuela's Chavez says he'll share oil wealth' B9). Cuba has already benefited from this preferential treatment in exchange for medical doctors and training.

One important question that is omitted from reports following the Hong Kong WTO talks is whether Cuba will continue to be excluded from this new and promising configuration of global resistance at the international level. Given that some of the most acute problems are caused by big pharmaceutical companies that pillage and patent the ancient herbal medicines and health knowledge of indigenous peoples, it would be interesting to consider how Cuba's advanced health care system and highly developed homeopathic pharmaceuticals might benefit other poor countries.

One of the many contentious issues at WTO talks is TRIPs (trade-related intellectual property rights). India's Trade Minister Kamal Nath questions the relationship between trade and intellectual property, and the very notion of knowledge being reduced to individual (corporate) property, crucial distinctions that the TRIPs title slyly elides: 'Recognition of rights to biological resources and traditional knowledge, as opposed to private intellectual property rights, is certainly a development issue' (Nardi, 'WTO Special: The TRIPs Traps for Health and Knowledge' 1). There is barely a trace left of the Convention on Biological Diversity in the 2005 WTO document, signaling the powerful bias of corporate interests in an institution that claims to promote trade among the world's nations, to the benefit of all. In this area of the talks, too, the line was drawn between the U.S. and WTO on the one side, and public health experts and leading NGOs including Médecins sans frontières [Doctors without Borders] on the other. Richard Lloyd, head of the Britain-based Consumers International, charges that 'the recent decision by the WTO General Council to approve a flawed and highly criticized amendment to the TRIPS on exports on generic medicines shows the WTO is ignoring those with expertise' (ibid. 2). 'Before TRIPs, international laws on patents, especially in developing countries, would not allow the patenting of food and drugs and other essential products' but due to pressure from American and Japanese multinationals, TRIPs was introduced against the will of developing countries (ibid. 2).

Business interests clearly override health interests for the WTO, since 'TRIPs requirements make it very difficult for governments to obtain medicines, including in emergency situations like an epidemic' (ibid. 2). We can consider the latest threat of an avian flu pandemic as a case study in how BigPharma harnesses ancient indigenous knowledge and then withholds benefits from the poor people whose knowledge the drug is derived from. The drug Tamiflu that is currently being hoarded in anticipation of this pandemic 'is a sort of updated version of an ancient Chinese treatment for coughs and flu. The fruit of the star anise trees is the starting point in the manufacture of this "modern drug" ' …'Hoffmann-La Roche (Roche), the Swiss pharmaceutical company which produces Tamiflu … received a world wide commercialization licence in the Unites States. Stocks of Tamiflu are in great demand and Roche is backlogged for years into the future. World health authorities including the UN's World Health Organization are urging Roche to license other companies to make the drug. But the company is resisting, claiming the drug-making process takes a year, that it would take new makers three years to get tooled up, and that the main ingredient is in limited supply' (ibid. 2).

Why is the WTO so often referred to in relation to the International Monetary Fund (IMF) and the World Bank (WB) despite its claim of being a democratically organized institution? One of the reasons might be that the 2005 WTO document 'obliges developing nations to sweeping negotiations to further open their markets in services like banking, insurance and utilities, which could signal another wave of privatization and deregulation like that championed by international financial institutions such as the World Bank and the International Monetary Fund' (Mekay, 'WTO Special: Subsidies Concession' 2).

Globalization from below imagines a far different reality, exemplified in physicist Vandana Shiva's advice: 'what would be best for farmers everywhere —in Europe, Africa, Asia, and in my country, India—is a focus on relocalizing production and consumption, and on meeting the needs of everyone, rather than corporations, rich consumers and amorphous "global markets" ' ('Relocalization Not Globalization' 248).

Litigation Instead of Legislation

1. Lawsuits Against Corporations: The Only Consequence They Understand?

Even in domestic cases, corporations like General Motors have been known to estimate the cost of a lawsuit for fatalities to be worth the savings on not implementing safety measures. In a well-documented case of fires caused by fuel tanks of certain models of cars being placed too close to the rear bumper, a GM engineer's report estimated that each fuel-fed fatality cost GM $2.40 per automobile. Conclusion?: 'The cost to General Motors of ensuring that fuel tanks did not explode in crashes, estimated by the company to be $8.59 per automobile, meant the company could save $6.19 ($8.59 minus $2.40) per automobile if it allowed people to die in fuel-fed fires rather than al-

ter the design of vehicles to avoid such fires' (Bakan 63). This chilling reminder of the dangers of self-regulation by corporations that calculate only
financial profits to themselves and their shareholders leads one to wonder how
much crasser the calculations are when involving poor, racialized people in
foreign countries.

Increasingly, state governments are allowing corporations to create private and quasi-regulatory regimes to set national and international standards
and rules. Jack Donnelly's assertion that 'few direct negative human rights
consequences are apparent at the moment' as a result seems to contradict the
mounting evidence of international abuses, and reveals that theoretical discourses on human rights often lack rigorous empirical documentation of
abuses ('Human Rights, Globalizing Flows' 238). His suggestion that human
rights governance be extended to representatives of NGOs and social movements is sound, but there is no indication of how those legal jurisdictions
would allow this development to happen, especially in the light of growing
corporate authoritarianism.

To complicate the issue further, clauses to protect workers contained in
international trade agreements are interpreted by mercenary government officials as protectionism on the part of First World trading partners, given that
some Third World leaders see their own citizens as their prime commodity and
want no legalistic interference in exploiting them: 'Malaysian representatives
have asserted, for example, that social clauses are not meant to help workers
but to stop foreign investment in developing countries' (Pangalangan 100).

A recent victory for transnational human rights has set an important precedent that might be more effective in the world of business than all the UN
norms and recommendations on corporate ethics put together. The corporations most implicated in massive rights violations, including executions, rape,
and genocide, tend to be oil and gas extractors since their operations often involve protection of their sites by armies and other 'security' forces in countries
run by repressive governments. In April of 2005, California-based Unocal Corporation agreed to pay damages to Burmese villagers after Unocal was charged
with assisting and encouraging government soldiers to torture, murder, and
rape them to facilitate Unocal's building of a gas pipeline. Corporation executives often represent these cases of egregious abuses as nothing more than the
price of doing business. In Unocal's case, the oil company actually argued that
the allegations of forced labor, murder, rape, torture, battery, forced relocation

and detention fell within their insurance policies' 'personal injuries coverage' and sued both its primary insurer and its re-insurers!

About two dozen such cases have been filed against multinational corporations for committing or being complicit with foreign governments in committing extraordinary brutality: 'Although about half have been dismissed, usually on procedural grounds, another dozen are still pending. Defendants include some of the largest and most profitable companies in the world: Royal Dutch/Shell, Chevron Texaco, Coca-Cola and Exxon/Mobil' (Eviatar 1). A series of federal court rulings in California established that corporations might be sued in the U.S. for assisting or encouraging human rights abuses in foreign countries, even if they are multinationals. While experts say that only international standards can get corporations to follow the same rules, the U.S. will not support the UN's set of norms since they are not enforceable. Furthermore, these companies do not seem the least bit concerned about their reputations because their image is manufactured by advertising and has no relation to their actual practices. The courts are left to rule on individual cases, forcing companies to give greater consideration to the political risks involved in doing business with repressive governments. What remains to be seen is whether damages will simply be incorporated into corporations' budgets and whether these costs will be considered to outweigh the benefits of doing dirty business.

2. Corporations Sue Governments and Citizens Pay

NAFTA's notorious Chapter 11, the first 'investor state clause' in any international agreement, is producing its first corporate victories over democratically legislated environmental and health rights. The Canadian government faces several lawsuits from American-based multinational corporations costing hundreds of millions of dollars in compensation, which is becoming known with no little irony as the 'Pay the Polluter Principle' ('Trade Case Study: Ethyl Corp and MMT' 2). According to this clause, corporations can sue governments for compensation when their property is 'expropriated' or when governmental measures are 'tantamount to expropriation.' In the new lingo, expropriation has nothing to do with a state's seizing or confiscating private property for public use, as the following case study makes clear.[1] Ethyl Corporation is the Virginia-based manufacturer of MMT, a manganese fuel additive that reduces car engine knocks. The product is controversial because it is believed to be a dangerous neurotoxin capable of producing Parkinson-like symptoms, and also disrupts car pollution control systems, and emissions tests' outcomes. MMT is used only in the U.S. and Canada, but is banned in California, and the U.S. Environmental Protection Agency has banned its use in formulated gasoline. Given that some scientists think that the product has adverse health effects, Canadian legislators wanted to ban the use of MMT as well, but the Canadian Environmental Protection Act does not recognize the precautionary principle, which protects users from potential adverse affects, and Canada ruled that there was inadequate data on the health risks of MMT. The Canadian government sought the next best solution by banning the import and transport of the substance. Enter Ethyl Corp. with boxing gloves, high-powered lawyers, and Chapter 11 of NAFTA. The result was a $251 million lawsuit against Canada in compensation for not being able to transport MMT between provinces, interpreted as 'expropriation' since this measure will reduce the value of Ethyl's MMT manufacturing plant, hurt its future sales, and harm its corporate reputation.

Amazingly it is not the company's distribution of a potentially hazardous substance that tarnished its reputation, but the government that brought these concerns to the public's attention. The issue of the company's reputation is complicated by its 'storied past' as described by Signy Holmes. In the '20s, workers in Ethyl's New Jersey plant experienced hallucinations and convulsions, which may have led to the deaths of five people. It took the U.S. government 50 years to finally ban tetraethyl lead in gasoline. 'Meanwhile, that lead had been finding its way into all sorts of awkward places, from water and soil to the brains of children' (Holmes 2). As if the accusation against the Canadian government of tarnishing Ethyl's reputation weren't ludicrous enough, the company complained that the legislative debate itself constituted an expropriation of its assets because public criticism of MMT damaged the company's reputation. The implication for freedom of speech is that common people, health professionals, scientists, politicians, and journalists do not have the right to discuss such matters and can even be held responsible and liable for casting doubts on a company's product. Such a position is in direct opposition to the UDHR's Article 19, which articulates everyone's 'right to freedom of opinion and expression,' a right that includes the 'freedom to hold opinions without interference and to seek, receive and impart information and ideas through any media and regardless of frontiers.' Moreover, Article 18 of the UDHR guarantees the right to 'freedom of thought [and] conscience,' which in any civil society that is advanced technologically will necessarily entail evaluating conscientiously the consequences of technologies and their by-products.

What is the American government's reaction to the Ethyl Corp. situation with its outright attack on democratic rights principles enshrined in the UDHR? Several sources report that 'Far from worrying about the implications of such actions, U.S. trade officials have argued that the ability of investors to use legal threats to influence legislative debates is a healthy innovation that will prevent governments from passing laws that violate international agreements' ('Ethyl Corp. sues Canada' 4). What kind of laws? In this case, environmental laws that would protect the earth and humans from toxins, laws that are congruent with Article 3 of the UDHR regarding everyone's right to 'security of person.'

The implications are far-reaching. Ethyl did win its case, though the compensation to be paid by the Canadian government was lowered to CDN \$20 million, which nevertheless could have been spent on more worthwhile causes like health or education. This decision set a precedent 'whereby the legal right of corporations to be compensated when public health regulations affect a company's bottom line is given the same weight as the public's right not to be harmed by industrial toxins' (ibid. 3). We note that, in this case, the company's rights seem to have outweighed the public's right to enact the precautionary principle, whereby substances would have to be proven safe before they could be introduced into the environment. On top of paying this unprecedented amount, the Canadian government wrote a letter of apology to Ethyl stating that 'there is no scientific evidence that MMT poses a threat to human health or the environment' (Barlow 2), as if a government could determine such a scientific problem, thereby betraying the scientific community and the public that the government is supposed to represent. Furthermore, 'this could send the message to investors that seeking compensation from the public for the cost of complying with environmental regulations constitutes a legitimate business strategy' ('Ethyl Corp. sues Canada' 3). A business strategy such as this might see windfall profits reaped via purely litigious, non-productive means and divert vast amounts of money better spent on priorities pertaining to any number of issues. Lest we feel sorry for governments being caught in what looks like a double bind—being sued for huge amounts for trying to protect public health and environmental rights— '... the reality is that federal governments are often willing to "lose" these cases in order to discipline provincial, state or municipal governments that have adopted progressive social and environmental policies. Where federal governments do not have the legal or political power to reverse such legislation, it can allow the "external" intervention of NAFTA to act on its behalf' (Greenfield 2).

Important democratic principles related to process, representation, transparency, and accountability are overwritten by the legal process involved in determining the outcomes of these lawsuits: 'NAFTA cases are settled by a secret tribunal, whose decisions supersede the decisions of individual governments even though the tribunal is not elected and is not accountable in any way to the public' (Holmes 3). Moreover, 'The records of the NAFTA tribunal are not publicly accessible and the decision is legally binding' (Sforza and Vallianatos 3).

The Ethyl Corp. is just one of the many victories for corporations against national sovereignty, elected governments, the rights of citizens, and a sustainable future. Another disturbing lawsuit in September 2000, lost this time by the Mexican government to the American company Metalclad, cost Mexicans $15 million for trying to stop the building of a hazardous waste treatment plant on a site that lies on top of an ecologically sensitive alluvial stream. The residents had already been forced to take the law into their own hands—brandishing machetes—against the previous dump owner who refused to obey federal orders to close it down in 1991. The site, located in Guadalcazar County in the state of San Luis Potosí, therefore has a history in which the actions of residents sought the enactment of federal legislation that is effectively rendered null and void by the NAFTA. Community efforts and national laws to protect the environment are defeated by NAFTA, and so too are multilateral environmental accords like the 1983 La Paz agreement between the U.S. and Mexico. While this agreement was designed to help reduce hazardous waste dumping in Mexico, and to encourage waste management, the proliferation of *maquiladoras* in the 'free' trade zone along the U.S.-Mexico border is producing vast amounts of waste that most companies do not manage or ship back to the U.S. in accordance with the La Paz agreement and Mexico's own 1988 General Law for Ecological Equilibrium and Environmental Protection. The ruling in favor of Metalclad could have two negative implications: 'First, it will likely result in a "regulatory chill" discouraging Mexico from imposing new regulatory standards for hazardous waste treatment facilities. The case also seems to have contributed to an investment chill on the part of foreign corporations...' (Clapp 3).

Canadian corporations contribute their share to undermining environmental protection and perverting the legal system to potentially force governments to pay polluters to stop polluting. The Canadian company Methanex sued the U.S. over a Californian ban on the gasoline additive MTBE, a suspected human carcinogen. The company argued that the ban is tantamount to expropriation and that it should be compensated CDN$1.6 billion. One positive move to involve environmental specialists and the public in such decisions resulted in March 2004 in the first intervention by NGOs—in this case, the International Institute for Sustainable Development (IISD) and U.S.-based Bluewater Network, Communities for a Better Environment, and the Centre for International Environmental Law—to present *amicus curiae* (friend of the court) briefs. 'In addition, following a second request by the potential *amici* in January 2003, the Tribunal issued a procedural order in June 2003 indicating that the hearings on the merits would be open to the public. This important decision was then applied through the medium of live, closed circuit television broadcast of the proceedings in World Bank facilities...' (Mann 12). While this is still a greatly reduced interpretation of 'public,' the Methanex case has been pivotal in at least starting to make the process more transparent, accessible, and accountable.

The NAFTA governments (Canada and U.S. thus far) have indicated they expect all of their future cases to be open to the public, and other recent investment agreements (those with the U.S. as a partner) include rules on open access to documents and proceedings and *amicus* submissions (Mann 13). While these developments are promising, civil society must work to exclude the concept of regulatory expropriation from international agreements.

> This involves reinstating the primacy of national regulations on public health, health care, education, environment, community development, employment protection, trade union and labour rights, natural resources (e.g., water), genetic resources (e.g., seed), etc., over and above trade agreements...with regard to investment rules on regulatory expropriation our immediate priorities must be:
>
> 1. Severely restrict the definition of expropriation.
>
> 2. Narrowly define the meaning of property so that it cannot be interpreted to include market-determined commercial asset value or future profit earnings.
>
> 3. Expand the definition of 'public purpose' that allows for expropriation without compensation. Therefore regulations on the social sectors listed above should be treated as a legitimate public purpose. (Greenfield 4-5)

What Needs to Be Developed and How?

Clearly improving one's lot in life as an individual, community member, national and even global citizen is a human right. But who gets to decide what kind of development most benefits local communities and the majority world, and how it is implemented? As we address in the Introduction, should we simply accept the terminology that labels countries as either 'developed,' or 'underdeveloped,' more recently modified to 'developing'? Is 'developing' just the politically correct version of 'underdeveloped' or is it a universal ad for global exploitation as the wave of the future?

Vandana Shiva and other majority world thinkers and activists challenge consumer-societies' view of what even constitutes poverty.[2] Supporters of sustainable development argue that subsistence farmers living in small villages may look poor to people who measure well-being in terms of how many cell phones, computers, televisions, and designer shoes one owns. Clear distinctions have to be made between simply forcing the neo-liberal agenda of unlimited economic growth and excessive spending on all peoples of the planet, and, the kind of sustainable development that would enable the majority world to secure their collective well-being. The further danger associated with the rhetoric of sustainable development, in which development trumps sustainability and is hijacked by neo-liberalism, must be thwarted. (Think pesticide-spewing lawn companies that form 'green' environmental associations and lobby groups to represent their corporate interests.) In reality, true human development undermines expedient distinctions between haves and have-nots, since a sustainable future would no longer divide the world into a simplistic 'us' versus 'them' paradigm.

In perfect sync with developmentalist mythmaking is a political rhetoric that speaks of 'mutual benefit,' giving the impression that the First World and big business have the generous will and ability to eliminate poverty through unfettered global trade, and such technologies as the genetic engineering of crops: fund-speak, trade-speak, and rights-speak all being more sophisticated and nuanced spin-offs of Orwell's Newspeak. This rhetoric is contradicted by hard facts like the appalling level of majority world debt (the 47 poorest and most indebted countries in the world owe approximately $422 billion) and the real economic power of rich nations to alleviate that debt (the WB and IMF could afford to cancel 100% of debt owed by the world's most heavily indebted and poorest countries *without jeopardizing their operations* [our emphasis; Steger 43]). Moreover, issues around cancellation of debt and increase of foreign aid don't account for other structural problems that lead to exploitation, including the transfer of tax-free profits from developing to developed nations via transnational subsidiaries; the transfer of mineral, oil, and other natural resource revenues; and the major issue of servicing debt and the net cost of that servicing over time. At what point beyond the payback amount of the initial loan can a debt be considered as paid? In many cases of developing world debt, the cost of servicing the loan far exceeds the initial value of the loan.

Another important point of confusion is that, while most manufacturing jobs seem to have moved to third world countries, the means of production and the profits belong to multinational corporations, and not to the countries in which they are merely operating. Furthermore, the 'ability of countries to convert export success into rising incomes—and so into improved living standards and poverty reduction—depends not just on the volume of production and export, but also on a value-added—a measure of wealth created. It is value-added through manufacturing production that has the biggest bearing on the distribution of global income and the benefits of trade. The bad news from a global distribution perspective is that the balance of power in world manufacturing has barely changed after 25 years of global integration' (UN *Human Development Report 2005* 118). So for instance, *maquiladoras* in poor countries are not just foreign-owned but designed to create low value-added by limiting most of the work to assembling imported parts for re-export.

In terms of human rights, the workers in poor countries are not much better off than were those who labored on colonial plantations. Arundhati Roy's account of her attendance at the 2000 World Water Forum in which the notion of the human right to water was connected to commercialization of water access is telling: when 1 billion people globally lack access to potable water, the market decides to charge them for the water they don't have. The economic right of the market overrides the human right to a life necessity in spite of the appalling contradiction Roy describes: 'No one values water more than a village woman who has to walk miles to fetch it. No one values it less than urban folk who pay for it to flow endlessly at the turn of a tap' (*Power Politics* 41).

The dominant version of globalization produces such contradictions and does so in the name of the empowered at the expense of the poorest denizens of the planet. The tentacles of corporate globalization have encompassed the planet in a very short time span due to the global hyper-acceleration of trade, militarization, and corporate media, supported by communications technologies that circulate virtual capital and equity via keystrokes and binary codes. Moreover, globalization has proliferated the number of 'private global actors' who are 'frequently the most egregious violators of rights' and are 'accountable to no one and to no institution or state' (Pollis and Schwab 'Globalization's Impact' 215).

The impunity and lack of accountability of these global actors, described in numerous examples throughout this book, are a significant obstacle to improving the lived experience of rights worldwide. And the confusion between life rights and market rights we have described in this section accounts for the gap between the rhetoric of rights espoused by the overdeveloped world and the reality of rights lived by the majority world.

The Racist Foundations of Developmentalism

Globalization-from-above relates to forms of exploitation and abuse of human rights with a long history. The economic theory of mercantilism prevalent between 1500 and 1800, especially in England and France, can be seen as an early expression of this economic trend. Its main tenet: exports create wealth for a nation while imports diminish it. Only raw materials not available in European countries should be imported from the colonies at deflated costs. All goods should be manufactured in Europe (thereby creating many industrial jobs, at subsistence wages) and then sold back to the colonies at a high price. Where do the colonies get the money to pay for manufactured goods? Clearly not from their exports of raw materials, but from the slave labor that keeps their economies running without having to pay anyone to do the work. Once this form of slavery is abolished, the countries that go from being colonies of European powers to neo-colonies of globalized power gamble away their economies on loans with high interest rates forced on them by that same globalized power. Just as during the colonial period commerce and industry came to represent the progressive hope of the future, today globalization and development serve the same purpose: but what is genuine progress and development?

People 'deprived' of McDonald's (which spends over $2 billion a year on advertising its image alone) and cell phones, people who live in simple housing where climate allows, with access to land on which to grow the crops they need to feed themselves, drinking water, fishing, and other activities indigenous to particular regions, may not consider themselves poor. Referring to such communities as 'underdeveloped' or 'developing' implies that they are inferior to 'developed' countries and need to change their ways and to keep striving towards the illusive goal and definitive accomplishment of being 'developed.' Sadly, many mega-projects foisted upon such communities have devastating consequences for both the local people and the environment, and negate a whole array of fundamental rights from individual freedoms and the right to human dignity, the right to national sovereignty and democratic decision making involving all citizens, to the global right to protect and equitably share the earth's resources.

Fake Development Based on Mega-Projects

The Narmada Valley Dam projects have been called 'India's Greatest Planned Environmental Disaster' and will displace approximately 1.5 million people from their land in three states, not to mention the annihilation of biodiversity that will occur due to inundating thousands of acres of forests and agricultural land. Arundhati Roy challenges the State's position that building these dams is in the national interest of development by asking 'How can you measure progress if you don't know what it costs and who has paid it?' The WB had supported one of these dams, the Sardar Sarovar project, with a loan of $450 million, but in this case acted more responsibly than it had in the past by organizing an independent study group to assess the impacts. Once it became clear how grave the environmental and social consequences would be, the WB withdrew the loan. The indigenous population of this area stood firm against the Indian government; they organized massive marches, rallies, and hunger strikes, and declared that they would stay on their land and drown when it was flooded. Roy observes that 'no one has ever managed to make the WB step back from a project before. Least of all a ragtag army of the poorest people in one of the world's poorest countries,' suggesting that perhaps the public attention received by 'Narmada Bachao Andolan, The Save the Narmada Movement' had at least as much to do with the Bank's decision as the scientific assessment. Unbiased scientists, environmentalists, human rights activists and members of the local movement agree with Roy that 'big dams are obsolete...they lay the earth to waste. They cause floods, waterlogging, salinity; they spread disease. There is mounting evidence that links Big Dams to earthquakes.' Unfortunately, even after losing the WB loan, the government with the support of the Supreme Court continues to move ahead with the projects, instead of looking at sustainable energy sources. This ongoing battle demonstrates that development is political and, is inextricably involved in human rights issues (Kapadia).

Fundamental to the politics of globalization-from-above is the division of first and third world countries into lenders and debtors, thereby perpetuating structural violence. Development aid given to poor countries by the WB and IMF are 'negotiated' with the countries' governments without consulting the citizenry. Loans based on structural adjustment programs are designed to mimic first world industrial development. In order to show that they are in a position to repay their loans, debtor governments must give up virtually all sovereignty. These so-called development programs usually involve privatizing public and government institutions, severely reducing state budgets by slashing social programs and government support of health and education, raising sales taxes, devastating subsistence farming by forcing farmers to grow cash crops for export, and further endangering the hungry poor by reducing food and agricultural subsidies.

Developmentalism robs people of their human rights as it denies them democratic participation in determining their collective destiny. The loans are even conditional upon removing trade taxes and tariffs, thereby denying poor countries the right to protect their fledgling institutions and industries. This arrangement is doubly hypocritical: first world countries had always taken strict protectionist measures during crucial phases of their own industrial development, yet they deny this form of economic planning to countries that most need it. Furthermore, foreign investment most often generates foreign profits, and benefits only the elite—government, military, and corporate officials—of the debtor country because they are in a position to divert funds and to ignore the needs of the majority.

The racism internal to many countries also divides the elites from the majority along color lines, even if membership is determined more by class and income. In Latin America, for instance, the pecking order is *criollos* on top, the light-colored people who claim to be descended from purely European ancestry; then the *mestizos* of mixed heritage whose economic level and class-consciousness tends to influence whether they acknowledge their indigenous roots or identify with the elites; and at the bottom of the pyramid are the poor *mestizos*, the Native peoples and those of African descent. The most significant divide in this pyramid is the one separating the tiny minority at the top from everyone else. The elite in all countries are cosmopolitan: they shop, invest, and travel all over the world; they send their children to prestigious schools in the North/West; they hobnob with the rich and powerful of first world countries. All this creates a serious identity crisis with overwhelming consequences for their nations: they can completely disassociate themselves from their fellow citizens to the point of viewing them as sub-human work mules when they are compliant. When the majority does try to stand up for its rights, the elite views them as enemies and terrorists out to steal the elites' birthright to wealth and power.

Haiti's Debt Crisis: A Parable of Exploitation

The systemic indebtedness of the majority world is a crucial aspect of globalization and developmentalism. The latter is based on a disastrous mix of long-term debt and insidious structural adjustment programs that compromise sustainable, independent majority world economies. First World loans based on adherence to market principles that benefit its own interests are part of a deep-seated neo-colonial global structure that disempowers majority world economies. Much ado was made about cancellation of a small amount of majority world debt at the July 2005 G8 Summit at Gleneagles Scotland, with worldwide Live 8 musical/media events led by Bob Geldof and Bono of U2 creating a buzz of anticipation at the global level. Some $40 billion of debt for 18 countries, 14 of which were African, was cancelled. To put that in context, African debt alone stands at some $200 billion. Shortly after the agreement in September 2005, Britain was criticized for accepting a 1.7 billion pound debt repayment from Nigeria alone, more than the entire amount of aid Britain gives to Africa a year (Seager). The Gleneagles agreement has been compromised by lack of a timetable or, for that matter, a percentage-based structure for sharing out the cost of this payment among G8 members. At the time this book was going to press, reports were surfacing that indicated the likelihood that the agreement was at best going to be deferred, at worst cancelled altogether.

Majority world debt issues are extremely serious, but also entirely resolvable: 'spread over 20 years, the cost of canceling the debts of the 52 Jubilee 2000 countries is only one penny a day for each person in the industrialized world.' In 2000 it was estimated that 7 million children a year die as the result of the majority world debt crisis; the 52 indebted countries of the Jubilee 2000 with a population of over a billion people have a debt burden of close to $509 billion, an amount less than the total worth of the world's 21 wealthiest individuals; and had debt 'been canceled in 1997 for twenty of the poorest countries, the money released for basic healthcare could have saved the lives of about 21 million children by the year 2000, the equivalent of 19,000 children a

day' ('Third World Debt'). In 2005 Anup Shah, in the essay 'The Scale of the
Debt Crisis,' noted the following short history of increases in patterns of global
indebtedness:

- In 1970, the world's poorest countries (roughly 60 countries classified as
  low-income by the World Bank), owed $25 billion in debt. By 2002, this was
  $523 billion;

- For Africa: In 1970, it was just under $11 billion. By 2002, that was over half
  [of the amount owed by the 60 low-income countries as classified by the
  World Bank], to $295 billion;

- Debt owed to the multilateral institutions such as the IMF and World Bank
  is currently [2005] around $153 billion;

- For the poorest countries, debts to multilateral institutions are around $70
  billion;

- $550 billion has been paid in both principal and interest over the last three
  decades, on $540 billion of loans, and yet there is still a $523 billion debt
  burden.

These and other appalling statistics make the issue of debt a crucial locus for
addressing deep structures of global inequity.

Exploitation clearly underpins structures of debt, and the Haitian example is
particularly instructive for how it shows the profound hypocrisy and cynicism
that lie behind systemic majority world indebtedness. Yves Engler has pointed
out that 'According to the Haiti Support Group, "Haiti's debt to international financial institutions and foreign governments has grown from U.S.$302 million in
1980 to U.S.$1.134 billion [the CIA now estimates Haiti's debt to stand at
U.S.$1.2 billion]…About 40% of this debt stems from loans to the brutal Duvalier
(Papa and Baby Doc) dictators who invested precious little of it in the country.
This is known as 'odious debt' because it was used to oppress the people, and, according to international law, this debt need not be repaid." ' Furthermore, the colonial and political history surrounding Haiti's longstanding debt crisis is
instructive. Now one of the poorest countries in the world, Haiti was also the first
country in the Western hemisphere to gain short-lived independence from colonial oppression, and was home to the first successful slave revolution in history.
Beginning in 1825, some 22 years after gaining independence, Haiti was forced to
pay France 150 million francs or some U.S.$22 billion in today's purchasing
power to recompense former slave owners in France for their property 'losses.'

It gets worse than just this extraordinary spectacle of colonial pillage in which free men had to pay off the colonial power responsible for their former enslavement. Haiti, as shown by Yves Engler and Anthony Fenton, was also forced to enter into usurious agreements with French banks that lent them the money for the reparations and had to give preferential treatment to French commercial enterprises: 'Under the threat of invasion (12 warships armed with 500 cannons were sent) and exclusion from international commerce, the first payment of 30 million francs was made. In order to make this payment the government was forced to shut down every school in Haiti. Some have called this the very first structural adjustment program' (Engler and Fenton 103-04). The effects of this imposed colonial debt were immediate and long-lasting, and included the increased ruralization of the Haitian economy and culture, and a long-term debt situation in which 'late into the 19th century, payments to France consumed as much as 80% of Haiti's national budget' (ibid. 104). This has been a venal stain on the country that just a few short years before had coined the slogan *'Liberté, égalité, fraternité'* and that years later would welcome dictator Jean-Claude (Baby Doc) Duvalier.

Moreover, rights and social justice structures, always a question of re-source allocation, were profoundly affected with long-term damage wrought on structures of governance, education, and the like: in 2005 AI documented a range of abuses and violations in Haiti including extrajudicial killings by po-lice; torture and ill-treatment that included child victims; arbitrary and illegal arrests; inhuman prison conditions; death threats to human rights advocates; impunity for past rights abuses; and violence against women including gang rapes. In 2005 this sad litany was only an echo forward of the seeds sown by the economic pillage of Haiti. In 1947, 122 years after the first payment, the last payment was made to the U.S. who had bought the debt from France during its 1915-1934 occupation of Haiti. And adding to the historical irony of it all were the U.S. machinations that lay behind the toppling of Aristide's government, which further exacerbated the already serious rights situation in Haiti.

The structural damage to the Haitian economy caused by the debt, which effectively created a long-term form of economic slavery and vassalage, was in-calculable and is behind the ongoing social, cultural, and political crisis cur-rently in evidence in the country. Engler and Fenton argue that there is a clear tie-in between former President Jean-Bertrand Aristide's 2003 decision to seek reparations from France for the $22 billion it exacted from Haiti and the coup that deposed Aristide shortly thereafter, with the incoming unelected president (Gérard Latortue) declaring shortly after he took power that the claim for restitution was 'illegal, ridiculous' (104). One must ask how the historical amnesia that afflicts shallow analyses of the sources of Haiti's problems, so often reduced to a racialized and racist discourse of blame, is itself a global affliction that applies to other situations of global colonial exploitation. Until that memory is restored with some degree of honor and integrity on the part of the First World that has so benefited from these forms of colonial debt, rights and social justice outcomes for the poorest nations and people in the world will be seriously compromised. As part of this restoration we would include the elimination of majority world debt and the implementation of meaningful, reparative aid programs.

For the majority world, the right to development is unthinkable without the right to be free from unreasonable debt structures that are the result of colonial exploitation. The parable: until the First World acknowledges and takes concrete action on the deep historical structures of debt and inequitable economic abuse that have crippled the majority world, global structures of meaningful social justice will be impossible.

Imitating the First World Model: A Recipe for Global Extermination

If all countries did miraculously attain the level of cancerous growth, measured only in terms of the GNP (Gross National Product), the planet would be stripped bare of all resources, poisoned, and buried under a global garbage dump that would push it right over the brink of total collapse. Measuring a nation's well-being in terms of GNP is an extremely one-sided and myopic approach to development, and one that is designed to ignore all human rights. In fact, according to this indicator, all disasters can be tallied up in terms of business profits. As feminist economist Marilyn Waring argues, the GDP (Gross Domestic Product) adopted by the United Nations to measure and compare the economic well-being of countries 'counts oil spills and wars as contributors to economic growth, while child-rearing and housekeeping are deemed valueless' ('Marilyn Waring').

By the same token, the environment only counts in terms of how it is being used to create products, while the value of clean air to breathe, clean water to drink is not factored into a nation's well-being, even though they are crucial for human life. The darker side of this warped view of the world leads to corporations trying to convert air and water into products for sale, in direct contradiction of the commonsensical view that free access to the basics needed to sustain life is a fundamental human right. Finally, peace does not register on the GNP system of measure because it doesn't produce anything but happiness, the invisible grounds for healthy productivity, while war is great for business because it involves the production and sales of expensive weapons, and huge contracts for rebuilding bombed-out cities and national infrastructures afterwards.

Environmental Footprints: The Northern Sasquatch (from Eduardo Galeano's 'To Be Like Them')

'A few countries squander resources that belong to everyone. Crime and delirium of the society of waste: the richest 6 percent of humanity devours a third of all the energy and a third of all the natural resources consumed in the world. Statistical averages show that one North American consumes as much as fifty Haitians. Of course, such averages can't summon up a resident of Harlem or Baby Doc Duvalier, but it's still worth asking: What would happen if the fifty Haitians suddenly consumed as much as fifty North Americans? What would happen if the immense population of the South devoured the world with the voracious impunity of the North? What would happen if luxury goods and automobiles and refrigerators and TV sets and nuclear power plants and electrical generating stations proliferated in the South in such a crazy fashion? In ten years all the oil in the world would be used up. And what would happen to the climate, which is already close to collapse from global warming? What would happen to the land, the little bit left after erosion? And the water, which a fourth of humanity is already drinking contaminated by nitrates and pesticides and industrial waste laced with mercury and lead? What would happen? It wouldn't happen. We would have to move to another planet. This one, worn so thin already, couldn't handle it.

The precarious equilibrium of the world, which teeters on the brink of the abyss, depends on the perpetuation of injustice. The misery of many makes possible the extravagance of the few. For a few to continue consuming more, many must continue consuming less. And to make sure the many don't cross the line, the system multiplies the weapons of war. Incapable of fighting poverty, the system fights the poor, and its culture—dominant and militarized—blesses the violence of power.

The American way of life, founded on the right to waste, can be lived by dominant minorities in dominated countries. Its adoption en masse would be the collective suicide of humanity.

It's not possible. But would it be desirable?'

How does the UN respond to the contradiction Galeano describes? Numerous declarations and conventions filled with reasonable but very general recommendations have been drafted and signed: the United Nations Convention on Climate Change, the Convention on Biological Diversity (all but erased from the 2005 WTO documents), the Forest Principles, the Rio Declaration and the establishment of the Commission on Sustainable Development. These declarations are severely undercut when the most powerful country in the world, the biggest polluter and devourer of resources, refuses to sign, because co-operating with the rest of the world would diminish its privilege. Even if the U.S. did sign on, these documents on such basic and urgent measures as reducing emissions of climate-altering greenhouse gases are *not* legally binding.

The Right to Food: Opportunity or Binding Obligation?

Hunger cannot be measured in terms of how much food is available in the market, because it depends on a person's entitlement to food, but also to health care, education, safe drinking water, and adequate sanitation. According to the UN's *Human Development Report 2003*, there were 400 million hungry people in the world, and in many regions the situation has worsened. A 2005 report presented in Rome at a meeting of the Committee on World Food Security identifies 36 hunger hot spots in the world, 23 of them in Africa. The problem is neither food scarcity, nor overpopulation, though in some regions these factors do have an impact. War is now the leading cause of world hunger with the effects of HIV/AIDS and climate change not far behind (CBC News 'War leading cause of hunger').

The main problem is political in nature: If all the food produced worldwide were distributed equally, every person would be able to consume 2,760 calories a day (more than the needed amount, taking young children into account). To some, this might sound like a communist plot: how could all that food be distributed equitably around the globe? But people could actually grow more food to feed themselves if they weren't displaced by armed conflict or forced by structural adjustment plans and other international agreements to grow cash crops like coffee. Small-scale rural development projects to improve the production levels of farmers would keep huge numbers of people from flocking to urban centers where they lose control over feeding themselves and have no legal entitlement to food. Furthermore, the devastating effects of global warming are most acutely felt in drought-prone countries even though they are not the ones causing the large-scale pollution responsible for this global threat.

In response to the problem of world hunger, delegates from 182 nations met at the World Food Summit in Rome, Italy, in 2002. The U.S. was the only country to oppose the right to food and ended up having a nefarious effect on the drafting of the final document, after having refused to sign both the Final Declaration of the 1996 World Food Summit and the 1966 International Covenant on Economic, Social and Cultural Rights. The official U.S. position views world hunger as a business opportunity for bioengineering corporations, without any consideration for protecting biodiversity, not to mention the need for a precautionary approach to new technologies that may have adverse health effects and devastating impacts on the world's ecosystem due to cross-pollination from engineered crops. 'Opportunity' becomes the operative word in the U.S. arguments against viewing food as an entitlement both in terms of strengthening the arbitrary practices of the WB, IMF, and transnational corporations, and in terms of maintaining the vague and unenforceable wording of the Declaration of Human Rights, which recognizes only the *opportunity* to secure food, clothing, housing, medical care and necessary social services. Clearly when pitted against each other, the masters of the universe are better able to grab their opportunities than are the poor and hungry whose opportunity 'one might imagine, may be gained by purchasing lottery tickets at the local convenience store' (Rosset).

The Protection of Water Rights by Indigenous People around the World

It is telling that the mass media do little to inform people about one of the greatest looming disasters in human history: a water shortage that will inevitably result in massive death for all life forms dependent on this finite resource. Fuzzy understanding of ecology leads to vague assumptions that water is continually replenished through precipitation. In fact, fresh water equals less than one half of one percent of all the water on Earth and millions of people depend on aquifer pumping, a practice that depletes many of the last remaining reservoirs[3]: 'Fresh water is renewable only by rainfall, at a rate of 40-50,000 cubic kilometers per year' (Bigelow and Peterson 284). Currently more than 5 million people, mostly children, die every year from bad drinking water (ibid.), and more than 1 billion people lack access to safe drinking water. Like food, water could be a sustainable resource if only agricultural and industrial practices operated on sustainable methods. Yet 90 percent of the Earth's fresh water goes to industry: mostly high-tech manufacturing of such products as silicon chips, oil, and industrial agriculture. Instead of imagining ways to reverse this suicidal trajectory, many governments and global bureaucracies promote privatization and deregulation as solutions, thereby selling this most basic of human rights to corporations that ultimately will decide who gets water based on who can pay. Existing trade agreements like 'NAFTA and the WTO already define water as a "commodity" and have rules that require governments to permit water exports under certain conditions' (ibid.). This is in direct contradiction of the General Comment agreed upon in November 2002 by the United Nations Committee on Economic, Cultural and Social Rights, which declared that the 'human right to water entitles everyone to sufficient, safe, acceptable physically and affordable water for personal and domestic use' ('Water for health enshrined as a human right').[4] Furthermore, the same declaration unequivocally states that 'Water is fundamental for life and health. The human right to water is indispensable for leading a healthy life in human dignity. It is a pre-requisite to the realization of all other human rights' (ibid.).

Chile and Bolivia are two of the countries where governments have privatized water thereby making access prohibitively expensive to their own citizens, especially in the case of their impoverished indigenous populations. Despite (or given) the fact that Chile's government under Pinochet was a fascist dictatorship, such a neo-liberal agenda was openly embraced and the resulting 1981 Water Code stipulated that water is a commodity, or 'tradable good,' and that people had to register their right to water with the state. This policy especially threatened indigenous Mapuche communities whose territory actually contains 98 percent of the source and trajectory of water. The concept of selling this precious resource is so alien to most indigenous people that it came as a shock to them to find out that governments had withheld information from them on how legally to register their rights to water in their *own* communities.

In the case of Bolivia, this affront to indigenous conceptions of communal holdings of resources led to violent conflict. The WB was fully implicated in turning over 'the management of the Cochabamba city water and sewage system to a single-bidder concession of international water corporations in 1999-2000. Under the arrangement, which was to last for 40 years, water prices increased immediately from negligible rates to approximately 20 percent of monthly family incomes. Citizens' protests were eventually met with an armed military response that left at least six residents dead. The protests continued until the consortium was forced to flee the country' (Lutz 'Indigenous Peoples and Water Rights' 13). The outrageousness of the situation in Cochabamba entailed Bechtel, the company involved, attempting to tax farmers for rainwater they freely collected from the sky and water bills for the poor going up by extraordinary amounts (60 to 90 percent).

Similarly, in Kerala, India, the town of Plachimada put a stop to the hydropiracy of the Coca-Cola plant that had contaminated groundwater wells with waste and had dramatically lowered the water table as a result of extracting 1.5 million liters per day. Coca-Cola's operations caused serious health hazards via water contamination and radically transformed access to the precious resource, with women having to walk miles to get clean water due to the 'drought-aggravated' water crisis. Public interest litigation, which is based on fundamental rights principles that limit private and commercial ownership of key public resources (like air, water, seeds, forests, and so forth), was used to put an end to the corporation's exploitation of Plachimada's water resources, but only after a concerted effort by local women that led to much wider alliances with national and international activists.[5]

Indigenous communities, whether in India or Bolivia, do not limit their agency to simply protesting these abuses. In Latin America, they put forward water reforms through a strategy called '*protesta con propuesta*' [protest with counter-proposals] emphasizing the community-based, social, and economic aspects of water. These local efforts to reverse decisions that would make water a luxury commodity are blossoming into multilateral, international solidarity networks that further strengthen the power of the sane. A good example of this is the 'Water Law and Indigenous Rights Program (WALIR), [which] began analyzing local water management systems and water rights in Andean countries in relation to official legislation. WALIR consists of academic partners in Bolivia, Chile, Ecuador, Peru, Mexico, France, the Netherlands, and the United States; NGOs; water users' federations; and grassroots movements' (Boelens and de Vos 20).

Water issues are not limited to poor countries, and the case brought against their own government by aboriginals living in the U.S. makes it clear that people must struggle to defend these most basic rights issues within the boundaries of the wealthiest nations. On 7 January 2006, the International Indian Treaty Council (on behalf of the Pit River Tribe of Northern California, the Yupik City of Gambell, the Gambell Common Council, and The Alaska Community Action on Toxics) submitted a formal Human Rights Complaint against the U.S. to the Special Rapporteur on the Right to Food of the UN Commission on Human Rights.[6] Fish is the traditional food of these people, but EPA and other environmental reports warn women of child-bearing age that 'one in six women in America have unsafe levels of mercury in their bodies and more than one in three children are at risk from mercury exposure in the womb. If a pregnant woman in the U.S. eats two meals of six ounces of fish...every week, there is a 50/50 chance that her child will get a harmful dose of methyl mercury' (Saldamando 26-27). These cases highlight the connections between dangerous contamination and the prevalent practice of environmental racism. Abandoned mines leaching mercury into water, various contaminants produced by oil corporations, the dumping of military toxins, and the results of weapons testing all conglomerate on lands inhabited primarily by aboriginal and other economically disadvantaged people, but the case of Northern California also shows that contamination traveling by water knows no boundaries.

Displaced and Dispossessed: The Rights of Migrants

Never before in history have so many people been forced to leave their regions to escape poverty, famine, war, and political and ethnic persecution. According to the UN, approximately one out of 35 people live outside of their country as refugees or migrants. This amounts to 175 million migrants worldwide, comparable to the entire population of Brazil. From the perspective of international trade, migrants are economic entities to be moved around to suit the needs of corporations, businesses, and individuals who benefit from their cheap labor. The flow of migration is represented hypocritically by mainstream media as a threat to livelihoods, security, and even white supremacy within first world countries, as if their economies weren't built on the backs of cheap laborers.

The UN General Assembly addressed the dehumanization of so many people in 1990, in the form of the UN Migrant Workers Convention, which stipulates that migrants are entitled to the same political, economic, and social rights as all human beings. Migrants are often represented as vagrants who invade countries that enjoy social services, in order to take advantage of welfare benefits to which they should not be entitled. The media disseminates this misconception to keep the unemployed and disenfranchised citizens of first world countries from examining the real causes of their own diminishing rights and incomes. The truth of the matter is very different: far from expecting handouts, migrants are people who are helping themselves and each other, and have the largest impact on global well-being. Even the IMF estimates that migrants send more than $70 billion a year in the form of remissions to their families. 'This capital flow, which gets directly to people in need, is greater than all governmental aid to developing nations' (Heartland Alliance for Human Needs and Human Rights).

The hypocrisy is further entrenched in the split between the sender countries that have ratified the UN Migrant Workers Convention, and the receiver countries—including the U.S.—that see more benefit in denying migrant rights, and have predictably refused to sign.

Free Trade Zones for Corporations/Indentured Servitude for Workers

Maquila and sweatshop workers around the world testify about the abysmal working conditions to which they are subjected, and strive to organize themselves in order to stop the human rights abuses regularly occurring in the Free Trade Zones. The fact that most of these workers are women, often in countries where there is widespread acceptance of sexism, plays a role in how parasitic corporations choose the host countries with the most vulnerable workforces. Applicants to these jobs are grilled with questions that break all the rules normally protecting people from discrimination: they are asked if they are married, pregnant, or nursing. They are often forced to take a pregnancy test on the spot. Preference is given to single young women, and even those who get pregnant after being hired are limited to two short bathroom breaks on which they are often accompanied by a supervisor. All this occurs during shifts that last 12-16 hours, which many workers spend on their feet the whole time. The wages they receive, for what seems like internment in a labor camp, barely cover rent and food.

In the northern Mexico *maquila* zones, companies sometimes give workers corrugated metal and scraps of wood and cardboard, expecting them to hammer together their own lean-tos to live in. On the factory floors, workers are constantly harassed to speed up production, increasing the danger of injury. Loud music is often blasted at them all day/night long and they are given amphetamines to encourage a frenzied pace. Workers are often subjected to toxic compounds and fumes with minimal safety equipment, under the supervision of higher-ups with no training in such matters, whose role is simply to harass (often sexually) and threaten workers.

An investigation by the *Guardian* into gangmaster culture—that is, the labor agencies that control the conditions of employment for foreign workers in the UK—came to the conclusion that 'Supermarkets, catering chains and processing plants...[operate] a system dependent on subcontracted labour that permits not only the abuse and underpayment of foreign workers, but also identity fraud, large-scale tax avoidance, benefit fraud, crime and violence' (Lawrence).

This finding occurred in spite of the Morecambe Bay, Lancashire, tragedy where 23 Chinese cockle pickers in the UK died as a result of illegal employment practices in February 2004. Gangmaster culture has insured, in Felicity Lawrence's words, that foreign workers 'are effectively operating outside civic society.' The rights, in other words, of vulnerable workers are often trampled upon in the space between legal and national cultures, where so much business gets done on the basis of exploitative practices that contravene rights covenants.

Migration from Mexico and Central America to the U.S. has created a veritable 'low-impact' war zone along the 2,000-mile border, resulting so far in about one migrant dead for every mile. Operation Gate Keeper (and its many versions depending on what segment of the border/time line we consider) reinforces what would be the safest points to cross, thereby forcing people to take greater risks by crossing through arid wilderness where they often perish from dehydration. In countries where human rights do not even play a minor role in how migrants are treated, death can come at the abusive hands of employers, who are not held accountable. As documented in the film *Modern Heroes Modern Slaves* that tells the stories of Sarah Balabagan and Flor Contemplacion, various nations (mostly Arab) send an estimated (low) 700 body bags a year through to a potential (high) 40 a week back to the Philippines, containing the remains of Filipina nannies and maids beaten to death or otherwise mistreated.[7] Even in the so-called democracies of the receiver countries, a report by The Regional Network of Civil Organizations on Migration cites arbitrary arrest, indefinite detention, inconsistent access to health care, and poor physical conditions in detention centers, and a lack of due process guarantees during the deportation process.

Labor Rights in the New World Order

Human rights abuses in the sphere of labor are not limited to any geographical region. The division between First and Third Worlds (not to mention the Second World, usually referring to the former Eastern bloc countries) is overly simplistic, especially when it comes to discussing labor rights and abuses. Citizens of the wealthiest countries are indoctrinated to believe that their democracies are legally bolstered by extensive rights documents that protect the individual. Looking at just the U.S. and Canada, the documents, labor codes and laws are certainly there in writing, and go back several decades: 'In 1938, at the height of the Great Depression, Congress passed legislation to prevent employers from exploiting the nation's most vulnerable workers. The Fair Labor Standards Act established the first federal minimum wage. It also imposed limitations on child labor. And it mandated that employees who work more than forty hours a week be paid overtime wages for each additional hour. The overtime wage was set at a minimum of one and a half times the regular wage' (Schlosser 73). These terms are identical in the Canadian Labour Code, so what happened?[8]

Whether examining the fast food and meat-packing industries dependent on migrant workers and the most disenfranchised citizens of Northern countries, or classy, high-profile advertising firms in major cities, we find that employers routinely break all the basic labor regulations, both at the national and global levels. In the garment industry, a U.S. Department of Labor survey found ' "the overall level of compliance with the minimum wage, overtime and child labor requirements of the Fair Labor Standards Act is 33 percent"—in other words, 67 percent of the garment industry workplaces did not comply with the law. Such systemic unlawfulness is not unique to the garment industry, however. Corporate illegalities are rife throughout the economy' (Bakan 75).

In jobs in which salary and benefits are calculated on an hourly basis, managers systematically ensure that workers do not get a full forty-hour week, in order to rob them of benefits. In higher paying white-collar jobs, however, where salary is calculated on an annual basis, employees are expected to work as long as it takes to get the job done. This often involves working more than eight hours a day and even on weekends, facilitated by home-use of computers, email, and other communication technologies that blur the boundaries between work and every other aspect of life. Even well educated people who are reasonably well informed about government and the legal system accept this violation of their own rights, buying into the work ethos (because an ethic it isn't!) that the company's profits and the shareholders' interests completely obliterate their own human rights as workers.

How the rights of minimum wage earners are violated is somewhat easier to understand: obviously the most vulnerable workers feel intimidated by management because they know that they are dispensable—easily replaced by people who won't 'make trouble' by asking that their rights be respected. But when it comes to skilled office workers relinquishing their rights without complaining, there are clearly some powerful ideological constraints at work, so effectively disseminated through media that erasing laws and human rights becomes naturalized. A comparative study of indigenous workers in Latin America and workers in Pittsfield, Massachusetts reveals that despite having more formal education, the U.S. workers are far more accepting of having their rights violated than their poor and often illiterate Latin American counterparts. This is because many Americans, regardless of their class/income status, have internalized the self-interest of the elite as the only explanation of how the world works.

American anthropologist June Nash notes that Bolivian miners who were laid off organized the March for Life to oppose the closing of mines in 1986, were highly critical of IMF-imposed plans that undermined nationalist solutions, and stood firm on their right to grow coca as a new source of income. In stark contrast: 'although General Electric workers have experienced in their own lives the movement of capital overseas and the destruction of the industrial base, I found a lower level of consciousness of their interdependence in the global system than in Bolivia. In interviews of a few laid-off workers in 1991 the majority justified the reduction in employment and layoffs of thousands in terms of the decline in profit' (xviii). Nash goes on to observe that in Pittsfield, the only workers who organized to fight for their rights were the most marginalized, those working in competitive firms (as opposed to corporations), mostly women, many of whom were single mothers. Canadian historian and novelist Ronald Wright asserts that 'hope, like greed, fuels the engine of capitalism' and quotes John Steinbeck as saying that 'socialism never took root in America because the poor see themselves not as an exploited proletariat but as temporarily embarrassed millionaires…nowhere does the myth of progress have more fervent believers' (123-4).

How Much Say Do We Have in Our Governments' Trade and Investment Decisions?

In Western media, articles marveling at Chinese entrepreneurship and transnational buying power also express a barely veiled fear reminiscent of Medieval Europe's terror of Mongol hordes and its U.S. manifestation in the form of laws passed in 1889 to prevent the 'yellow peril.' Many more articles focus on China's changing and growing economy than on its record of war crimes, crimes against humanity, genocide, mass murder, enslavement, and systematic torture. Though China committed all these crimes in Tibet, as did 'Indonesia in East Timor and, in its past, in Bali and Java…China is certainly not alone in its human rights violations and crimes against humanity' (McMurtry 234-5). Given the anti-communist thrust of Western media, most people nevertheless have heard about serious rights abuses in China, and even those Western politicians who most fervently promote trade with China must speak to that public knowledge. They handle this by insisting that trade is a vehicle for democratizing totalitarian regimes.

This simplistic, paternalistic notion is based on the assumptions that global trading regimes are truly democratic, and that our goodness will rub off on the Chinese once the dynamics of free market trading force them to be more like us.

This is assuming a lot, especially when global trade has less to do with truly democratic principles and more to do with how managed democracies can maximize profit for a small elite. Why wouldn't the same recipe for salvation work for Cuba then? Why do powerful democracies impose trade sanctions on some countries to punish them, while they welcome other countries into the brotherhood of democratic capitalists in hopes of reforming them? Clearly, China knows how to play the game that Cuba is not willing to engage in quite so wholeheartedly.

China has opened the floodgates to foreign investment and massive corporate penetration. This, despite the fact that China executes approximately 5,000 to 12,000 people annually (more than the rest of the world combined), many of them belonging to ethnic minorities, led out directly from their 'trials' (often presided over not by a judge, but by a state official who has little or no legal training) to the execution grounds, making any appeal process impossible. There are over 65 crimes that are punishable by death including tax fraud, bribery, and vandalism. There is mounting evidence that capital punishment in China is becoming a lucrative business in the trade of human organs, and that the victim is killed in a medically controlled way to cause the least impact on the targeted organ, usually sold to a wealthy foreign patient awaiting the transplant in a nearby hospital.

Presenting his findings before the Subcommittee on International Operations and Human Rights, Michael E. Parmly, Principal Deputy Assistant Secretary of State, warned that 'the lack of transparency in the Chinese criminal justice system, the secrecy that surrounds prison executions, and the removal of organs make actual documentation of the practice impossible. However, the anecdotal and circumstantial evidence regarding the practice of removing organs from executed prisoners for sale to foreigners and wealthy Chinese is substantial, credible, and growing' (1). Harry Wu, the Chinese human rights activist 'and others claim that the Chinese Government takes organs from 2,000 executed prisoners a year. That number is growing because the list of capital crimes in China has been expanded to accommodate the demand for organs' (Scheper-Hughes 'Organ Trade' 4). This cynical business practice has led scholars and politicians worldwide to speculate that the number of prisoners executed will keep increasing in accordance with the profit principle of this death industry.

From the perspective of the consumer who does not want to be complicit in human rights violations, it is often impossible to avoid buying a product made in China. Try finding an electric beater that is not. Even if you manage to, thereby scoring a small personal victory, you are complicit with massive rights violations through your country's involvement in transnational trade agreements that are not compliant with international law.

A similar ethical bind plagues citizens whose governments invest millions of dollars of our taxes and pension plan contributions into industries that we may oppose: 'through the Canada Pension Plan (CPP), millions of working Canadians are now being forced to invest their retirement savings in the top four prime contractors for Star Wars 'Missile Defense,' namely Boeing, Lockheed Martin, Raytheon and TRW (owned by Northrop Grumman, [which has more than 125,000 employees, and operations in all 50 states and 25 countries]. These four corporations are estimated to have received about 60% to 70% of all the contracts for so-called "Missile Defense." All four rank within the top five U.S. weapons contractors. CPP investments in the "Big Four" were worth about $20 million as of September 30, 2004 (the latest figures available from CPP Investment Board, CPPIB)'(Sanders).

Throughout this book, we underline that rights declarations and conventions are in the majority not legally binding and are difficult to enforce. Labor laws, on the other hand, are legally binding yet business (including government) has found countless ways of violating workers' rights. Transnational corporations have worked very hard to squash labor unions and have succeeded to a large extent. The rise of enormous corporations in all areas of business, the concentration of power in so few hands, and the freedom to pick up and move across borders if expected to comply with national laws, all make it that much easier to enforce new business practices based on 'the pathological pursuit of profit and power' (Bakan). And in the contexts we describe in this section, it is worth remembering that the International Labor Organization 'estimates that approximately two million workers lose their lives annually due to occupational injuries and illnesses, with accidents causing at least 350,000 deaths a year. For every fatal accident, there are an estimated 1,000 non-fatal injuries, many of which result in lost earnings, permanent disability and poverty. The death toll at work, much of which is attributable to unsafe working practices, is the equivalent of 5,000 workers dying each day, three persons every minute' (Kick 90).

Fostering Labor Rights through Fair Trade and Solidarity Networking

Those who believe that smaller is better can still promote genuine local development around the globe through communications that are both democratic and globalized. The Internet is a virtual battleground when it comes to organizations promoting their often diametrically opposed versions of civil liberty and security, for instance. The Zapatista uprising in response to NAFTA as the last straw after over 500 years of oppression has been called the first postmodern revolution, in large part due to the Zapatistas' technological savvy in disseminating their views around the world through the Internet. The communiqués sent electronically to major newspapers, world leaders, and other oppressed groups and individuals not only contradicted everything published by the main Mexican press, but did so in a way that left little doubt as to which side was being truthful and justified in its actions.

This is the beauty of self-expression (in this case collective) and being able to voice your own story instead of being misrepresented by state and corporate power through their mouthpiece: mainstream media. The Zapatistas were also effective in drawing attention to how local farmers and the environment are destroyed by large agribusinesses and the trade agreement that brought the Mexican economy to total collapse. One of their many initiatives to improve their own lot without government intervention and international development aid (which of course they don't qualify for since they are branded by the mainstream media as terrorists or insurgents) is to engage in fair trade. Many indigenous groups have turned the disadvantages associated with having to grow cash crops such as coffee and cocoa into a sustainable and equitable livelihood by networking with international organizations that market fair trade products and guarantee a stable minimum price to farmers regardless of market and weather conditions. These democratic trading practices are not culture-specific and are spreading throughout all regions of the world with such initiatives as community-supported agriculture.

Globalization-from-below movements everywhere network to promote direct action, participatory democracy, and equitable trade. So far, the positive results of these efforts are far more tangible than all the good intentions expressed in the UN Global Compact whose ten principles (sound familiar?) attempt to put a human face on globalization. The ten principles, spanning human rights, labor standards, environment, and anti-corruption, contradict the most cherished profit-making practices of transnational corporations, and therefore are unlikely to be embraced by them.

Vandana Shiva sums up how many global citizens view the current state of affairs, which implicates governments and transnational corporations: 'The bankruptcy of the dominant world order is leading to social, ecological, political and economic non-sustainability, with societies, ecosystems and economies disintegrating and breaking down' ('The Living Democracy Movement' 115). These indicators of imminent disaster are more meaningful to the majority than are stock market indicators measuring the profits of a tiny minority. But since most media are owned by parent companies in the business of transnational trade, media aggressively mediates a world that denies the experiences of the majority, substituting them with fictions of progress. Governments have shown themselves to be so deeply complicit with these fictions that many people are re-thinking their relationship to the state, and what it means to be a citizen subjected to the state (which in turn is subjected to transnational trade regimes). A local, but globally representative example of how governments support transnational corporations instead of their own citizens can be seen in how the Canadian government and Canadian military industries scratch each others' backs in the form of donations of millions of dollars to each other (Coalition to Oppose the Arms Trade [COAT]).

Members of civil society are also coming to realize that peace, justice, and sustainability are interdependent, yet systematically compromised by governments in tandem with transnational corporations. And people everywhere (except in mainstream media) are coming to the conclusion that the future of all life on earth depends on global solidarity movements aimed at creating/sustaining cultural formations that are radically different from the one dictated by the new world order. 'We are diverse—women and men, adults and youth, indigenous peoples, rural and urban, workers and unemployed, homeless, the elderly, students, migrants, professionals, peoples of every creed, colour and sexual orientation. The expression of this diversity is our strength and the basis of our unity. We are a global solidarity movement, united in our determination to fight against the concentration of wealth, the proliferation of poverty and inequalities, and the destruction of the earth. We are living and constructing alternative systems, and using creative ways to promote them.' (Fisher and Ponniah 'Social Movements' Manifesto' 346).

While the scope of these numerous movements makes them sound abstract—especially since they are never validated on TV or through other forms of corporate media—it is important to remember that they are made up of people working locally and networking globally to promote diversity and justice, most often in specific contexts.

The G8 summit meetings held behind closed doors, protected by barricades crowned with razor wire, and guarded by Terminator Droids are pathetically dwarfed by democratic meetings such as the World Social Forum (WSF) and the popular meetings at which the majority shares common concerns, against and alongside every official meeting held to plot their oppression.

Envisioning Global Well-being Based on the Fulfillment of Human Rights

The most positive aspect of globalization is that it has facilitated some forms of democratic communication allowing people to see beyond their own immediate circumstances. It used to be a common argument to say that criticizing Western privilege by Westerners was hypocritical because we all enjoy the standard of living and freedoms that capitalism affords us. This argument inevitably condemns people to regimes of truth: socialism vs. capitalism, or more narrow partisan politics: liberal vs. conservative, democrat vs. republican. The collapse of the Soviet bloc has reduced the viability of this reductive mindset. But more importantly, since people are becoming aware of how their privilege depends on others being exploited and denied their human rights, another concept of citizenship is starting to emerge. On the one hand, the citizens of the richest countries cannot deny their inevitable complicity with the structures that make our lives so easy. But that consciousness of complicity need not lead to cynicism or abjection. Once people move from identifying only with their nation and think of themselves as global citizens, the old dichotomy of 'us' versus 'them' starts to open up to new possibilities along with the borders across which democratic ideas and practices can then flow.

The 2004 Nobel Peace Laureate, Wangari Maathai, is a Kenyan woman and founder of the Green Belt Movement who focuses on women and children, since women are the primary caretakers of the environment and their families. While women's work tends to be devalued or completely ignored by conventional economics, Maathai makes it clear that their 'domestic' duties include subsistence farming, and that they are the first members of many rural communities to notice environmental degradation because it impacts directly on their access to firewood, clean water, balanced diets, shelter and income. The fact that the Norwegian Nobel Committee explicitly links environment to democracy and peace in the granting of this award is important for bringing global attention to Maathai's insights. These include how international economic arrangements are unjust and connected to bad governance in debtor countries as well as a lack of democratic space at both national and global levels. Her work also connects the dots between deforestation, climatic instability, and contamination in soil and water (usually resulting from bad national governance prompted by international economic institutions) and how this all contributes to excruciating poverty. The Green Belt Movement in Africa, which by 1997 had planted over 20 million trees *that survived*, is committed to cultural biodiversity, especially with respect to indigenous seeds and medicinal plants, thereby giving a global voice to those who oppose corporate patenting, bioengineering, and BigPharma monopolizing of local cultural knowledge regarding food and health (Maathai).

In the area of economics, the GNP is losing currency in favor of a more humane and inclusive system of measurement: the Genuine Progress Index which takes into account sustainability, well-being and quality of life, and social and natural capital. The GPI assigns value to assets like population health, educational attainment, community safety, voluntary work, and environmental quality. This technical change in how statistics are gathered also indicates a fundamental paradigm shift with global repercussions. While the GNP ignores the violation of human rights, these are necessarily registered on the Genuine Progress Index. The UN has adopted this system of measurement, together with the Human Development Index, which still nonetheless relies heavily on GDP.

But again, until governments and international funding bodies also base their decisions on the most inclusive indicators, development will continue to benefit corporations at the expense of the majority of the population and the environment. In the end, no amount of money will save the few wealthy pockets of population once our global life-support system is exhausted, and unable to provide clean air, water, and food. That is the true bottom line.

Notes
1. The new expansive definition of 'expropriation' currently used by corporations is a legacy of the Reagan administration, and for several decades has been the political project of a well-organized corporate movement known as the 'takings movement' or 'takings project.' 'Under Reagan, right-wing judges and lawyers used a series of Supreme Court cases to redefine the meaning of the "takings clause" in the Fifth Amendment of the U.S. Constitution. This clause reads: "...nor shall private property be taken for public use without just compensation." By applying an expanded definition of "private property" and "taking," it was ruled that government regulations which limited the commercial value of investment projects or restricted profit earnings could be treated as acts of expropriation' (Greenfield 3-4).

2. Dr. Vandana Shiva founded the Research Foundation for Science, Technology and Ecology in Dehra Dun, Uttar Pradesh, India, in 1982. As the site's homepage states, the Foundation works on biodiversity conservation and protecting people's rights from threats to their livelihoods and environment by centralized systems of monoculture in forestry, agriculture and fisheries. For reports on community defense of human rights see the Navdanya site run by Shiva.

3. According to a report by The Kerr Center on the Ogallala Aquifer (underlying approximately 225,000 sq. miles in the Great Plains region of the U.S.: the High Plains of Texas, New Mexico, Oklahoma, Kansas, Colorado, and Nebraska), 'The abuse of the Ogallala Aquifer for the last thirty years together with the wasteful depletion of soil symbolized by the Dust Bowl, matched by the decline of America's historic independent farmer, signals that today's conventional farming cannot continue indefinitely into the future' (28).

4. A General Comment 'is an interpretation of the provisions of the International Covenant on Economic, Social and Cultural Rights' ('Water for health enshrined as a human right'). In this case, the declarations of the General Comment meant that the 145 countries to have ratified the Covenant 'will now be compelled to progressively ensure that everyone has access to safe and secure drinking water and sanitation facilities—equitably and without discrimination' (ibid.).

5. Public interest litigation is predicated on natural rights shared by all life forms: 'to share in nature's wealth, to ensure sustenance—food and water, ecological space, and evolutionary freedom' (Shiva *Earth Democracy* 62). For a more complete description of what happened at Plachimada, see Shiva's *Earth Democracy*, 168-72.

6. One of the details of the Complaint to the United Nations Rapporteur states that 'approximately 26,000,000 pounds of mercury were used in gold ore recovery in Northern California, mostly in the Sierra Nevada and the Klamath-Trinity Mountain areas...Clear Lake, the traditional homeland to Pomo Indian fishing communities, contains 100 tons of mercury alone' (Saldamando 28).

7. Gina Mission, a writer/reporter living in the Philippines, states: 'Some 700 workers, mostly women, die each year following mistreatment by their employers, according to recent figures released by the Filipino House of Representatives Committee on Overseas Foreign Workers. But women activists say the mortality figure is likely to be even higher. An anonymous source at Ninoy Aquino International Airport says that 40 foreign workers arrive home in coffins each week. Most cases of death and abuse against female overseas workers occur in Arab countries.'

8. 'Since 1919, 183 international conventions on labor have been signed. According to the International Labor Organization of these, France has ratified 115, Norway 106, Germany 76 and the U.S. ...14. The country at the head of globalization follows only its own rules, making sure that its corporations can operate with impunity in their hunt for cheap labor and their conquest of territories which their dirty industries can contaminate at whim' (Galeano, 'Los derechos de los trabajadores' [Workers' Rights']).

Chapter 3

All Human Beings Are Equal: The Commonality Of Minority And Majority Rights

The perceived conflict between minority and majority rights is often used to obscure the ways in which social justice is unevenly distributed globally. While there are many points of disagreement between Western and majority world concepts of human rights and dignity, the polarization of individual and majority rights clouds the real issues. The rights of women and children—the majority of world population—do not infringe on the rights of indigenous people, gay, lesbian, bisexual, and transgender people, disabled people, refugees and immigrants—all considered minorities. When any of these people's rights are violated or abused, the resolution to such injustice must be guided by the basic principle that all human beings are equal in their diversity.

Given the concise format of this book, it is impossible to devote chapters to each group whose rights are systematically violated in specific ways. We do not want to bracket these groups' rights, thereby giving the impression that they are marginal, or special interest lobbies, as the elite like to label dissenting voices. It is also important to understand that individuals cannot be reduced to one isolated aspect of their being, even when discrimination tends to stereotype and target people in this way. We tend to view these groupings as such because numerous documents and working groups address specific rights in order to target them more effectively: the Convention on the Rights of the Child (ratified November 1989), the International Convention on the Elimination of All Forms of Discrimination Against Women (CEDAW) and the Optional Protocol to CEDAW (December 2000), the

International Covenant on Economic, Social and Cultural Rights (1966), the UN
Working Group on Indigenous Peoples (1993), Draft Declaration on the Rights of
Indigenous Peoples (expired without ratification on December 31, 2004), and the
UN Permanent Forum on Indigenous Issues.

In practice, many of the issues addressed in human rights covenants and
conventions overlap. What most of these groups, including lesbians, gays, bisexuals and transgender people (LGBT) share is that they are marginalized by
an elite, predominantly made up of powerful men who erect their privilege over
everyone else's rights. Admittedly, the groups identified in this way are diverse
and when their problems and interests are reduced to political agendas these
are bound to exclude and to clash: indigenous women and queer natives are
struggling against male supremacists within their own local cultures, on top of
those dominating the global elite. A boy child may be subjected to paternal
abuse, and simultaneously initiated into sexual dominance to later take on his
father's role and privileged position. A gay man can 'pass' for straight or just
'neutral Man' and choose to reap the benefits of male supremacy on certain occasions, even if this involves hurtful suppression of his rights and desires.
Conservative and fundamentalist women attack reproductive rights and other
freedoms sought by their sisters, and so on.

Human rights cannot be reduced to a numbers game in which majority interests override all others' rights. For example, even if heterosexual people make up
the majority of the world population, this fact should not have a negative impact
on defending sexual diversity rights; equality does not mean sameness and must
be defended in relation to diversity first and foremost. The 'moral majority' is a
dangerous concept; it is misleading to assume that large masses of people are in
agreement on every aspect of an issue, even if a consensus is perceived and represented by the media or by politicians. Furthermore, large masses of people can be
misinformed and manipulated by various institutions and mass media. Liberal
democracies conceive of freedom based on the individual, yet when it is conve-
nient to exclude, marginalize, or scapegoat a certain group of people, the idea of
consensus is invoked. The same way in which 'minority' group platforms narrow
down their members' identity to focus on a single aspect, the concept of 'majority'
also erases the undeniable differences among individuals perceived as belonging
to the majority on any given issue.

A concrete example of the hypocrisy of denying individual rights on the
basis of perceived majority beliefs can be examined in the debates around
same-sex marriage. When in the former Eastern bloc individual rights were

trampled on in favor of majority rights, the West interpreted this injustice as the tyranny of the masses. But now in Canada and elsewhere, some politicians are ignoring the fundamental concept of equality, arguing that the majority of their constituents are opposed to same-sex marriage. If the majority of their constituents expressed a preference for living in all-white communities and thereby banished people of color beyond their gates, would that form of exclusion be viewed as democratic? In dealing with human rights and minorities, politicians' pandering to majority bias is not democratic, but rather is analogous to how corporations violate human rights on the basis of benefiting shareholders at the expense of larger principles.

The notion of 'majority' hides many different forms of power dynamics and inequality, the most obvious one being men's supremacy. The privileged circle of powerful men that divvy up power on a global scale can include token members whose communities are marginalized: that is the meaning and power of hegemony, which is what binds a society together without the use of force. The political dominance of the patriarchal elite is perceived as natural, or is not perceived at all. Majority rule is the myth that obscures the fact that small elites made up of men hold most of the power in the world: the power to make decisions that affect the lives of every inhabitant of the planet. Decisions to provoke wars, to invade countries, to allot huge portions of national budgets to war or military instead of to social programs, to pollute the environment. Even though virtually all politicians, world leaders, CEOs, and bankers are men, gender identity usually goes unnoticed when discussing the worst problems plaguing the earth.

While the elitist power of men is the most pervasive expression of privilege in every country in the world, the word 'patriarchy' rings abstract and theoretical, like a specialized term used only by academic feminists. Privilege and power extends to manipulating and purging language of words that incriminate the elite: 'What can such a word as "human" mean when its collaboration with "man" and "men" throughout the history of *man*kind has become obvious?' The masculinist concept of 'human' would have us believe that ' "*he*," as an unqualified generic pronoun, can be used correctly to include "*she*"...Imagine a world of *yang* and *yang* instead of *yin* (the female principle) and *yang* (the male principle)—a concept which in China never offers two absolute oppositions—and you will have the inhuman (hu)man-constructed world of Frankenstein' (Trinh 66-7). The global hegemony of patriarchy is just such a world with profound implications for how those who are not part of its immediate interests are treated inequitably.

Human Rights and Sexuality

Reducing Women to Their Bodies

> Women constitute half of the population of every country. To disre-
> gard women and bar them from active participation in political, so-
> cial, economic and cultural life would in fact be tantamount to
> depriving the entire population of every society of half its capability.
> The patriarchal culture and the discrimination against women, par-
> ticularly in the Islamic countries, cannot continue for ever.
> —Shirin Ebadi, Nobel Peace Prize Lecture, Oslo, December 10, 2003

Ebadi's assertion that approximately 50 percent of every country's population is
female is becoming inaccurate especially in India and China (though not limited
to these countries), where sex-determination tests are used to target female fe-
tuses for abortion. Where such technology is inaccessible, newborn girls are often
simply killed, drowned in a bucket of water like unwanted kittens. This practice,
observed primarily in China, also resulted from the state restriction on reproductive rights, stipulating one child per couple, which for economic and traditionally
misogynistic reasons translated into a preference that the one child be a son. According to Vandana Shiva, this form of systemic violence rooted in patriarchy is
being exacerbated by globalization. In the past, and in the least 'developed' or
globalized regions today, women were and still are productive community members, often the primary farmers practicing sustainable agriculture. Once the ecological approach to farming is replaced by globalized agribusiness using
chemicals and heavy machinery on large monoculture farms, men take over and
women are socially devalued and seen as a burden. Demographic statistics show
that there are 60 million 'missing' women in the world, and that half of them are
Indian, as a result of the growing business in female feticide.

The dowry system in India grew out of this change of women's status
from productive family member to burden. Previously the groom's family paid
a 'bride price,' wealth that stayed in the hands of women, but now the tables
have turned and the bride's family pays to get rid of her, and is often extorted
for additional payments that they are unable to make. This misogynistic practice results in more than 5,000 Indian women becoming victims of dowry
deaths annually. The money is no longer an investment in women's productivity and sustainable community management, but is squandered on luxury
consumer goods by the groom's family, thereby destroying the foundations of
community, sustainability, and threatening the very survival of women. A re-

port issued by the Ministry of Health and Family Welfare in Delhi states that '[T]he city continues to decimate females at inception, in the womb and currently before conception. The alarm bells were ringing in 1991 and the 2001 census sounds the death knell for the female half of our population' (cited in Shiva *Earth Democracy* 137).

Shiva examines how the convergence of patriarchies and fundamentalisms (both religious and market) replace 'women-centred worldviews, knowledge systems, and productive systems that ensure sustenance and sharing [with] patriarchal systems of knowledge and the economy based on war and violence' (ibid. 133). Her complex critique of this convergence can be applied to other regions where violence against women is state sanctioned, without reducing that violence to a question of religion, as the Western media tend to do in their generalizations about Islam. The following case study shows how religion is invoked and perverted to justify the domination of a small male elite that holds power over their community through terror.

In 2002, 28-year-old Mukhtaran Bibi (also known as Mukhtar Mai), a member of the Gujjar tribe, was gang-raped at gunpoint on the orders of a village council (*jerga*) in her village in Meerwala, Pakistan. Her crime? According to reports, her teenage brother had befriended a girl from the higher-caste Mastoi tribe and was accused of having had 'illicit relations' with her, thus offending the Mastoi's collective honor. Men from the Mastoi tribe sodomized the boy and, when he threatened to reveal the rape, the Mastoi men assembled the tribal council, accusing the boy himself of rape. The boy's family was then told that the Mastois would forgive the boy if his sister, Ms. Bibi, came before the council to plead for clemency. When the sister arrived before the council, four Mastoi men gang-raped her in a nearby house—on the orders of the council and with armed guards stationed to prevent her family from rescuing her. Ms. Bibi was forced to walk home covered in a torn shirt, jeered by villagers. Punishment was meted out on Ms. Bibi with the expectation that she would commit suicide, thus restoring honor to the Mastoi. When she refused and prosecuted her four attackers and two members of the village council, six men were initially sentenced to death, then five of them had their sentences later acquitted (because of apparent lack of evidence, despite the public nature of the crime), and a sixth man had his death sentence commuted to life imprisonment.[1]

In June 2005, when Ms. Bibi tried to leave Pakistan to accept an invitation from AI to visit the U.S. to tell her story, the Pakistan ambassador to Washington,

Jahangir Karamat, intervened to attempt to repress Ms. Bibi's right to travel out of the country, a right guaranteed under the UDHR. Ms. Bibi was placed under house arrest, and for several days was imprisoned, had her cell phone removed and was virtually disappeared until international pressure was brought to bear on the situation. Ms. Bibi was one of hundreds of women who are raped or gang-raped in Pakistan each year, a crime that usually goes unreported and un-punished, according to the Pakistan Human Rights Commission ('Mukhtaran Bibi'). The story illustrates the brutally skewed cultural logic that oppresses women in Pakistan and other parts of the world, what HRW calls a 'global social epidemic,' and the disproportionate power of the patriarchal system in which women continue to suffer the consequences of men's actions. In Bibi's case, no amount of relativist argument allowing for local cultural standards as the norm for determining equitable justice or rights can justify what occurred as a function of her gender and its relation to patriarchal power.

What sets women apart from the other groups that demand specific rec-ognition of their rights? While we cannot engage in an extended discussion of how women's status has been defined throughout history, it is unavoidable to ask why men have reduced women to the status of children (in terms of legal rights), who in turn have been reduced to the status of animals (in different re-gions and historical periods), although this hierarchy is already skewed and represents Western notions of (hu)man dominance. This division of life is re-flected in the mandate of humane societies established in the late nineteenth and early twentieth centuries, which was to protect children, women, and ani-mals. Is it enough to say that these groups are simply vulnerable? The notion of vulnerability focuses the attention on their shortcomings, and away from the root of the problem: the abusers, and their anthropocentric, male-centric, hierarchical worldview.

Women's bodies have been colonized throughout history. Their capacity to be penetrated and impregnated has dominated and even determined their cultural status. In human life, biology is always subjugated to cultural prac-tice, and only if this reproductive and nurturing capacity of women is cultur-ally interpreted as vulnerability, denigrated as inferiority, will it function as such. Women are the majority, and yet are subjected to unequal treatment in every country in the world, without exception.[2] HRW paints a startling portrait of the world rights situation for women in terms that show their exploitation and inequality:

Combatants and their sympathizers in conflicts, such as those in Sierra Leone, Kosovo, the Democratic Republic of Congo, Afghanistan,
and Rwanda, have raped women as a weapon of war with near complete impunity. Men in Pakistan, South Africa, Peru, Russia, and
Uzbekistan beat women in the home at astounding rates, while these
governments alternatively refuse to intervene to protect women and
punish their batterers or do so haphazardly and in ways that make
women feel culpable for the violence. As a direct result of inequalities
found in their countries of origin, women from Ukraine, Moldova, Nigeria, the Dominican Republic, Burma [Myanmar], and Thailand are
bought and sold, trafficked to work in forced prostitution, with insuf-
ficient government attention to protect their rights and punish the
traffickers. In Guatemala, South Africa, and Mexico, women's ability
to enter and remain in the work force is obstructed by private employers who use women's reproductive status to exclude them from work
and by discriminatory employment laws or discriminatory enforcement of the law. In the U.S., students discriminate against and attack
girls in school who are lesbian, bi-sexual, or transgendered, or do not
conform to male standards of female behavior. Women in Morocco,
Jordan, Kuwait, and Saudi Arabia face government-sponsored discrimination that renders them unequal before the law—including discriminatory family codes that take away women's legal authority and
place it in the hands of male family members—and restricts women's
participation in public life. (HRW 'Women's Rights')

To this list of abuses faced by women the world over we can add further extreme forms of injustice, including honor killings which occur in the Middle
East, Pakistan, and Bangladesh, and Female Genital Mutilation (FGM) which
is practiced in nearly thirty African and Middle Eastern countries, leading to
severe health problems for women and babies during birth, often ending in
death. The sheer pervasiveness of these human rights abuses makes them
seem like the natural order of things.

Historically rape has been a weapon of war, designed to humiliate the individual woman, her family and community, and even her nation. This is especially true in countries where a woman's worth is measured by her chastity,
and where rape therefore is not a singular event, committed against an individual, but an everlasting form of social stigmatization. The stigma is sometimes

even branded into visible parts of women's bodies such as their hands after they have been gang-raped in secret camps, a practice that has been observed in Darfur (Joffe-Walt 2). Increasingly, rape is committed by soldiers not only upon storming a community, but in highly organized rape camps where women and children are interred to endure the abuse for long periods of time. Many mass rapes in Bosnia-Herzegovina have occurred in such camps where women were forcibly held and raped by Serbian soldiers: 'Rape camps are often situated in former coffee houses and restaurants. Their names symbolize both the traditional and the modern': *"Vilina Vlas"* [Nymph's Hair/tresses], *"Kafana Sonja"* [Coffeehouse Sonja], *"Laser"* and *"Fast Food Restaurant."* For women, these places are *pakano na zemlji* [hell on earth]. In many camps, the majority of the female victims have died, either from gunshots, bleeding as a consequence of gang rape, or by suicide motivated by shame' (Olujic 2). 'Every year, thousands of Vietnamese women and girls are transported to China. Most are made to believe they will find good jobs and marriage prospects there. Once they reach China, however, many end up as beggars, forced labourers or prostitutes...according to Vietnamese authorities, more than 20,000 women and children have been transported to China in the past 10 years for forced marriage or prostitution' (Chelala).

More recently in 2003, a string of rape camps was discovered in northern San Diego County. The news has been slow to emerge since the illegal victims, young women and even underage girls, are too terrified to testify against their captors and are often deported back to Mexico by U.S. authorities without receiving counseling, health care, or any other form of compensation or support. 'Over the last few years, police say they have busted numerous sex trafficking rings in northern San Diego County ...To the trafficker, the children are expendable, resusable and resellable, and that makes them a commodity' ('Fields of Shame: Sex Slavery Exposed' 2-3). Given the covert nature of these operations and the highly professional tactics associated with organized crime, the estimated numbers vary widely: according to NBC 4, 'Every year, as many as 2 million women and children are smuggled out of their home countries and sold into slavery—at least 100,000 end up right here in the United States. Many come to Southern California' (ibid. 1). This source reports that the traffickers prostitute the women to large groups of migrant workers, though there is no concrete evidence so far that Mexican migrant workers are raping their compatriots while non-Mexican men are uninvolved in the business. The 2005 federal statistics are more conservative and estimate that as many as 17,500 sex slaves are smuggled into the U.S. annually. Uneducated girls are enticed to believe that the traffickers will deliver them to safe, well-salaried jobs as chambermaids or nannies in the U.S. Otherwise, they are simply kidnapped. Once they are smuggled across the border, many are taken directly to illegal brothels in New York, where pimps threaten and beat them, force them to become addicted to crystal meth and cocaine, and prohibit any communication with their families or anyone else who could expose the operation (Bode 1-2).

Women and HIV/AIDS

Women's right to safe sexuality and sexual autonomy is not attainable without the basic right to economic security.

The World Health Organization (WHO) identifies the following issues as particularly urgent:

- poor reproductive and sexual health, including a higher risk of infection by HIV;
- neglect of health needs, and clinical management models based primarily on men;
- 'all forms of coerced sex—from violent rape to cultural/economic obligations to have sex when it is not really wanted, increases risk of microlesions and therefore of STI/HIV infection';
- harmful cultural practices, including female genital mutilation;
- sexual abuse, particularly by adult men who seek ever-younger partners in order to avoid infection, or, as is often the case in India, in order to be 'cured.'
  (Source: World Health Organisation Fact Sheet no. 247)

Legal regimes and inheritance structures also serve to discriminate against women. Women whose husbands have died of AIDS are regularly rejected, without recourse, by both their own and their husband's families, and their property is frequently taken from them. Children who have lost parents to AIDS together with their inheritance rights have to take on hazardous labor including prostitution, as well as being forced to live on the streets.

'The relationship between abuses of women's rights and their vulnerability to AIDS is acutely clear in Africa, where 58 percent of those infected with HIV are women. Infection rates among adolescent girls and young women in much of Africa are strikingly higher than those of their male counterparts, exposing the disturbing reality that young women face appalling levels of abuse and discrimination ('HIV/AIDS and Human Rights' HRW, 'HIV/AIDS in Africa' and UNDF for Women [UNIFEM]). Early marriage means that young girls are forced to have sex when their bodies are not fully developed and hence are subject to greater risks of tearing and abrasions, making them that much more susceptible to HIV infection.

'In Senegal, men who were surveyed believed that female circumcision was advantageous as it 'rationalizes women's desire and helps women resist men.' Female circumcision has been shown to increase women's risk of contracting HIV/AIDS. In several countries in sub-Saharan Africa, almost half of all girls aged 15-19 did not know that a person who looks healthy could be infected with HIV and could transmit it to others. In Uganda, domestic violence prevents women from freely accessing HIV/AIDS information, from negotiating condom use, and from resisting unprotected sex with an HIV-positive partner, yet the government has failed to take any meaningful steps to prevent and punish such abuse. In Kenya, simply because of their gender, many women AIDS victims sink into poverty and will die even sooner because customs condone evicting women from their homes and taking their property upon their husband's death. In Zambia, orphan girls are often sexually abused at the hands of their guardians, including family members and teachers. In South Africa, the government is lagging in its commitment to provide post-exposure prophylaxis to rape survivors, and girls are deterred from attending school because of high rates of sexual violence and harassment.'

(HRW 'HIV/AIDS and Human Rights')

Indigenous women are the most marginalized and most widely ignored group in the world. To some extent, this is because the women's movement and people of color groups have agendas that are inevitably narrow in order to address problems related to a specific aspect of identity. Localized agendas cannot account for the multilayered identities and diverse experiences of women on a global scale. Indigenous women, for instance, have been critical of the Beijing Draft Platform for Action coming out of the UN's Fourth World Conference on Women because they note its many blind spots regarding how First World development models exploit the South. These women say that the overemphasis on gender discrimination actually depoliticizes many of the problems faced by majority world women. For example, they point out that equal pay and equal status is made possible in the First World because its economy is built on extracting cheap resources and labor from the majority world (Lutz 'Indigenous Women's Voices').

Even in the face of this complex web of rights abuses, women and their supporters rally to stop the violence, and also network globally, on the basis that this violence connects with other problems created by globalization-from-above. Just one instance, among countless worldwide, of solidarity and determination to enact human rights is the World March of Women and the

Women's Global Charter for Humanity adopted in Kigali, Rwanda, in December 2004. After not having received a single concrete response from the IMF, WB and UN to 17 practical demands for the elimination of poverty and violence against women drafted in 2000, the 5,500 participating groups in 163 countries and territories continue to hold annual marches and public education activities. In 2005, women of the World March organized a Relay to send the Charter around the world. They also transmitted the Charter's message in a patchwork quilt that was gradually pieced together as the Charter was relayed from Sao Paulo, Brazil, stopping in 53 countries, to arrive in Ouagadougou, Burkina Faso. Such international efforts uniting communities of common concern, despite enormous distances and huge gaps between their living standards, are addressing the previous fragmentation of women's movements. The Women's Global Charter for Humanity is rooted in the knowledge that women's justice includes diverse constituencies, the environment, and an expansive vision of human well-being.

Juárez and Vancouver: Violence against Indigenous Women

Indigenous women across the Americas suffer much higher rates of sexual assault and murder than other women, abuse that is usually perpetrated by non-indigenous men. In Canada, 'Indigenous women between the ages of 25 and 44 with status under the federal Indian Act, are five times more likely than other women of the same age to die as the result of violence' (AI *Stolen Sisters* 23). And '70 percent of all violent crimes against Indigenous people in the U.S.—and 90 percent of sexual assaults—are reported to be carried out by non-Indigenous people' (ibid. 26). There are many striking similarities between the disappearances of primarily indigenous women in Ciudad Juárez and disproportionately high numbers of aboriginal women in Vancouver's Eastside and along the 'Highway of Tears,' a section of Highway 16 between Prince George and Prince Rupert in British Columbia. There are 61 women missing from this area and at least 500 indigenous women have been murdered or disappeared and presumed dead across Canada: 'Approximately 370 women have been murdered in the last decade in Ciudad Juárez and neighboring communities in the industrial zone along the U.S.-Mexico border. Officials acknowledge that at least 70 other women remain missing, although some activist organizations in the region put that number as high as 400' (AI 'Stop the Killing'). Documentary filmmakers like Audrey Huntley and Christine Welsh chronicle the many stories of the missing and presumed-dead indigenous women and the missingwomen.net website continues to compile and document these cases (Hunter 3).

In a documentary film entitled *Señorita extraviada/Missing Young Woman*, Mexican filmmaker Lourdes Portillo interviews a woman named María whose testimony implicates the police force of Juárez in the torture, rape, and murder of young women working in the maquilas. This woman was detained in a police station where a female police officer tried to sexually assault her. When María refused to co-operate, she was beaten and threatened by a group of officers who showed her photographs of women being tortured and raped by police officers who stood around in a circle watching, laughing, and taking turns, after which they doused the victim in gasoline and set her on fire. These horrific images are corroborated by the findings of charred remains of women's bodies and clothing scattered in the desert just outside of Juárez. Politicians, including the governor, have publicly blamed the disappeared women, accusing them of dressing provocatively, of frequenting dangerous clubs, and of being prostitutes who are undeserving of protection. The police routinely destroy material evidence, such as clothing and shoes, and in some cases, the remains of the wrong women are given to the families of the disappeared.

By contrast, in Canada, private persons commit the assaults and murders, and police investigations are often racially biased and abnormally slow, rarely concluding with an arrest. Rapists and murderers also practice racial profiling, and choose those victims who are socially most marginalized and least likely to receive police protection. In this context, race, gender and class are inseparable, making indigenous women historically the most vulnerable people in both countries. Violence against women is seldom represented as a human rights issue, and in Canada's case, this might explain why Canada has yet to ratify the Inter-American Convention on the Prevention, Punishment and Eradication of Violence against Women. Both the UN and AI have criticized Canada for not fulfilling its duty of due diligence, which 'means that a state must take reasonable steps to prevent human rights violations, use the means at its disposal to carry out serious investigations, identify those responsible, impose the appropriate punishment and ensure that the victim receives adequate reparation' (AI *Stolen Sisters* 7).

A long history of discriminatory policies such as 'revoking the legal Indigenous status of Indigenous women who married non-Indigenous men have already been found by the UN Human Rights Committee to have violated minority cultural rights' (ibid. 8). Such policies have resulted in indigenous women becoming separated from their communities, becoming dependent on their husbands, and ultimately becoming more vulnerable especially in cases where those marriages ended in divorce, leaving the women with children who were also denied status and had no connection with their native communities. In 1985 these policies were finally repealed through a successful complaint to the UN Human Rights Committee.

In the case of *maquila* workers in Juárez, they are often poor indigenous women who go north in search of work and, instead of crossing the border into the U.S., remain in the 'free' trade zone.

These factories are owned and operated primarily by Canadian and U.S. companies, and also seem to be implicated in the murders of hundreds of women. Portillo's film reveals the highly suspicious practice of taking photographs of the most attractive young women in the *maquilas* on a regular weekly basis. It is not clear whether they were led to believe that they were being considered for a better position in modeling, but what seems plausible is that the victims were actually selected from these photos by the murderers, suggesting that plant officials are also implicated.

The murders of Canadian and Mexican indigenous women result from the historical structural violence of condemning them to live in poverty, of denying them the education that could lead to safer jobs, of non-indigenous men viewing them as dehumanized sexual objects, and of repeated evidence that their lives do not matter enough to the police, government, or to their fellow citizens to demand justice. Just one example from countless of how structural violence operates is the fact that 'Indigenous run child services programs receive 22 percent less funding than provincially-funded counterparts serving predominantly non-indigenous communities' in Canada (ibid. 17).

Anna Hunter describes the root cause of this form of violence as being structural and systemic, clarifying that the problem can only be fully understood by considering the legacy of colonization of aboriginal women: 'colonial practices take many forms and varieties that stretch beyond government actors to include those with institutional capacity to legitimize the colonial order, including educators, media personnel, lawyers, judges, police officers, literary authors and publishers, historians and scientists. The cumulative result of the insidious phenomenon of colonization is the extreme marginalization of Indigenous women from the social safety nets of society' (1-2).

The Marginalization of Gender Diversity Rights

We, African lesbians, gays, bisexuals, and transgender people, do exist—despite your attempts to deny our existence. We are part of your countries and constituencies. We are watching your deliberations from our home communities, which are also your home communities. We demand that our voices be heard...

Across Africa, we face human rights abuses [that] threaten our safety, our livelihoods, and our lives. That we are targets of such abuse proves that we exist—states do not persecute phantoms or ghosts. It also proves the necessity for action to safeguard our real situations and our basic rights.

African lesbians, gays, bisexuals, and transgender people confront harassment from police; abuse by our neighbors and our families;

and violence and brutality—sometimes punitive rape—on the streets. We are discriminated against in the workplace. Some of our families force us into marriages against our will, in the hope of changing our inmost selves. Some of us, among them the very young, are evicted from our homes because of prejudice and fear. (HRW *The Johannesburg Statement on Sexual Orientation, Gender Identity, and Human Rights*, 2004)

During World War II, lesbians and gay men were targeted by the Nazi regime. However, while they were amongst the millions murdered in concentration camps, when the United Nations drew up the Universal Declaration of Human Rights in 1948, no recognition was made of discrimination or other human rights abuses on the grounds of sexuality. Since then, there has been no international human rights standard that has addressed sexual orientation or gender identity.

In the spring of 2003, the UN Commission on Human Rights discussed a draft resolution on 'Human Rights and Sexual Orientation,' which would have as its aim for 'all states to promote and protect the human rights of all persons regardless of their sexual orientation' (Baird 30). The resolution was proposed by Brazil, seconded by South Africa, and supported by more than 19 countries. However, a coalition of five countries—Pakistan, Egypt, Libya, Saudi Arabia and Malaysia—introduced amendments (supported by the Vatican) that would have removed references to discrimination on the basis of sexual orientation, rendering it meaningless. Discussion on the issue was postponed until the UNCHR's 2005 session.

Anti-homosexuality laws, in various guises, remain in some 80 countries, and homosexuality is punishable by death in nine (Iran, Afghanistan, Saudi Arabia, Mauritania, Sudan, Pakistan, United Arab Emirates, Yemen, and the northern provinces of Nigeria). Even where laws are not strictly enforced they create an atmosphere wherein queers and transgender people are demeaned, even where they are not subject to persecution, harassment, and extortion. Such laws persecute people who identify as queer, but there is also a long history, rooted in the same ideologies, of discrimination against those *perceived* to be gay, lesbian, bisexual or transgender. Moreover, the criminalization of 'sodomy' (a term used to describe 'unnatural' sexual behavior, or 'crimes against nature') has been shown to have political implications: in 1998 Anwar Ibrahim, Deputy Prime Minister of Malaysia, was arrested on charges of 'sexual misconduct, corruption and threatening national security' (AI *Crimes of Hate* 18), charges that were, according to AI, politically motivated. Ibrahim was severely beaten whilst in custody, and Mahatir Mohamad, Prime Minister of Malaysia, referred to him as a 'sodomist, unfit to rule the country' (ibid. 18).

GLOSSARY

REMEMBER...

THE HIV VIRUS CANNOT BE TRANSMITTED THROUGH SHAKING HANDS, HUGGING, TOUCHING, KISSING, PETTING COUGHING, SNEEZING, SWIMMING POOLS AND TOILETS, EATING UTENSILS OR FOOD, SHARING BEDS, BED LINEN AND CLOTHES, OR THROUGH MOSQUITO BITES.

THE HIV VIRUS IS TRANSMITTED (PASSED FROM ONE PERSON TO ANOTHER) THROUGH THE EXCHANGE OF HIV-INFECTED BODY FLUIDS THROUGH:
- UNPROTECTED (WITHOUT A CONDOM) SEXUAL INTERCOURSE WITH SOMEONE WHO IS INFECTED
- UNSTERILISED EQUIPMENT, INCLUDING NEEDLES, SYRINGES, RAZOR BLADES AND OTHERS THAT HAVE BEEN PREVIOUSLY USED BY SOMEONE WHO IS INFECTED.
- TRANSFUSION OF INFECTED BLOOD OR BLOOD PRODUCTS THAT CONTAIN THE HIV VIRUS.
- AN INFECTED MOTHER TO HER CHILD DURING PREGNANCY, AT CHILDBIRTH OR THROUGH BREAST-FEEDING.

EVERYONE HAS A RIGHT TO INFORMATION, INCLUDING HIV/AIDS RELATED INFORMATION. WE NEED TO BE INFORMED AND SPEAK OPENLY ABOUT HIV/AIDS TO PREVENT INFECTION AND TO HELP THOSE ALREADY INFECTED.

PEOPLE LIVING WITH HIV/AIDS HAVE A RIGHT TO BE TREATED WITH RESPECT AND DIGNITY. YOU SHOULD TREAT PERSONS LIVING WITH HIV/AIDS LIKE EVERYONE ELSE.

FREEDOM FROM DISCRIMINATION FOR ANY REASON (RACE, COLOUR, SEX OR RELIGION, THE OPINIONS YOU HAVE, WHERE YOU COME FROM, WHETHER YOU ARE HEALTHY OR ILL, AND WHATEVER YOUR SEXUAL CHOICES) IS A HUMAN RIGHT THAT EVERYONE SHOULD ENJOY AND ALL SHOULD RESPECT.

ALL GOVERNMENTS ARE RESPONSIBLE TO PROMOTE AND PROTECT HUMAN RIGHTS. GOVERNMENTS SHOULD NOT DISCRIMINATE.

PEOPLE LIVING WITH HIV CAN HELP EVERYONE BETTER UNDERSTAND HIV AND AIDS AND NOT BE FRIGHTENED OF IT. THEY CAN HELP OTHERS TAKE STEPS TO PROTECT THEMSELVES AND THEIR LOVED ONES

DISCRIMINATION IS WRONG AND UNFAIR. IT IS A VIOLATION OF ANOTHER PERSON'S RIGHT. THOSE WHO DISCRIMINATE SHOULD BE HELD RESPONSIBLE FOR THEIR ACTIONS...

STAND UP FOR HUMAN RIGHTS. TAKE ACTION AGAINST HIV/AIDS DISCRIMINATION! YOU CAN MAKE THINGS HAPPEN!..

HRW noted that following the release of its report on homophobic violence in Jamaica, which detailed harassment of both men who have sex with
men and HIV/AIDS outreach workers, the Jamaican Police Federation called
for sedition charges to be made against HRW and local HIV/AIDS and queer
advocacy groups. The JPF also denied that the police had any role to play in
protecting against homophobic violence, and endorsed homophobia as 'good
moral values' (HRW 'Letter Urging Jamaican Government').

Nonetheless, many countries do prohibit discrimination on the grounds of
sexual orientation. South Africa and Ecuador have included a prohibition in
their constitutions. The European Charter of Fundamental Rights (2000) prohibits discrimination on the grounds of sexual orientation, as do nations including Australia (many states of which specifically protect transgender people,
although certain regulations depend on whether 'the person is a recognized
transgender person who has had surgical intervention'), Brazil, Mexico, Canada
and Argentina. The ongoing criminalization or social marginalization of homosexuality should also be considered dangerous insofar as it helps to perpetuate
the spread of HIV/AIDS.

Human Rights and HIV/AIDS

Minoritized populations afflicted with specific diseases related to sexuality suffer discrimination in ways that are deeply systemic. Perhaps no better example of this exists
than in the case of the HIV/AIDS pandemic in Africa, which has devastated a broad
swath of the population across age, class, cultural, gender, and sexuality boundaries.
Like the rights of the disabled and of the aged, discussed elsewhere in this chapter,
HIV/AIDS presents a limit case on the rights horizon: what are the rights of people afflicted with the disease and how do these rights mark yet another expression of the
idea that all humans beings must be treated equally in their diversity?

Fundamental Rights:

...a strong and clear public health rationale exists for the protection of human
rights and the dignity of infected persons. For example, if it is the common
practice that HIV infection, or simply suspicion of infection, leads to a stigmatization of the person or group, or to discrimination vis-à-vis the concerned
(such as the loss of employment or obstacles to access to education), these
persons will undoubtedly actively try to avoid detection and, as a result, lose
contact with health and social services.

This reluctance to seek assistance out of fear of stigmatization and discrimination in turn not only exacerbates the difficulty of preventing infection but also runs counter to any educational and outreach efforts in this context. (Lawson 31; citing a Report of the Secretary General of WHO on measures taken to protect human rights and prevent discrimination in the context of HIV/AIDS)

According to HRW, HIV/AIDS has claimed 22 million lives and infected over 60 million persons since the 1980s. But in addition to the disease itself have been the human rights violations it has prompted: sexual violence and coercion of women and girls, abuse of sex workers and injecting drug users, stigmatization of men who have sex with men, and violations of the right to information on HIV transmission. HIV/AIDS spreads with efficiency in prisons due to sexual violence, and lack of access to condoms, harm reduction measures for drug users, and information. And importantly, human rights violations stigmatize persons with the highest risk of infection, marginalizing them and limiting their access to information and treatment.

HRW notes that the U.S., despite being the world's leading donor to HIV/AIDS programs, has in recent years supported prevention programs that promote sexual abstinence and marital fidelity, censoring information about condoms. Moreover, in many countries political and/or religious (notably in the Roman Catholic Church) leaders 'have associated condoms with sin or sexual promiscuity, implying that people who use condoms lack the moral fortitude to abstain from sex until marriage.' The Holy See 'explicitly objects to condom use and at times has publicly distorted scientific information about the effectiveness of condoms against HIV.' The consequence is that vast numbers of people at risk of HIV/AIDS have no access to condoms, or even basic HIV/AIDS education (HRW 'HIV/AIDS & Human Rights').

The goal of realizing human rights is fundamental to the global fight against AIDS. And in a world facing a terrible epidemic—one that has already spread further, faster and to more devastating effect than any other in human history —winning the fight against AIDS is a precondition for achieving rights worth enjoying. (UNAIDS, Peter Piot, UNAIDS Exec Director)

The UNAIDS website notes that HIV/AIDS is a security issue, 'whether one is looking at the more traditional meaning of security (threats to defence of the state, with those threats emanating from other states) or the newer concept of "human security" which, in its Human Development Report 1994, the United Nations Development Programme (UNDP) defines as: "safety from constant threats of hunger, disease, crime, and repression. It also means protection from sudden and hurtful disruptions in the patterns of our daily lives—whether in our homes, our jobs, in our communities or in our environments." '

The virus has also destabilized societies and the state through its decimation of families and households, as well as undermining economies, including agricultural development as adult farm workers sicken from the disease. It has also proven to be an issue of national security: in some nations, infection rates in the military are as much as five times that of the civilian population. In the case of China, for instance, the potential threat of the virus is enormous, especially because the government has a record of persecuting AIDS activists.

A 2005 HRW report entitled 'Restrictions on AIDS Activists in China' documents how China is jailing and persecuting dozens of AIDS activists, violently closing the Orchid AIDS Orphanage in Shangqiu City, Henan (established in 2003 by AIDS activist Li Dan),[3] using violence against AIDS protestors, blocking websites with information about the prevention of AIDS, and imprisoning staff working at AIDS organizations. This despite the fact that the virus is expected to infect close to 10 million Chinese by 2020, thus potentially creating the largest HIV-positive population in the world.

By 2010, more than 10 million Chinese may become infected with the virus: 'One of the epidemic's epicenters is Henan province, where more than one million people have become infected with HIV following the selling of contaminated blood by provincial officials in the 1990s. None of the officials involved has been punished, and some have even been promoted,' while NGOs battling HIV are harassed by the Chinese government, always suspicious about organizations that it cannot fully control (Chelala).

HIV/AIDS and Homophobia

Amnesty International notes that some governments (including governments in the Caribbean) have claimed that 'sodomy' laws are necessary for the prevention of HIV/AIDS. Linking HIV/AIDS to homosexuality is factually inaccurate, discriminatory, and acts as a barrier to effective HIV prevention work. HIV/AIDS workers have consequently been detained and harassed while distributing condoms to sex workers, for example. It also makes prevention work in prisons almost impossible (AI *Crimes of Hate*).

International treaties, including the International Covenant on Economic, Social and Cultural Rights, oblige states to 'respect, protect, and promote the right of all people to the highest attainable standard of health,' which in turn requires states to 'refrain from limiting access to contraceptives' and 'people's participation in health-related matters,' to refrain from 'censoring, withholding or intentionally misrepresenting public health information,' and to prevent third parties from limiting 'people's access to health-related information and services' (HRW 'HIV/AIDS & Human Rights').

Repressive and Pro-active Responses to HIV/AIDS and the Outcomes

India

> In September 2004, the executive director of the Global Fund to Fight AIDS, Tuberculosis and Malaria, Dr. Richard Feacham, echoed numerous analyses in suggesting that India had surpassed the Republic of South Africa as the nation with the highest number of people living with HIV/AIDS in the world. Current United Nations estimates place the number of people living with HIV/AIDS in India at approximately 5.1 million; however experts have pointed to widespread underreporting of HIV/AIDS in India and believe the actual figure to be much higher. In most Indian states, sex is the main mode of transmission of HIV. (HRW 'HIV/AIDS & Human Rights')

Nonetheless, condom sales have dropped in India, and shortages have also been reported. More disturbingly, NGO workers serving vulnerable populations such as sex workers and men who have sex with men report regular harassment by police: 'Some police officers treat the provision of condoms to men who have sex with men as an act abetting sodomy, which is criminalized under section 377 of the Indian penal code. While prostitution is not criminalized in India, police reportedly have used condom possession as justification for harassing sex workers and outreach workers who encourage sex workers to use condoms.' Strict obscenity laws also act to limit the types of information that NGOs can provide on condoms. As abstinence-only programs have taken a wider hold, basic information about HIV transmission is still lacking: a 2001 survey cited by the World Bank 'found that 70 percent of women and 82.5 percent of men had "basic awareness" of HIV/AIDS; however, the World Bank also reported that "more than 75 percent of Indians mistakenly believe that they could contract HIV from sharing a meal with a person with HIV." '

Under a new health act, the Indian government lifted the prior administration's ban on condom advertisements on television in July 2004. 'However, further steps must be taken to ensure that condom promotion strategies work, especially for women. For example, violence or the threat of violence significantly impedes women's ability to negotiate condom use with their sex partners; however, the Indian government has failed to take the most basic steps to protect Indian women from violence. Rape within marriage is not recognized under Indian law, and there is currently no domestic violence law, although one has been drafted' (ibid.).

Brazil

Brazil's HIV/AIDS strategy has been widely cited as an example of a successful prevention strategy. This included local production of generic antiretrovirals (ARVs) for all people living with AIDS in the country, widespread dissemination of information and voluntary HIV testing, and government-supported programs for sex workers and drug users. The government has also been visible and active in promoting condom use, including supporting construction of a domestic condom factory. By 2003, UNAIDS estimated 660,000 people were living with HIV/AIDS in Brazil, significantly fewer than had been previously projected.

The country's aggressive policies have not been free of controversy, particularly from the Roman Catholic Church: 'In 2004, the government ran a public service message entitled "nothing gets through a condom" soon after which the Brazilian Catholic Bishop's Conference issued a statement saying that condoms were not 100 percent safe.' Moreover, USAID canceled a US$8 million grant to Brazil for condom promotion and marketing and HIV prevention materials without explanation, 'leading to speculation that the cancellation had reflected a change in USAID priorities away from condom promotion to high-risk groups' (ibid.).

Africa Is Slowly Dying...

Africa has been affected by HIV/AIDS far more than any other continent. Statistics for the end of 2004 showed that 25.4 million of the 39.4 million people in the world who are HIV-positive lived in sub-Saharan Africa. For the vast majority of people living in Africa, however, access to antiretroviral drugs for the treatment of AIDS is not available.

As the number of adults dying of AIDS rises over the next decade, an increasing number of orphans will grow up without parental care and love and will be deprived of their basic rights to shelter, food, health and education. In African countries that have already had long, severe epidemics, AIDS is generating orphans so quickly that family structures can no longer cope. Traditional safety nets are unraveling as more young adults die of AIDS related illnesses. Families and communities can barely fend for themselves, let alone take care of the orphans. Typically, half of the people with HIV become infected before they are aged 25, developing AIDS and dying by the time they are aged 35, leaving behind a generation of children to be raised by their grandparents or left on their own in child-headed households. ('AIDS Orphans—The Facts')

Voices from Africa

Sarah Okiri,

P.O. Box 288

Sondu, Kenya

> *I am 10 year old and I am the first boar. My mother died in 2000 and my father I left school when my mother sick to care my other sisters. I am working in somebody house to get food to eat. We find hard to play with children because they do not want us to. I do not WANT TO GO TO SCHOOL because teachers want money. 2 relatives of min died this year next Sondu Market. They worked in the bars and they were called Baby and Aomo. ('Africa Alive Postcards')*

> *I'm writing to you on a day I feel so down and feel that life can be unfair. Once again the virus has taken a friend, and a dear person to me. A person I got to share joy, laughter, and many other things with.*

> *She died in her sleep. I am hurting, you have no idea. I do not want to tell lies. I nursed this woman back to life last week. She was so cold and kept telling me to put on extra blankets. The room was so hot I was sweating from trying to make her warm. Even massaging her feet would not help. I had to go inside her blanket and sleep with her to try and bring her to at least the body temperature while waiting for an ambulance. I cannot believe that she did not make it!*

> *Fond regards, Thabisa*[4]

Upon the Hilltop

> I will shout myself hoarse
> A monster is ravaging, Decimating our population
> And if don't listen, we will be wiped out
> Listen, learn and live
>
> About its origin, that's immaterial
> It strangles, annihilates and drains the body, It emaciates to the bone
> Till the final knell of death
> Listen, learn and live
>
> Listen to the three commands of life
> If thou are not married, thou shall abstain
> If thou cannot abstain, thou shall use a condom
> If thou art married, thou shall be faithful to one wife
> And if thou shall not follow commandment three, thou shall apply the second
> Listen, learn and live.
>
> Go ye, preach these to all Africa, And ye shall live!
> —David Ndung'u Waweru (age 15, Kenya; 'Poems from Africa')

AIDS Facts from the African American Self-Help Foundation

It is believed that over 90% of all the world's orphans reside in the continent of Africa, where 80% of all AIDS deaths in the world have occurred and 70% of all new HIV infections also occur. Already, life expectancy has been seriously impacted, dropping drastically by half from age 68 to 34. Current statistics state that over 11 million have died—almost 3 million of them children.

Here are a few key facts and figures about the disease that has killed 18.8 million people since the beginning of the epidemic:

- "The HIV/AIDS pandemic is producing orphans on a scale unrivaled in world history," states a report by The UN AIDS Project.

- AIDS is the fourth leading global cause of death, according to UNAIDS.

- 24.5 million people are living with the disease in sub-Saharan Africa—compared to 900,000 in North America.

- In Africa, 20 percent more women than men are living with HIV.

- There are now 16 countries in which more than one-tenth of the adult population aged 15-49 is infected with HIV. In seven countries, all in the southern cone of the African continent, up to one adult in four is infected with the virus.

- So far, the AIDS epidemic has left behind 13.2 million orphans—children 15 years old or younger who have lost one or both parents to the disease.

- AIDS orphans are expected to number 44 million by 2010 (9 September 2000, *World Magazine*).

- At least one of every two 15-year-old boys in Kenya, South Africa, Zimbabwe, and Botswana is on track to die of AIDS.

- Thirty-four million people living in sub-Saharan Africa have been infected with HIV.

- Eleven and a half million of these people have already died. (One quarter of these were children.)

- In some African countries, about 25% of the pregnant women are infected with HIV.

According to AI, 'Women who breach society's rules of sexual conduct are frequently targeted for betraying the culture and identity of their own community. This is especially true of lesbian and bisexual women. Militarized societies tend to place even greater emphasis on the purity of their idealized women, as opposed to the "unclean" enemy.' Citing an example of how minorities are targeted to force a criminal consensus of the so-called moral majority, AI gives us the following horrific testimony: 'In late 2002, in the city of Medellín (Colombia), a 14-year-old girl was stripped in the street and a sign saying "I am a lesbian" was hung around her neck. According to witnesses, three men then raped her. Her body was found days later; her breasts had been cut off' (AI *Casualties of War* 2).

Clearly this girl was targeted, tortured, and killed in order to make a terrifying example of her gender orientation. All aspects of her being were brutally erased: she was a girl child most likely living in poverty (for the wealthy are usually protected from such cruelty); given that she lived in a Latin American country, she may also have been indigenous, mestiza, Afro-Latina, or mulatta. These different aspects of her identity were all subsumed under the sign hung around her neck by her homophobic murderers, whose actions violated her humanity with impunity. Only the perpetrator's identity can be reduced to his single-minded psychosis. Can such extreme expressions of homophobic hatred be countered by the notion of tolerance? What does it mean to simply 'tolerate' someone's difference?

Any discussion of gender diversity rights must examine the severe limitations of the concept of tolerance. What poet Audre Lorde has to say about difference is the very backbone of how we conceive of the universality of rights: 'Difference must be not merely tolerated, but seen as a fund of necessary polarities between which our creativity can spark like a dialectic. Only then does the necessity for interdependency become unthreatening. Only within that interdependency of different strengths, acknowledged and equal, can the power to seek new ways of being in the world generate, as well as the courage and sustenance to act where there are no charters' (90).

Gender Diversity in Australia

Historically, Australia has been relatively progressive in its human rights related to gender diversity. Women have been entitled to vote and stand for election since the first federal election in 1902. The colony of South Australia granted women the vote in 1895 (second only to Aotearoa/New Zealand), and was one of the first Commonwealth jurisdictions to repeal its 'sodomy' laws (1975). Same-sex relationships have been recognized as grounds for immigration sponsorship, and sexual orientation, as well as gender, have been successfully invoked to grant asylum to refugees. Most states also have anti-discrimination legislation protecting the equal opportunity not only of women, but also of queer and transgender individuals.

So what's gone wrong?

Despite apparently progressive laws being on the books, the Australian ideal of a 'fair go' for all has in practice been less than egalitarian. The first women were not elected to Federal Parliament, for example, until 1943. As of the 2004 Commonwealth election, 59 members of the two Houses were women, only 26 percent of seats. In the state of Tasmania, sodomy laws were overturned only in 1997 under pressure from the federal government and the UN Human Rights Committee. And Australia's increasingly restrictive approach to refugee claimants could soon impact the capacity to claim status for persecution because of sexual orientation.

Even as pay equity is a recognized principle of Australian law, indirect discrimination continues, particularly around maternity issues. The Federal Sex Discrimination Commissioner has noted that by August 2001, 70 percent of women aged between 20 and 54 were in the workforce. And yet despite being a signatory to the Convention on the Elimination of all Forms of Discrimination against Women, Article 11 of which recommends the introduction of paid maternity leave with social benefits, Australia is one of only 5 (of 163) countries not to have introduced paid maternity leave.

More overt have been governmental actions designed to undermine not only the rights of women, but those few attributed to queer and transgender people. Recent recognition of the right to same-sex partner benefits has been offset by unsuccessful attempts to restrict provision of assisted reproductive technology to heterosexual couples. A virulent public debate ensued.

A 2004 amendment to the Marriage Act extended the heterosexist definition of marriage to deny recognition of foreign same-sex marriages. Moreover, because Australian law does not recognize same-sex couples, they have no capacity to apply jointly to adopt. And while provisions exist for transgender people to amend official documentation, some, such as a requirement for surgical intervention, fail to acknowledge the complexities involved in gender transitioning.

What an analysis of the legal situation belies, however, is the effect of such unequal treatment in practice. Cases made under equal opportunity legislation are slow to resolve (again, the old problem of expeditious access to legal instruments that are effective and have the force of law, as we have seen in other human rights situations), and the tendency towards alternative dispute resolution measures such as conciliation has meant that substantive legal change occurs infrequently through the courts. A failure to address indirect discrimination means that many women find themselves making a choice between competing social obligations: to be successful at careers and to be mothers. And indirect attacks on queer rights by the Coalition government have affirmed an historic marginalization in a country whose national symbols celebrate male stereotypes. Think Crocodile Dundee. While gender diversity protections do exist, a truly equitable community is hard to imagine so long as public discourse remains so socially anti-egalitarian.

Why Same-Sex Marriage?

The strenuous debates over same-sex marriage, largely in developed countries, point to yet another minority rights issue in which the principles of equality in diversity are being fought over. Belgium, The Netherlands, South Africa, and parts of Canada have all extended marriage to include same-sex couples, either through legislation or the courts. Under the UDHR, all men and women have the right to marry and found a family. While the UDHR has tended to be interpreted in a heterosexist fashion, there is nothing on the face of it that precludes the support of same-sex marriage.

The right to marriage by same-sex couples is an important one symbolically and legally. Precisely because marriage is fundamental to the social structures of many countries, the continued denial of marriage to same-sex couples denies them full capacity in those societies. It is *not* a religious issue—provided that exclusions are drafted to protect religious freedoms, churches will continue to be free to discriminate against queer couples by refusing to sanctify their unions. Because marriage is also a civil issue, however, LGBT individuals will not attain equal rights unless their relationships have the same value as heterosexual couples.

Linked to this, the failure to recognize same-sex couples has far-reaching legal implications. Custody of children can prove complex, particularly in jurisdictions that refuse to allow joint adoptions by same-sex couples. Control over medical treatment may pass to a patient's family, rather than his/her partner. In addition there are tenancy, housing, tax, and inheritance issues that all favor heterosexual marriage, particularly where no alternative is offered to same-sex couples.

For transgender people, the marriage question is often even more convoluted: will they be able to marry in their preferred gender? At present this depends on whether or not the state in which they live allows them to change official documentation or not. While not all members of the LGBT community believe that marriage is necessarily an institution whose norms should be replicated by same-sex couples, in the absence of any choice, there can be no real equality.

Community Support, Dignity, and Rights for People with Disabilities

In societies in which a person's worth is reduced to his or her use-value, physical or mental disabilities can divest human beings of their human worth. While the principle of the equality of human beings is especially crucial in the protection of those who cannot stand up for themselves alone, people with intellectual and other severe disabilities require not just equal treatment, but special treatment. Intellectual disability (often coupled with physical ones) has been especially stigmatized in most 'developed' nations; historically, the Western obsession with Man's intellectual superiority to the animal kingdom (the basis of most philosophical discourse on everything from metaphysics to epistemology) inevitably segregates and ignores those humans who think and articulate thoughts differently from the standard of the ideal rational being, which is to say an idealized version of a heterosexual man of European descent.

In terms of attention from official international bodies like the UN, the rights of people with disabilities have been completely neglected until very recently. While such human rights instruments as the International Covenant on Economic, Social and Cultural Rights recognize and include the Principles for the Protections of Persons with Mental Illness and for the Improvement of Mental Health Care, these instruments have been underused in protecting people with disabilities. This serious omission in human rights thinking has prompted advocacy groups to urge the UN Human Rights Commission to address the negligence commonly practiced toward the most vulnerable members of any society. Advocacy and activism led to the drafting and adoption of Resolution 2000/51 calling for increased attention to the field of disabilities, an effort that has encouraged further research and detailed recommendations designed to hold governments accountable for the treatment of people with disabilities. In 2001, the UN General Assembly adopted Resolution 56/168, which initiated a formal UN process for drafting a specialized convention. Since 2003, member nations of the UN have been working to draft a Convention on the Rights of People with Disabilities.[5]

One of the most important watchdog and advocacy groups is Mental Disability Rights International (MDRI). Their findings show that people with intellectual disabilities tend to be victims of the worst conditions leading to heinously inhuman and degrading treatment. They cite numerous cases of extreme human rights violations, especially in countries with limited financial resources, often resulting from such factors as structural adjustment plans that we have been outlining in this book. Social services are the first to go in economies on the brink of collapse. And within social services, those that relate to the care of individuals who cannot advocate for their own rights (due to severe disabilities or to having been stripped of those rights without due legal process) are on the very bottom of most states' list of priorities. Children and adults with intellectual disabilities tend to be categorized within institutions, the ones with the greatest needs for protection ironically subjected to the worst imaginable neglect: abandoned face-down in cribs without any human contact, tied to wheelchairs and beds, kept in cages too small to allow them to stand—conditions that are not limited to the Third World (Rosenthal and Sundram). These testimonial images are so horrific that they recall the treatment received by animals in the most squalid zoos. Institutionalized people often receive dangerous and improperly administered medical treatment, including electro-shock 'therapy.' Institutionalization also leads to the loss of skills and an inevitable turning inward for those deprived of human contact.

The most far-reaching of the many valuable recommendations proposed by the Yale Declaration is to 'explore alternatives to the use of guardianships such as mentors and citizen advocates...The legal principle of substitute decision making should be replaced, wherever possible, by supported decision making' (ibid. 475). Rather than viewing the rights and dignity of people with disabilities as exceptional, human rights thinking would benefit most from the challenge posed by those whose survival and dignity implicates the community directly in collaborative decision making.

Working with the intellectually and physically disabled, listening to what they need and desire, learning from a perspective that has been denied and silenced historically—this is where the theory and practice of social justice intersect on the ethical horizon. The extent to which a community integrates its disabled members and the support systems it devises to aid with this process are the ultimate measure of that community's spiritual health and humanity. In this regard, the rights of people with disabilities reinforce the rule of thumb we propose at the beginning of the book: namely, that the baseline measure of rights occurs in relation to how they are meaningfully applied to the most dis-possessed, disempowered, and victimized.

The Rights of the Aged

A quote from *Africanews* of Kenya sums up how the elderly were once respected and honored in Africa and, it would be correct to add, in most parts of the world:

> In Zambia, like in many other African countries, the old have always been cherished. Many people regard the elderly as reservoirs of wis-dom, custodians of social values, culture, and tradition. However, the status of the elderly in Zambia is eroding by the day. They are rapidly becoming destitutes [sic], as the current socio-economic sit-uation can no longer allow most families to take care of them. (Tembo and Sibanda 1)

While the various regions of the world are marked by different historical trends, one common feature of the general attitude toward the elderly is that they are not a source of wisdom, but a burden. In affluent countries where adult children could afford to take their aged parents into their homes instead of institutionalizing them, the trend is to preserve the nuclear family and to distance grandparents, even those who are not critically disabled, often at great financial cost to the family. As in the case of the disabled, even if elderly people's basic physical needs are met in nursing homes—and they often are not—their lives deteriorate significantly in emotional and psychological terms when they are ghettoized and have little or no meaningful contact with people of different ages. In poor countries where nursing homes are not an option for the majority, 'the elderly are being physically, financially, and mentally abused and neglected, mostly by their children' (ibid. 1).

The extended family is weakening all over the globe, in poor countries just as in post-industrial countries, leaving the elderly to fend for themselves with varying degrees of state support. While many countries have medical plans, social security, pension plans, and other forms of support, these are be-ing stretched to the limit and severely eroded due to the changing demo-graphic of a steadily increasing number of elderly people. Even in the poorest African countries, there is now a decline in the birth rate, improved health care provisions, and a moderate decline in mortality. Yet ironically, these indicators of health improvement spell disaster for the elderly. According to one forecast, 'if the current trend of lowering birth rates and lowering death rates continues, by the year 2050 one out of five people will be aged 60 years or older' ('Human Rights Explained'). These factors are quoted in most reports on the reasons for lack of support for the elderly, but it would be fair to question a system that allocates proportionally enormous funds to the military complex instead of social welfare.

Despite the international scope of the UN, 'the General Assembly...urges the support of national initiatives on ageing...so that: Appropriate national policies and programmes for the elderly are considered as part of overall development strategies' ('The Human Rights of Aged Persons' 3-4).

In some countries like Canada, government responsibility is further broken down to the provincial level, making the standardization and enforcement of rights for the aged even more difficult. The province of Manitoba is just getting around to introducing a bill of rights for the 9,000 people living in nursing homes with new rules stipulating such basic rights as 'the right to refuse medication and treatment, the right to meet with legal representatives as often as necessary and to meet privately with friends and family' ('Manitoba introduces nursing-home bill'). Such bills are crucial, especially given that in most homes the provincial standards are not posted and available only on request. Interpretation of the standards is loose particularly as a result of serious understaffing, creating uncomfortable and even humiliating circumstances. In Alberta, one of the wealthiest provinces, residents of nursing homes protested being bathed only once a week, and being abandoned on the toilet for half an hour. In one case, Marie Geddes went on a hunger strike to protest the lack of staff and may have died as a consequence. Treating human beings as just another variable to achieve cost-effectiveness has led to such absurd practices as washing and dressing residents at 3 a.m., five hours before breakfast, clearly showing no regard for normal sleep patterns and a human schedule ('Alberta's ailing homes').

The elderly are perceived as easy targets and are increasingly the victims of a wide range of crimes, from fraudulent business deals to violent burglaries. Media images contribute to the discrimination against the elderly, often representing them as comically confused and socially useless. Elderly women make up the majority of the most aged and are especially vulnerable, often the victims of neglect and of physical and psychological abuse. One of the most extreme cases of a negative image generating human rights abuses occurs in northern Ghana where 'elderly women accused of being witches have been forcibly banished to a place where they must live under deplorable conditions. The existence of the Gambaga Witch Camp says as much about how Ghanaians view elderly women as their fear of being affected by witchcraft' (Safo 2). Adequate medical care is also a serious problem in most parts of the world; in the West, big pharmaceutical companies fight to maintain high prices for their drugs, and even in affluent countries many people are without drug plans. In poor countries, hospitals discriminate against the aged, prioritizing the younger patients for treatment. Elderly people worldwide find themselves living in poverty after having worked all their lives. Some cannot even afford bus fare to travel to distant clinics for health care. Many are subject to physical and emotional abuse that remains largely out of the public eye in institutions charged with their care. And perhaps most tellingly, the elderly, as a global demographic group, have by far the highest rate of suicide, with elderly men especially at risk: 'Worldwide, men 75 and over have a suicide rate of 55.7 per 100,000, while women in the same age group have a rate of 18.8' (Kick 92-3). Implicit in such an extraordinary suicide rate is the extent to which the other issues raised in this section contribute to such a degraded quality of life that it drives many to their deaths.

In response to the violations of human rights and dignity described above, the rights of aged persons can be broken down into three main categories: protection (similar to that of children and people with disabilities, who need more protection since they depend at least partially on others' support); participation (ensuring that they are actively engaged in society instead of being isolated and disempowered); and image (the need to define a more positive idea of the identity and capabilities of the elderly) ('Human Rights Explained'). Some of the commitments made at conferences and rights documents aimed at ensuring the rights of the elderly are the UN General Assembly Proclamation on Ageing, the International Conference on Population and Development in Cairo, the World Summit for Social Development in Copenhagen, the World Conference on Women in Beijing, and the Habitat II Conference in Istanbul.

Children: Our Legacy and Our Future

Children have been one of the last groups to have their rights addressed specifically in a UN Convention (1989), the most widely ratified treaty in the world with only Somalia and the U.S. absent from the signatories.[6] This long delay may be due to the fact that abuses suffered by children can be interpreted as directed at other aspects of their identities like gender, ethnicity, poverty, and so forth. In Western societies, children are seen as symbiotically attached to their parents, especially mothers, and therefore only recently have their rights been considered as specific. Given the current state of social chaos in many parts of the world, children are abandoned or kidnapped and forced to live on the streets, to serve as soldiers in military forces, and to work under brutal conditions as bonded laborers, slaves, and prostitutes.

In addition to the social pressures that children suffer because of adult behaviors, *The Lancet* reports that approximately 10 million children, one-third the population of Canada, die each year 'most from preventable causes and almost all in poor countries. Six countries account for 50% of worldwide deaths in children younger than 5 years, and 42 countries for 90%.' Moreover, the same report emphasizes 'the importance of undernutrition as an underlying cause of child deaths associated with infectious diseases, the effects of multiple concurrent illnesses, and [the] recognition that pneumonia and diarrhoea remain the diseases that are most often associated with child deaths' (Black, Morris, and Bryce). The global apartheid that separates the rich from the poor, the majority world from the First World, effectively condemns these 10 million children to death. And poverty has dramatic effects on the family life of children. According to a 2004 study by the ATD Fourth World (*How Poverty Separates Parents and Children*), many children are condemned to separation from their families due to poverty, thus causing significant damage to their own social development as well as to the societies in which they live as a whole.

It is clear that even those who have parents, but are living in poverty, have no protection from what we commonly view as conditions afflicting adults. The UN Convention recognizes children's vulnerability and calls for special safeguards by reason of the child's physical and mental immaturity. In the global scheme of things, this nurturing view of children is limited to those living in rapidly shrinking affluent and stable situations. Even in an affluent country like Canada, a record number of children are being taken away from their parents (as a result of alcoholism, drug addiction, and consequent neglect and abuse of their children) to be placed in foster homes. AI records global case studies relating to such abuses as political killings and extrajudicial executions, disappearances, death penalty for juveniles, torture, unfair trials and arbitrary detention, together with the extreme vulnerability of children during war, which creates children refugees and asylum seekers.

In Brazil and many other countries, street children are seen by powerful elites as non-human, as criminals—which they are often forced to be—and as a danger to society. These children are consequently persecuted, tortured, and killed by security forces and death squads, 'There are many millions of street-children worldwide; 20-30% of them have no adult or family links at all, even though many are as young as five or six' (AI *Childhood Stolen* 56). Members of death squads are sometimes off-duty police officers or just neighborhood vigilantes who consider that they are providing a social service condoned by politicians. In the case of Baixada Fluminense, a ring of poor industrial cities around Rio de Janeiro, a death squad member called Nilmo asserts that even politicians who publicly oppose vigilante-style executions as part of their political platform secretly approve of the practice, as high up the ladder as President Lula da Silva. Killing petty thieves, rapists, drug-dealers, vagrants, and ex-cons is seen by some as a reasonable form of grassroots justice, especially in regions that as recently as 50 years ago did not have any public services including policing. Following a recent massacre of 29 people, most of them women, children, and gainfully employed young men, public outcry finally got results: 'on May 19, 2005, 11 police officers were charged with first-degree murder, attempted murder, and taking part in gang activity' (Blore). While men, especially those directly involved with death squads, claim that they greatly reduce crime and make the streets safe for women and children, most women are less convinced and worry that their children may be the next victims.

According to a macabre logic, street children are exterminated because they are seen as having no future; they have absolutely no status as consumers, hence businesses even pay hired killers to cleanup the streets by targeting children whose only means of survival depends on begging, drug trafficking, shoplifting, and pick-pocketing. Article 7 of the Convention on the Rights of the Child is especially poignant in this respect: 'The child shall be registered immediately after birth and shall have the right from birth to a name, the right to acquire a nationality and, as far as possible, the right to know and be cared for by his or her parents.' Children are born into such extreme poverty that their conditions are fraught with all the dangers of a war zone, part and parcel of what is being called the Fourth World War even in areas where there is no recognized armed conflict. In such extreme circumstances, they are often abandoned without being named or registered. Ironically, the unidentified corpses are sometimes offered names by unrelated families so that their burials can be recorded.

Some NGOs focus on the elimination of child labor, but it is important to take into account that adults who live in poverty and are unemployed are forced to send their children to work. Social activism that succeeds in shutting down businesses that employ children can endanger them further, by driving them into more hazardous underground jobs and prostitution. Child poverty cannot be alleviated without addressing the root causes of their parents' poverty. Too often, the abuse of children's rights is seen as a Third World problem without recognizing that not only are wealthy countries and transnational corporations implicated directly in how children are treated around the world, but abuses also happen within their own borders. Only eight states in the world are known to have executed minors, and they include the U.S. Children in poor countries are abducted for adoption in the U.S. and Europe, and there is mounting evidence that the poorest among them are even killed for the trafficking of their organs, also characteristically destined for wealthy recipients.[7]

More than 300,000 children are currently recruited into armed forces worldwide, facilitated by the UN Convention, which was watered down to make the minimum age 15 instead of 18 years (UNHCR 'The World of Children at a Glance'). Often these children are as young as six, and an estimated 30 percent are girls who suffer sexual abuse from members of their own units (AI *Casualties of War* 3 and AI *In the Firing Line* 13). There is now an international effort, in the form of the Draft Optional Protocol to the Convention, to raise the age to 18 years in order to protect children from participating in armed conflict. Predictably, this protocol 'is opposed by several powerful, developed countries, like the USA. The UK's Ministry of Defense also opposes this move' since their own minimum age is 16 years (UN 'Convention on the Rights of the Child').

According to UNHCR figures, affluent and powerful countries are not contributing enough funds to help with emergency relief or AIDS, which has killed more than 3.8 million children and orphaned another 13 million.[8] A huge improvement could be achieved in protecting children's rights and well-being: 'if developed countries met an agreed aid target of 0.7 percent of their gross national product, an extra $100 billion would be available to help the world's poorest nations' (UNHCR 'The World of Children at a Glance'). But as we discuss in the context of development, the exclusive use of GNP as an indicator of economic progress ignores global well-being and the huge social profit of saving lives.

The skewed view of progress associated with GNP cannot take into account the fact that children are the future, and that no genuine progress is possible if their lives and well-being are threatened by poverty and war, in a global system that sacrifices them to corporate profits. AI lists several concrete measures for governments to implement in order to protect children's rights. Many of these measures rest on the simple distinction that children be treated with the special care needed by those who have not reached full maturity when they are in detention or in contact with the justice system; that they be given adequate support for rehabilitation and reintegration into society after having suffered abuse, and that they be protected against hazardous labor, military recruitment, and sexual exploitation (AI 'Children—10 Steps for Implementing Children's Rights').

Civil society must adamantly oppose the techniques of corporate media and the military to erase children's deaths by referring to this destruction of the future as 'collateral damage' and 'anti-personnel' in the case of weapons technologies like land mines.[9] According to AI, public opposition to land mines convinced many military leaders to accept the ban on landmines, and in some cases even to support it. We cannot depend on the military to self-regulate how children are treated in war, and government initiatives to protect children from indiscriminate attacks happen only in response to massive public disapproval (AI *In the Firing Line* 98-9).

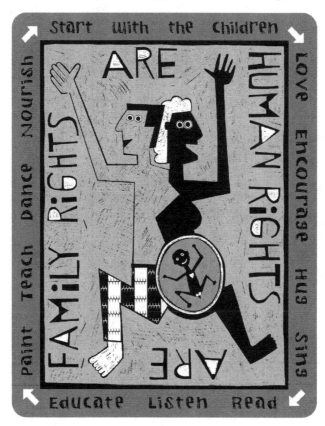

Racism and Structural Violence

> Race begins with the thought of immortality and conformity; racism begins when we put into action practices that indicate that society is permanent, that identities are known and fixed, and that human nature has reached the point where change is no longer necessary. Race is when some specimens are declared perfect and all others are judged by this exacting standard. —Cecil Foster

> The idea of 'race,' which most anthropologists and demographers consider to be a biologically insignificant term, has enormous social currency. Racial classifications have been used to deprive many groups of basic rights and therefore have an important place in considerations of human inequality and suffering…There is an enormous difference between seeing people as the victims of innate shortcomings and seeing them as the victims of structural violence. Indeed, it is likely that the struggle for rights is undermined whenever the history of unequal chances, and of oppression, is erased or distorted. —Paul Farmer

One of the subtlest and most widespread expressions of racism is embodied in the very notion that race pertains to people of color, and that consequently the problem of racism belongs to them. A perhaps more nuanced version of this view holds that racism is promoted by individuals who simply need to be educated, controlled or punished for this form of anti-social behavior. But, as a HRW report points out, 'the reality of racism does not turn on the definition of groups that are oppressed, or on the much disputed concept of race itself, but may be driven largely by the perceptions of the oppressor' (HRW 'Racial Discrimination' 2). The 'oppressor' refers to institutions, policies and agendas, to people with power over many, to systems primarily. We have noted elsewhere that in European and Anglo-American traditions there tends to be a reductive focus on the individual as fount of good and evil, and how individualism ignores history and collective memory. The amnesia that plagues the isolated individual obscures the fact that certain groups of people have been enslaved, disenfranchised, and disempowered by global political and economic systems. While individual xenophobes certainly pose a threat to racialized people, governments and media use this tactic to divert attention away from their own racist policies and practices.

Structural violence refers to the long-lasting effects of historical discrimination; it is an approach widely used by liberation theologians to draw the connections between oppression and poverty, the connections that elites try to erase. One telling example of this kind of erasure is the U.S. and white-governed South Africa's failure to record mortality data by socioeconomic status, substituting race for class, though 'results showed that, by whatever indicators of class one might choose (level of education, income, or occupation), mortality rates are related to social class' (Farmer 45).

Rights Lite: Mexico's Indigenous Communities' Fight Continues

Oaxaca, Mexico: Communiqué of September 18, 2004: 'It is now 72 hours since 14 of our brothers and sisters have been delivered to different state prisons, and 104 hours since they were forcibly removed with clubs, teargas, explosives and water guns from our squatters' protest in front of City Hall and the Church of Santo Domingo; 104 hours since they were beaten and tortured. Political prisoners all receive the same treatment in prison: offences, abuse, assault, that is what our brothers and sisters have received in prison.' (email sent by CIPO)

Seemingly benign tourism of the type one finds in Oaxaca, Mexico, can be a dangerous cover-up for rights abuses. This we discovered firsthand when we spent six weeks in Oaxaca in 2004. A large painted banner and columns of enlarged color photographs showing victims lying in pools of blood immediately caught our attention on our first trip to the Zócalo, or main plaza, at the tourist heart of the city. A young native woman sat behind a makeshift table covered in pamphlets, hand-woven *huipiles*, and a few bags of local fair-trade coffee. When asked for information, she handed us a homemade business card identifying her organization as CIPO-RFM (Consejo Indígena Popular de Oaxaca 'Ricardo Flores Magón' [Popular Indigenous Council of Oaxaca, followed by the name of a Zapotec playwright, essayist, journalist, and activist who died in a prison in Kansas in 1922]). Members of CIPO live in remote villages in the mountainous regions surrounding Oaxaca, and their obvious poverty contrasts violently with the paradisal land-of-plenty images that make the tourism culture here thrive.

Having given up all hope of ever having their human rights recognized and getting government officials to make good on their various promises for development funding, native people came from isolated rural areas to set up what they call a '*plantón*' (a kind of squatters' protest camp) in two of the main church squares. From there, they occupied government offices until they again received more promises for immediate payment and action on a number of human rights violations including the severe beatings and murders depicted in the photographs on display.

This particular *plantón* was strategically planned to coincide with the *Guelaguetza*. The term 'guelaguetza' is a Zapotec word meaning a system of mutual aid practiced in native villages whenever a communal project needs to be completed. Traditionally, the communal work would be followed by a celebration, but in the urban context, only the festive aspect of this deeply democratic practice has been appropriated and highly commercialized. The natives involved in the *plantón* lived, cooked their meals, wove, and handed out pamphlets in the square, surrounded by the trendiest and most expensive boutiques selling indigenous-made products to tourists.

The owners of these businesses, the editor of the local newspaper (with the laughably inaccurate name, '*El Imparcial*' [The Impartial]), and anyone else identified with the elite were all outraged at what they considered to be trespassing by the natives. They were accused of scaring away tourists (though we saw only foreigners approaching them to pick up pamphlets to inform themselves about the conflicts), and of smelling badly (and who wouldn't without access to bathing water!). Neither the business owners nor the editor of '*El Imparcial*' noted the irony of the situation.

When natives have been reduced to commodities and national emblems —makers of fine woven rugs, baskets, ceramics, clothes and jewelry—natives of flesh and bone can be ground into the dirt by police, paramilitaries, government officials, and the business class. Native art stands in for a remote ancestral past appropriated by the Mexican government as an emblem of national identity. Recently, Vicente Fox, even further removed from the native communities than his predecessors, implemented educational reforms that cut native studies out of the curriculum.

Many Canadians associate the movement for native rights in Mexico with the Zapatistas who, on the eve of NAFTA (January 1, 1994), started an armed struggle against the Mexican government, the ruling class of the state of Chiapas, and neo-liberalism generally. Since then, there have been conflicting reports on the effects of NAFTA on the Mexican government, largely depending on whether you consult politicians and specialists who measure only economic growth or those who scrutinize the bigger picture: the level of unemployment, underemployment, homelessness, poverty, erosion of labor laws, impact on the environment, and the continuing abuse of human rights. What many of us wouldn't have heard about are the systematic human rights violations in other regions of Mexico.

We dropped by the CIPO compound in a poor barrio of Oaxaca where their squatted headquarters are located on land reclaimed from encroaching non-natives. Raúl Gática is one of their most threatened members, and has suffered numerous beatings and tortures and is under constant death threat by local paramilitaries. This staunch rights activist showed us around the site that included a low building with offices, a residence under construction with rooms for native children from villages who could stay there while attending university or college in the city, a projected café and restaurant that will serve traditional dishes (much of the food grown on the premises and the members' communal lands), and a cultural center aimed at attracting students, scholars, activists, and anyone who wants to learn about the unthinkably rich native culture in Oaxaca and social justice issues around native rights. Kids played in the common areas and offices, no weapons were seen anywhere (unless a computer connected to the web is seen as such), and conversations in different indigenous languages mixed with the aromas coming from pots cooking traditional stews.

Now shift the scene to the State Commission on Human Rights where lawyers work in elegant offices guarded by police. Their help is often needed against corrupt *caciques* (local leaders) representing state interests in collusion with their own private interests against those of their communities. Yet the lawyers from the State Commission on Human Rights complain about how it is next to impossible to travel to those villages, and even more impossible to understand the local politics in order to make any recommendations, which are rarely acted upon anyway. A recent report by a group of students studying human rights at the Autonomous University in Mexico City confirms the charges of indigenous people taken as political prisoners on 14 September 2004, in Oaxaca and the collusion of the state's Human Rights Commission. After interviewing some of the detained, the students affirm: 'after having heard the testimonies of Margarita García García, Habacuc Cruz Cruz and Dolores Villalobos Cuamatzin, we do not have the slightest doubt that they are political prisoners since they are detained because of their social struggle and not for any crime committed. And in fact, we consider them as hostages by the authorities who have them in prison, not only to punish social struggle, but also to intimidate their comrades and society in general.' The students express shock at discovering that 'one of the members of the public organization that is supposed to defend human rights (the State Commission for Human Rights of Oaxaca) could have instead violated them, and demand the president of the State Commission for Human Rights to restrain the disguised acts of repression committed by his personnel ('Report from the Commission of Human Rights of the Universidad Autónoma').

This is 'rights lite' at work, and it happens as a function of trade agreements like NAFTA that produce these shadowy state bureaucracies to pacify concerns about the rights exploitation that underpins economies based on cheap labor. Rights lite: create a toothless bureaucracy that legitimizes the state's control over human rights issues. And at the same time do not act on virtually every recommendation made by such commissions, thereby maintaining the status quo through inaction. Hopefully the bearing witness by students and human rights activists will influence both the Mexican government and its trading partners to radically reform human rights organizations in order to end the collusion among police, politicians and corrupt human rights bureaucrats, thereby putting an end to the abuse systematically targeted at the indigenous population.

It is impossible to have an honest discussion about racism without examining history in order to understand the legacies of slavery and caste discrimination. While Westerners are quick to condemn the caste system in such countries as India, they are less likely to recognize the striking similarities of intent and effect in their own histories. Structural violence in this case refers to the historical fact of building the capitalist economy in the Americas on the enslavement of Native Americans and Africans, and then further disadvantaging these people through segregation (a term that seems to have a softer tone than 'apartheid,' only because of American bias). However, the 'Jim Crow' Laws enforcing segregation in most U.S. states from the 1880s to the 1960s were anything but soft. Named after a black character in minstrel shows, these minutely detailed laws covered all aspects of private and public life, and forbade even the promotion of equality in Mississippi: 'Any person...who shall be guilty of printing, publishing or circulating printed, typewritten or written matter urging or presenting for public acceptance or general information, arguments or suggestions in favor of social equality or of intermarriage between whites and negroes, shall be guilty of a misdemeanor and subject to fines not exceeding five hundred (500.00) dollars or imprisonment not exceeding six (6) months or both' (' "Jim Crow" Laws' 3).

What can freedom of speech, democracy, and a host of amendments to the American Constitution regarding liberty and equality possibly mean in the face of this kind of structural violence? Acknowledging the civil wrongs of a racist past is the first step towards eradicating racism. Toward this end, on June 13, 2005, the U.S. Senate gave a formal apology for having prevented any anti-lynching legislation from being passed, thereby contributing to the epidemic lynchings that plagued the U.S. from 1890-1952. And in Philadelphia, Edgar Ray Killen, a Baptist minister and suspected Ku Klux Klan member, will stand trial for the 1964 murder of three civil rights activists. These cases reveal the political roots of racism and the human rights violations that result from bad government. Legislation or lack thereof impacts all aspects of social life. According to Senator Mary Landrieu of Louisiana, lynching 'was a community spectacle and an act of domestic terrorism...she recalled that lynchings were often festive occasions where children were let out of Sunday school to celebrate and railways offered cut-rate tickets for out-of-town spectators. Picture postcards of the victims' bodies were quickly printed and sold as souvenirs' (Freeman 'Righting the Civil Wrongs'). 'Between 1882 and 1968, more than 4,700 people, most of them black, were killed by vigilante mobs who took the law in their own hands against alleged criminals or simply to settle scores or punish blacks who were considered uppity' (ibid.).

Lest we think that slavery, racism, and segregation are limited to U.S. history, let us consider a recent court ruling against Centre Maraîcher Eugene Guinois Jr., one of Canada's largest commercial vegetable farms located in the province of Québec. This particular case of racism involved black migrant workers who were ordered by the management to use a ' "blacks-only" cafeteria that lacked heat, running water, proper toilets, refrigeration and many other amenities' (Patriquin). According to the testimony of four of the approximately 100 workers treated this way, 'the black workers were verbally and physically abused on several occasions, and were the targets of graffiti reading "here are our monkeys" and "blacks are pigs" ' (ibid.). Amazingly, the company is seeking to appeal the ruling to pay the four complainants damages. The discriminatory practices described by these migrants are prevalent on large Ontario farms as well. Furthermore, law in Ontario prohibits organizing labor unions on farms, and since most agricultural workers belong to racialized groups, these laws are a form of structural violence. While the official rationalization would cite cost-effectiveness and efficiency as the objectives of this law, it is designed to keep racialized workers in a subordinate and disadvantaged position vis-à-vis their agribusiness employers. The apparent lack of racial conflict in Canada seems to have been the result of racist policies barring racialized groups from emigrating, but now that migrants and limited numbers of racialized immigrants have started to arrive, Canadians' sense of moral superiority to Americans must be challenged.

The profoundly damaging effects of belonging to groups that have been reduced to commodities and thereby dehumanized do not evaporate miraculously once slavery and apartheid are banned. Being forcibly uprooted and losing one's ancestral land and with it cultural continuity are enough to damage and even destroy a group's sense of identity. Consider by contrast how Euro-Americans cherish their history and trace their roots all the way back to Ancient Greece. While some communities have different forms of preserving cultural memory such as storytelling, this does not diminish the importance of the past in their making sense of the present. In fact, for many people, the past has an even more profound significance in terms of collective well-being in the present than does the Europeans' notion of history (often used to perpetuate the false story of white supremacy to justify conquest and empire).

In response to this global phenomenon of systemic racism, Durban, South Africa, hosted the United Nations World Conference Against Racism,

Racial Discrimination, Xenophobia and Related Intolerance (September 2001), which targeted five principal areas: caste discrimination, the protection of migrants and refugees, discrimination in the denial of citizenship rights, discrimination in criminal justice and public administration, and the matter of reparations. Reed Brody, Advocacy Director of HRW, declared that the 'victims of racism around the world expect more than empty talk—they expect action. This meeting needs to offer something to the refugee in Europe who is beaten up simply because he is a "foreigner," to the scavenger in India whose low caste prevents him from rising in life, to the Tibetan tortured by Chinese police, to the Palestinian under Israeli occupation, to the African-American child who is three times as likely to live in poverty as her white counterpart' (HRW 'Anti-Racism Summit' 1).

In accordance with the insight that we carry the past within us and need to right past wrongs in order to heal and progress, HRW expressed the hope that the conference would 'call for reparations to address the continuing effects of slavery, segregation, and other extreme forms of racism' and proposed 'the creation of truth commissions to examine how a government's past racist practices contribute to contemporary deprivation and to propose methods of redress' (ibid. 2). As we have seen in so many other instances in which U.S. interests are threatened by international human rights initiatives, the U.S. delegation left the summit justifying its refusal to participate with Secretary of State Colin Powell's announcement that 'the conference was bound to contain hateful language against Israel, and that negotiations would be futile.' Instead of staying to work with other member states to rectify any objectionable language, the U.S. fled from a forum where discussions about inequality, racism, and structural violence would force American delegates—together with all other members of the global community—to reflect upon their own problems and possible solutions (HRW 'Disappointment as U.S. Bolts' 1).

The trickle down effect of these international conferences has led to the establishment of truth commissions in various countries. The mandate of these commissions is to bring to light much-needed testimony from individuals whose stories cannot be replaced with statistical data, however useful that kind of empirical evidence is in gauging the effects of structural violence. Personal and collective stories include expressions of inevitable emotions in response to being victimized, giving this kind of truth a human dimension much more effective at communicating the speaker's dignity and defense of human rights than 'objectified' forms of information.[10]

The Ontario Human Rights Commission (OHRC) in Canada collected testimonials from victims of racial profiling, one of the most pernicious forms of racism in the province. Ontario's capital city Toronto is said to be the most multicultural in the world and its law enforcement has one of the worst reputations for discriminating against racialized people through what is deemed scientifically sound statistical evidence in the form of racial profiling. This practice 'involves a form of stereotyping based on assumptions that certain people are more likely to commit crime, or be a threat to public safety and security' (OHRC 'Statement on Racial Profiling' 1). Reading through the numerous testimonials of victims, their friends and families, collected in the OHRC report 'The Effects of Racial Profiling,' one begins to see the scope of the problem and the seriousness of the damage to racialized communities in ways that cannot be captured in purely second-hand, theorized reflections. There is no more powerful medium than people speaking up and offering on their own behalf advice on how to remedy a situation that adversely affects them.

Unfortunately, governments and law enforcement agencies rarely encourage this participatory approach. Members of the Muslim, Arab, and South Asian communities resent the fact that they are seen as communities to be looked into because they are suspected of posing a security threat. They understandably are insulted by being identified with terrorists when in fact they are just as concerned about security issues as anyone else. How much more productive would it be to engage them as members of a community of shared concerns, and to have them give their insights into the conflicts and possible solutions that government security agencies so often misunderstand with dire consequences (OHRC 'The Effects of Racial Profiling' 9).

As in the international arena, the reports and recommendations of Human Rights Commissions are not given much priority by provincial governments. The Ontario Human Rights Commission notes that 'many individuals in positions of leadership have still not taken action to address racial profiling.' Some steps have been taken, such as conducting a government review of the police complaints mechanism, the installation of cameras in police cruisers, and recent human rights awareness being undertaken by some policing services. But the OHRC concludes 'to date, however, we have seen little in the way of action or even response in other priority areas identified in the Report, including the recommendation that the government establish a racial diversity secretariat' (OHRC 'Statement on Racial Profiling' 1).

Equally discouraging is Canada's track record on bringing Aboriginal living standards up to national standards and those generally associated with an affluent country. A case of water contamination on the Kashechewan reserve in Northern Ontario in 2005 finally received extensive news coverage publicizing images and details of the appalling living conditions characterizing remote communities. According to Dr. Trussler, chief of staff at Weeneebayko General Hospital in Moose Factory, 'Nothing here is worth saving...The homes aren't worth saving. The nursing station is way out-dated. We need a hospital here, not a nursing station. It needs to be run to provincial standards, not federal standards, which are totally sub-standard. And we need to have a proper water-treatment facility...and the school needs to be replaced.' In response to the federal government's claim that there is no hepatitis A problem in Northern Canada and therefore no need to provide vaccines, Dr. Trussler retorts: 'This is absolute rubbish. There's 100 native communities in Canada currently under a boil-water advisory. Anytime you are under a boil-water advisory, there's probability you are going to run into hepatitis A sooner or later' (Rusk). The living conditions of Aboriginal people who currently also have the highest suicide rate in the world are testimony to the structural violence experienced by racialized and marginalized groups even in the wealthiest nations.

Notions of racialization are becoming more inclusive as we realize that discrimination against groups of people has little or nothing to do with biological factors or physical marks of racial or ethnic identity. This is the case with the caste discrimination prevalent in India against the Dalits (formerly known as 'untouchables') and the Burakumin of Japan. Over 250 million people suffer this form of discrimination also practiced in Nepal, Sri Lanka, Bangladesh, Pakistan and several African states. In response to the inclusion of caste discrimination in the World Conference Against Racism, the Indian government objected to what they called an 'external agenda' as if all Indians accepted the caste system, which the government represents as somehow intrinsic to Indian culture. This flies in the face of the efforts of hundreds of Indian human rights groups and NGOs dedicated to banning this form of discrimination, efforts that the Indian government has tried to sabotage on numerous occasions. As represented so powerfully in Arundhati Roy's novel *The God of Small Things*, Dalits live in a state of apartheid and have no legal recourse to defend themselves, since they not only lack police co-operation, but are often the victims of police brutality that is entirely sanctioned by the government. The concept of 'untouchable' is crucial in the process of othering the oppressed. Considered in light of Enrique Dussel's ethics of liberation and his insistence on the need for face-to-face recognition of the other's humanity in the proximity of that other's suffering body, it becomes clear how the interdiction to touch functions to distance and radically de-personalize the oppressed.

Paul Farmer, American doctor and academic, founds his medical ethics on liberation theology and its radical challenges to structural violence. He agrees with 'Jon Sobrino and others who believe that "the poor and impoverished of the world, in virtue of their very reality, constitute the most radical question of the truth of this world, as well as the most correct response to this question" ' (quoted by Farmer 202). Farmer wonders when the rubric of human rights will include all humans, and when First World nations will stop discriminating against poor humans using the logic of global markets. The most illustrative example of global structural violence comes in the form of unequal or no access to medical care. As Farmer points out, medical ethicists in affluent countries (that can afford to include ethicists in their medical budgets) spend most of their time debating whether to curtail surplus forms of intervention to prolong the lives of the terminally sick or even brain-dead.

Pharmaceutical companies concentrate on developing drugs for profit, while blatantly ignoring curable diseases that kill millions:

> Every affliction, even many of the indignities of normal aging, must have its response, as the therapeutic armamentarium grows and the desire for health makes the pharmaceutical industry the most profitable of all major industries. But inequalities of access and outcome increasingly dominate the health care arena, too. Every victory is marred by a troubling counter-story: protests of indigenous people against the Human Genome Project; grisly stories of organs stolen or coerced from the poor for transplant to the bodies of those who can pay; great enthusiasm, on the part of drug companies, for the development of new drugs to treat baldness or impotence while antituberculous medicines are termed 'orphan drugs' and thus deemed not worthy (based on profitability) of much attention from the drug companies. (Farmer 161-2)

Viewing racism from a global perspective focused on structural violence necessarily highlights some forms of racism for endangering the lives of entire communities that live in poverty due to global economic policies. Paul Farmer makes the point that identity politics in the academic world have tended to narrow the discussion of racism to elites at the expense of the vast majority of racialized people whose acute suffering cannot be separated from class and gender. Clearly, while all forms of racism must be challenged with a view to radically democratizing societies, those who are privileged regardless of their race should concentrate more of their efforts on the vast numbers of racialized people who are dying or barely surviving the multiple effects of discrimination. Those who simply accept the status quo and the injustice tend to do so at more than an arm's length from the suffering. The main conclusion of people like Farmer who work directly with destitute communities is that most problems are remediable. Interestingly, those who know through experience are the least likely to despair or sink into apathy. While specialized knowledge such as medicine is essential especially when practiced as it is in the Western tradition as emergency response, it is the general desire to know the truth about racism and poverty that will ensure access to the rights required to live with dignity.

Global Racism Squelches Haiti's Vision of Equality and Liberty

The most telling case of global structural violence directed against a racialized nation is that of Haiti, the poorest country in the Western hemisphere. A pervasive form of racism manifests itself whenever people assume that such places are disadvantaged simply due to lack of education, or high levels of corruption. While these problems are certainly contributing factors, they are the results of structural violence shaped by historical events and global relations with racist states. Citing the consequences instead of looking to the roots of poverty reveals an underlying assumption that racialized people are incapable of governing themselves and are in constant need of foreign aid. Close examination of histories written from the people's perspective, and not from that of their oppressors, discloses that foreign intervention causes and prolongs problems instead of alleviating them.

We need to be reminded of the Haitian revolution of 1804 during which a progressive view of racial equality emerged according to which all people who expressed solidarity and were willing to live in peace as equals with blacks were considered black, while those bent on enslaving and exploiting human beings were termed 'whitemen' regardless of the color of their skin (Foster 64-5). Haiti's was only the third written constitution in the world after the American and French, and the only constitution stating in no uncertain terms that the ideal nation would not be founded on race and racist exclusion. Haiti's constitution was the first to use the term 'brothers' to mean all human beings and to conceive of equality as being all-inclusive.

Haiti was seen by other American states as the greatest threat to racial and economic privilege, and the U.S. subsequently intervened to take control of Haiti's government to ensure that true liberty and human rights for all would not spread to the U.S. and through their many client states to the South. To the North, Canadian racist policies ensured immigration limited to Europeans (right up until the multicultural policies of the Trudeau government in the 1960s), and the segregation of First Nations people on reservations, an ongoing problem.

White supremacist Canadians prophesied that the U.S. would become another Haiti and decided to avoid race relations altogether by excluding and marginalizing non-whites. The U.S. government had refused to recognize Haiti's black government in deference to France and to protect its own stake in slavery.

The culmination of racist hypocrisy is to criticize a country's undemocratic government when in fact dictatorships are put and kept in place through American intervention. Such was the case of Jean-Claude Duvalier (alias 'Baby Doc') whose murderous regime had the support of Ronald Reagan's government during which time Haitian boat refugees were routinely returned to Haiti regardless of the torture and/or certain death many of them faced: 'approximately twenty-three thousand Haitians applied for political asylum in the United States. Eight applications were approved' (Farmer 36).

Haiti's first democratically elected government, led by liberation theologian Jean-Bertrand Aristide, was quickly aborted under mysterious circumstances, which involved the deposed president Aristide being flown to Africa, accompanied by 'military officials from the United States and France, acting in full knowledge of most Western nations, including Canada' (Foster 87). Mainstream media's complicity would explain why these circumstances remain a mystery. Prior to this coup, the Aristide government had organized a truth commission to ascertain the details of a massacre in the poor community of Raboteau. The process was judged by outside observers to be exemplary in terms of democratic legal procedure: 'The jury delivered guilty verdicts for sixteen of the twenty-two accused and convicted, *in abstentia*, all members of the Haitian high command, including many who had benefited from training in the United States' (Farmer 82).

Though the first of its kind in Haiti, the trial was ignored by North American media. Instead, they spread stories about chaos and corruption in Haiti. Furthermore, many of the countries harboring the criminals refused to co-operate and to arrest and extradite them. The U.S. obstructed the truth-finding process by stealing and then withholding crucial documents: 'When U.S. forces invaded Haiti in the fall of 1994, they drove trucks straight to the offices of the armed forces and the brutal paramilitary group, the Front for Haitian Advancement and Progress (FRAPH), hauling away documents, photos, videos, and other material that contained extensive evidence of egregious abuses of these forces, including gruesome "trophy photos" of FRAPH victims…They remain in U.S. government hands, under the control of the Department of Defense' (Hayner cited in Farmer 83).

Following the coup, 'the U.S. Coast Guard intercepted thirty-four thousand Haitians on the high seas; the majority of these refugees were transported to Guantánamo' where by their own accounts and those of independent observers they suffered sub-human treatment in surroundings that could only be described as a concentration camp (Farmer 56).

On the economic side of structural violence in Haiti, false development projects like Haiti's largest dam displaced about 3,000 farmers who now live in an isolated village that receives neither electricity nor water. The various forms of structural violence are interwoven, created and maintained by powerful individuals. Lest we see the widespread suffering of people as somehow inevitable or its alleviation as hopeless, Farmer reminds us that 'these afflictions are not the result of accident or a *force majeure*; they are the consequence, direct or indirect, of human agency. When the Artibonite Valley was flooded, depriving families…of their land, a human decision was behind it; when the Haitian army was endowed with money and unfettered power, human decisions were behind that, too. In fact, some of the same decisions makers may have been involved in both cases' (40).

Indigenous Women's Protection of Life Rights

The abuses to which children are subjected, the horrors produced by armies with unfettered powers, all discussed earlier in the chapter, remind us of the implications of patriarchy: a world order based on the power of men and a key determinant in the creation of global inequalities. 'Military culture typically prizes aggression and reinforces male stereotypes, while devaluing attributes traditionally associated with women' (AI *Casualties of War* 2). Stella Tamang, an indigenous woman from Nepal, chair of the Indigenous Women's Caucus of the UN Permanent Forum on Indigenous Issues, and chair of the South Asia Indigenous Women Forum, identifies the masculine and feminine qualities that relate to global conflict: 'Armed conflict is not the choice of women. It is undeniably a male-dominated, male-perpetrated game of aggression that claims innocent lives and displaces thousands of families. It is the men's creation to gain more power and more wealth. The worst pain-bearers of armed conflict are ultimately women and children' (Tamang 'Peace Teachers' 14). Her vision to end the suffering calls for global recognition of women's capacity to be peace teachers and conflict mediators. She criticizes the division of the world into the private realm to which women are relegated, and the public realm where men are thought to belong despite having shown themselves incapable of forging lasting peace agreements.

Speaking in a workshop on women as conflict mediators, Tamang makes it clear that majority world women and indigenous women conceive of their rights and their lives as inseparable from the lives of others: 'My presentation is to raise the voice of those women who are brave and are ready to die to protect and defend the children, the weak, and the elders, the animals and nature' (ibid. 14). To the common view of women's vulnerability, she responds: 'little is known about how women survive in conflict, how they protect and save the lives of thousands of children and elders, how they cope, and what they contribute toward rebuilding peace' (ibid. 14). To this end, she enumerates examples of the crucial roles women in indigenous cultures play as trusted and successful peacemakers, from the Maranao women in the Philippines and Arumanen Manobo women in Mindanao, to Maasai women, particularly the mothers of warriors who show their sympathy for both sides in the conflict, since as mothers 'they cannot afford loss of life' (ibid. 15).

Tamang contrasts these success stories with how women are restricted from official peace negotiations in the war between Nepal's Armed Forces and the Communist Party of Nepal-Maoist—how in two rounds of negotiations only the government side included one woman. Without women peacemakers, the talks invariably revolve around numbers, checks and balances in relation to weapons, territorial lines, power, laws and elections; that is, business as usual at the expense of any meaningful resolution. Tamang says that women show the human face of the conflict through their testimonies of the devastating human costs of war. Instead of negotiating power relations, the women's stories offer concrete, practical solutions.

In another case of a woman's contribution to peacemaking, Betty Bigombe, born and raised in Gulu, Uganda, is in the process of negotiating with Joseph Kony, rebel leader of the Lord's Resistance Army made up almost exclusively of children: 'According to the United Nations Children's Fund, 20,000 children have been abducted since the mid-1980s, driven by a potent mix of abuse and Mr. Kony's charismatic invocation of spirits into killing, mutilating and looting other civilians—even their own families' (Nolen 'Face to Face'). While Bigombe has a Harvard education and once held a government post in Mr. Museveni's government as minister for the pacification of the north, these are not the credentials that make her a sensitive and effective mediator. If anything, her previous involvement in the president's 'military solution' and the propaganda, repeated during 18 years of bloody clashes, that Kony's army is finished, brought Uganda no closer to a peace settlement.

Bigombe's power lies in her capacity as local resident and intelligent negotiator who does not represent the enemy but the terrorized refugees. Government arrangements to reach a ceasefire seem to have been intentionally obtuse, making the ceasefire next to impossible for the rebels to comply with, given the unreasonable deadline imposed on them allowing for no consultation among rebel leaders. Obviously, the government benefits financially from prolonging the war. Nevertheless, Bigombe managed to take two cabinet ministers into the bush for talks with Kony and made substantial headway through treating him with the respect that should be accorded to any fellow human being: ' "You've got to reach him at his level, have an ability to meet his personality," she said. "I laugh with him talk with him, all to get him to understand what he's doing" ' (ibid.). The fact that Bigombe does not stand to benefit from prolonging the conflict distinguishes her from most governments' officials. Her effectiveness is rooted in the belief that common people want peace and are willing to work toward that objective, however exotic their ideological rhetoric and cruel their acts of resistance. Finally her faith that 'there are no insurmountable situations' encourages mutual understanding, as opposed to the military might implicated in her former governmental directive to pacify only the other side. Bigombe's recognition of her adversary's basic dignity despite deep disagreement over Kony's strategies offers a radically different model not just for negotiating concrete peace treaties, but in theoretical terms as well. Her approach breaks down the binary of 'us' versus 'them' and recognizes that basic needs that go unsatisfied fuel rage and a thirst for revenge.

Majority world thinkers generally challenge the Western philosophical traditions in which Euro-centric and Anglo-centric views on human rights originate. In accordance with Arandhati Roy's observation that human rights discourse is being appropriated and reduced to limit the scope of our understanding of social justice globally, other majority world thinkers prefer to address human dignity as a more complex and inclusive approach to analyzing and responding to injustice. The Just World Trust brought together delegates from 60 countries to Kuala Lumpur in December 1994 to discuss Western global dominance and its impact upon human rights. In his introductory remarks to the conference 'Rethinking Human Rights,' Chandra Muzaffar challenges the view that Western 'democracies' are the beacons of human rights with what he calls the simple but fundamental truth that 'Western global dominance is, and has been, one of the greatest threats to the human rights and human dignity of human beings everywhere.' This recalls Ignacio Ellacuría's insight, that only the oppressed know the oppressor, which is also the insight fueling the Fourth World Movement briefly discussed in our final chapter.

The elites (corporate, military, media, and political) who marginalize and dehumanize people must be identified and systematically opposed in order to democratize the world, the only form of globalization that is sustainable. The lessons that the currently marginalized have to teach are crucial for any meaningful rights progress to be made globally. How prepared are the current hierarchies of government and state in the most developed countries to enable this democratic vision? In the honest answer to that question lies the enormous gap that rights must traverse in the years to come.

Notes

1. Ms. Bibi was awarded compensation by Pakistani President Pervez Musharraf totaling Rs.500,000 (approximately US$8,000), which she used to build two local schools (one for girls, the other for boys).

2. We are still far from achieving democratic politics even in countries that consider themselves politically enlightened, given that women are denied access to participation: 'around the world, women are seriously underrepresented in domestic politics, accounting for only 14% of national parliamentarians. There is little difference between industrial and developing countries. In most industrial countries—including France, Japan and the United States—women account for 10-20% of parliamentarians...a number of Arab states have no female representation' (UNDP, Human Development Report 2002 *Deepening Democracy in a Fragmented World* 16). Many countries have introduced quotas to accelerate women's parliamentary representation: 'they are in use in all 11 countries that have achieved more than 30% representation by women, from Sweden and other Nordic countries to Argentina...but quotas are primarily a temporary remedial measure, and are no substitute for raising awareness, increasing political education, mobilizing citizens and removing procedural obstacles to women getting nominated and elected' (ibid. 70).

3. Close to 100,000 children in Henan alone have been orphaned. By contrast, Cuba, which has the lowest rate of HIV infection in the Western Hemisphere, has had enormous success in restricting the spread of the virus precisely because it had both an effective screening process (it first detected the disease in 1985 in *internacionalistas* returning from service in Africa) and an effective education campaign (see Farmer 69-79 for a more detailed account of Cuba's response to the HIV/AIDS crisis).

4. This excerpt was taken from an educational website compiled from people whose lives have in some way been affected by HIV/AIDS (from the TeachersFirst.com site)

5. According to Mental Disability Rights International (MDRI), 'The U.S. government stands apart by stating that it will not sign such a convention. This position undermines the importance of the convention and puts the U.S. in danger of losing its place as a world leader on the rights of people with disabilities.'

6. A 'Youth Ambassadors for Peace' publication notes general hostility on the part of the U.S. toward the UN; some of it is attributable to the anti-communist paranoia that Noam Chomsky documents in U.S. media generally. Some apologists for the U.S. position charge that the UN Convention weakens national sovereignty and domestic policy, ignoring the fact that the Convention only makes suggestions and recommendations that cannot be enforced through any punitive means. A more shameful reason for U.S. opposition to the UN Convention on the Rights of the Child is that U.S. interests, both military and business, profit from activities that put children at risk. To cite a few: 'The United States provides arms, training, and money to countries that use child soldiers. This is strictly forbidden in the CRC but is a very profitable business for the U.S. government and U.S. corporations; the United States allows children to join the armed forces without parental consent at age 17, they begin recruiting programs through ROTC at the age of 8; the

United States was one of seven countries that, until the U.S. Supreme Court decision of March 1, 2005, allowed juvenile offenders to be executed; the United States has economic interests in countries where child labor is being used, consequently, business interests in the U.S. have placed their financial resources behind preventing the ratification of the treaty' ('UN Convention on the Rights of the Child' 3).

7. While anthropologist Nancy Scheper-Hughes does not refer specifically to street children here, she describes the business trend in marketing organs as follows: 'in general, the movement and flow of living donor organs—mostly kidneys—is from South to North, from poor to rich, from black and brown to white, and from female to male bodies' ('Organ Trade' 2). When she does address the possibility of trafficking in organs extracted without consent from the poor and from kidnapped street children, she treats it as 'rumor,' qualifying its ability as the 'weapon of the weak' to 'challenge and interrupt the designs of medicine and the state' ('The Global Traffic in Human Organs' 202). It is not clear why poor people's testimony should be interpreted in this symbolic way, given the concrete evidence of killings and removal of organs without consent reported by such organizations as The Preda Foundation (Upper Kalaklan, Olongapo city, Philippines), and The International Campaign against Child Trafficking (ICACT), which 'points out that children are not only trafficked for their organs and body parts but for a variety of illegal purposes, including sexual exploitation, adoption by childless couples, begging and transporting drugs,' not to mention child pornography (BBC 'Azerbaijan probes child-organ traffickers' 2).

8. Between 1994 and 1999, the UN requested $13.5 billion in emergency relief funding, much of it for children. It received less than $9 billion. In 1998 donor countries allocated $300 million to combat AIDS, though an estimated $3 billion was needed (UNHCR 'The World of Children at a Glance').

9. Although the U.S. first led the initiative to ban land mines, it retains 1 million deadly 'dumb' mines destined for Korea, and has approximately ten million stockpiled. While the U.S. has had a moratorium on export since 1992, it has refused to announce a moratorium or ban on the production of mines. Canada has been the leader in the ban movement and introduced a UN resolution supporting the treaty (Ottawa 1997), inviting all states to sign. None voted against, but the U.S. and Cuba abstained. The U.S. and other countries have opted to deal with these issues in a guarded and watered down way in order to reduce the impact on the arms industry. They have done this through the Conference on Disarmament, at which some members tried to negotiate a transfer ban on mines instead of a total ban on the weapon (HRW 'The Mine Ban Treaty and the Americas').

10. The Jesuit Jon Sobrino makes a similar case for the power of images, another form of bearing witness: 'Statistics no longer frighten us. But pictures of the starving children of Biafra, of Haiti, or of India, with thousands sleeping in the streets, ought to. And this entirely apart from the horrors that befall the poor when they struggle to deliver themselves from their poverty: the tortures, the beheadings, the mothers who somehow manage to reach a refuge, but carrying a dead child—a child who could not be nursed in flight and could not be buried after it had died. The catalogue of terrors is endless' (quoted in Farmer 8).

Chapter 4

Terrorism, Security, And Selective Rights In An Age Of Retributive Fear

The tragedy of 9/11 produced dramatic shifts in how developed nations' legal structures impact on human rights. The U.S. Patriot Act, a bill that permits major rollbacks of accrued civil liberties and a widely imitated piece of legislation in democracies like Canada and India, is only one of many new instruments that undermine rights under the guise of the so-called 'war on terror.' It is impossible, post 9/11, to speak of rights without addressing the massive campaign currently being deployed to undermine civil rights in the name of state self-interest and so-called 'security.' What would appear to be a small cadre of oligarchic interests are shaping state-interests along lines that 'secure' their goals. In many cases those interests may be reduced to economic outcomes such as the control of major oil-producing regions or the stimulation of slack economies via the arms/war industry.

Terrorists believe that anything goes in the name of their cause. The fight against terror must not buy into that logic.
—Kenneth Roth, Executive Director, HRW

The stage is being set for a full-scale assault on human rights.
—Arundhati Roy

Terrorism is to be condemned whether it includes state terrorism, individual terrorism or terrorism that justifies itself as part of a struggle for liberation. Movements using terrorist methods annul the missions to which they are dedicated and lose all claims to legitimacy.
—50th Congress of International PEN, 1987

Post-9/11 restrictions on rights were implemented ostensibly to create a more secure environment through the extraction of information from suspected terrorists (often using torture), the restriction of flows of human traffic across international borders, the increased surveillance of private citizens, the legal harassment of dissidents and critics, and so forth. In reality these restrictions do nothing of the sort. Instead they exacerbate injustices and the inequitable treatment of minority cultures, critical and oppositional voices, and the already disempowered, among numerous others. In this section we examine how the war on terrorism has been marked by degradations of achieved human rights and civil liberties—while acknowledging that terrorism potentially compromises all forms of established rights environments. It has become clear post 9/11 that terrorism poses two immediate threats to rights: one involves actual acts of terror and the other entails the response or backlash against those acts of terror, whether in restrictions on civil liberties in the name of security of person or in state interventions against terrorist-sponsored states in the name of state security.

Both threats derive from a culture of retributive fear. The culture of fear and paranoia that underlies the war on terror is not conducive to rights culture —if only because the war itself is such a crude instrument and is itself an opportunity to further abuse rights. No country has ever been bombed into democracy. Generally, wars' underlying motivations are at odds with meaningful rights outcomes within a global context that will require other means than brute force to resolve situations with profound historical and cultural roots. Moreover, the anti-terrorist legislation being deployed in the two nations most responsible for the war on terror (the U.S. and the UK, incidentally the two nations ranked at number one and four globally in terms of being leading suppliers of major conventional weapons) is being used to contain, deter, or shut down legitimate protests and critiques against state practices at odds with rights practices.

The 2005 HRW Report states that 'Washington's moral authority in the war on terrorism has been undermined by the abuse of prisoners in Iraq [referring to the Abu Ghraib prison scandal] and the secretive detention and coercive techniques used against prisoners elsewhere' with Ken Roth, the HRW executive director, noting that when the U.S. 'has set itself up as the defender of human rights around the world...[and] it fails to adhere to long-established standards, it lends seeming legitimacy to repressive practices pursued by other governments in the name of security' (quoted by McCarthy). Regardless of one's stance on the moral legitimacy of the war on terror as pursued by the U.S., the point is that significant abuses have taken place and that these are magnified by the position of the U.S., described by State Department spokesperson Richard Boucher 'as at the forefront of the defence and promotion of human rights around the world' (ibid.).

The legitimacy of rights as a moral force is compromised as soon as those who set themselves up as leaders in the sustenance and promotion of rights commit violations or abuses of rights. In the war on terror, numerous rights violations have occurred on a global scale that have not demonstrably or measurably made the world a better, safer place. Internecine guerilla warfare, puppet governments, the ongoing exploitation of resources to the benefit of multinational interests, and the restoration of Afghanistan as the main source of opium for the world have replaced the twin evils of the Taliban and Saddam Hussein and his cronies. Messy as the situation is and compounded by the moral relativism that produces simplistic 'us against them' positions, a key factor in how the war on terrorism has produced negative results is the change in internal policies of industrially developed nations with respect to their own citizens' rights. The damage done is even more profound when those seen to be in symbolic positions of leadership in relation to the promulgation of rights worldwide exemplify the ways in which rights, civil liberties and social justice backslide when confronted with state responses to terrorism.

Shortly after the so-called war on terror was launched, HRW noted in 2002 how on a global scale, governments were 'using the U.S.-led war on terrorism as an excuse to carry out repressive policies and crush...internal dissent' (quoted in BBC ' "War on Terror" Curbing Human Rights'), the key countries identified in the report being Russia, Uzbekistan, and Egypt. Further, the report noted how 'the United States and its Western allies are turning a blind eye to abuses in friendly countries in return for their support in the campaign against terror.' Thus, changes in the internal policies of leading rights nations produce changes in the internal policies of countries in which rights culture is less present, a tragic circumstance that contributes to an overall cycle of declining liberties as sanctioned by responses to terrorism. Or, as stated by Michael Ignatieff, 'To conduct a defense of liberal society in defiance of these precommitments [to rights culture within a liberal democracy] is to betray the order that is being defended, as well as the citizens whose security depends on that order' (*The Lesser Evil* 53).

The key problem in this notion relates to *how* the defense of rights ideals is undertaken primarily through military engagement and the enormous resources deployed to make such an engagement possible—and how, in the case of post-9/11 terrorism, the key source of the terrorists who apparently committed the actions, Saudi Arabian cells of Al-Qaeda, were very much secondary targets as opposed to Afghanistan and Iraq, both crucial to consolidating American oil interests. One must ask if similar resources to those deployed for military reasons had been reallocated for education, aid, building meaningful cross-cultural understanding, conflict resolution through diplomacy, and so forth would not a more constructive human rights outcome have prevailed? Are the effects of military investment, which contribute to the militarization of domestic space in the developed world, really appropriate means for solving complex problems with meaningful rights outcomes? Militarization has produced, among others, multiple forms of surveillance, instantaneous access to strategic communications, the arming of private citizens, the production of gated local and global communities, the ghettoizing of violence, game- and role-playing based on military models (the militarization of domestic, community space), the pollution of geographical space through the extensive use of depleted uranium weapons (among other chemical agents), which radiate both soldiers and civilians and leave a vast trail of invisible destruction in their wake, and most importantly, the massive redistribution of resources away from other strategies for sustainable survival. How can a vision of human rights survive, let alone spread, from such a death- and fear-driven culture?

From 'Campaign Against Depleted Uranium'

What is Depleted Uranium?

The misnamed 'Depleted' Uranium is left after enriched uranium is separated from natural uranium in order to produce fuel for nuclear reactors…While the term 'depleted' implies it isn't particularly dangerous, in fact, this waste product of the nuclear industry is 'conveniently' disposed of by producing deadly weapons. Depleted uranium is chemically toxic. It is an extremely dense, hard metal, and can cause chemical poisoning to the body in the same way as can lead or any other heavy metal. However, depleted uranium is also radiologically hazardous, as it spontaneously burns on impact, creating tiny aerosolised glass particles, which are small enough to be inhaled. These uranium oxide particles emit all types of radiation, alpha, beta and gamma, and can be carried in the air over long distances. Depleted uranium has a half-life of 4.5 billion years, and the presence of depleted uranium ceramic aerosols…[therefore] poses a long-term threat to human health and the environment.

Depleted Uranium at War

In the 1950s the United States Department of Defense became interested in using depleted uranium metal in weapons because of its extremely dense, pyrophoric qualities and because it was cheap and available in huge quantities. It is now given practically free of charge to the military and arms manufacturers and is used both as tank armor, and in armor-piercing shells known as depleted uranium penetrators. Over 15 countries are known to have depleted uranium weapons in their military arsenals—UK, U.S., France, Russia, Greece, Turkey, Israel, Saudi Arabia, Bahrain, Egypt, Kuwait, Pakistan, Thailand,

Iraq and Taiwan—with depleted uranium rapidly spreading to other countries. Depleted uranium was first used on a large scale in military combat during the 1991 Gulf War, and has since been used in Bosnia in 1995, and again in the Balkans war of 1999 [and again in 1991 and in the most recent post-9/11 invasion of Iraq].

> A sub-commission of the United Nations Commission on Human Rights appointed a 'rapporteur' to investigate the use of depleted uranium weapons among other types of weapons, after passing a resolution which categorized depleted uranium weapons alongside...nuclear, chemical and biological weapons, napalm, and cluster bombs as a 'weapon of indiscriminate effect.' [our emphasis]

The widespread diffusion of depleted uranium in faraway war zones (like Afghanistan, Kuwait, and Iraq post-9/11) that have been created as a function of the war on terror presents another rights enigma, producing disease, trauma, death, and long-term environmental damage. Robert Fisk has carefully documented the astonishing rise in the cancer rates of civilians in Iraq who lived in areas hit hard by DU munitions. Fisk managed to access a restricted letter from Paddy Bartholomew, the business development manager of AEA Technology, 'the trading name for the UK Atomic Energy Authority,' which states that 'U.S. tanks fired 5,000 DU rounds [in the Gulf war], U.S. aircraft many 10s of thousands and UK tanks a small number of DU rounds. The tank ammunition alone will amount to greater than 50,000 lbs of DU...if the tank inventory of DU was inhaled, the latest International Committee of Radiological Protection risk factor...calculates 500,000 potential deaths' (*The Great War* 735). Moreover, the tortured bodies of children and adults who die of cancers caused by DU remain uncounted as either victims of torture or casualties of war.

These staggering mortality implications in conjunction with the long-term environmental damage caused by indiscriminate use of these munitions amount to crimes against humanity and the earth, with civilians bearing the cost, yet again, of the long-term suffering associated with DU. Remember that the most basic form of right, upon which all forms of security are based, is to a secure environment, a secure ecology. Thus, the so-called 'war on terror' produces its own terrors, severely compromising rights for civilians who bear the burden of what is odiously termed 'collateral damage.' In the case of DU munitions that damage will be generational, wreaking both ecological and human havoc, and, of course, sowing the very seeds of irrevocable hate for the perpetrators that will make the world less secure.

The War on Civil Liberties: the UK, India, U.S., and Canada

Meaningful rights outcomes are severely compromised when the ostensible *defense* of rights becomes a selective *attack* based on retributive fear that serves imperial self-interest window-dressed as genuine concern for global rights.[1]

In the UK, the human rights watchdog group Liberty has analyzed anti-terrorism legislation in relation to both Ireland and, more recently, to Muslims living in the UK. A Liberty commentary in 1993 on the Prevention of

Terrorism Acts stated 'A suspect community has been constructed against a backdrop of anti-Irish racism. The community has suffered widespread violation of their human rights and civil liberties. As a consequence, the United Kingdom's reputation throughout the world in upholding human rights and civil liberties has been constantly compromised' (Liberty *Suspect Community* 3). After passage of the Terrorism Act 2000 and the Anti-Terrorism, Crime and Security Act 2001 'The similarities between the treatment and experiences of the Irish community at the height of the IRA threat and of the [1.6 million strong] British Muslim community today [2004], are striking' (ibid. 3).[2]

From internment to policing ('the number of Asians stopped and searched by police rose 41% between 2000/01 and 2001/02, and searches on black people rose 30% compared to 8% for white people in the same period' [5]), the cases of Islamophobia have significantly increased as a result of the legislative response to 9/11 with significant increases in assaults, vandalism, and hate messages transmitted via email, Internet and telephone (7). Moreover, the end result has *not* been to achieve constructive co-operation between UK authorities and British Muslims, that community becoming 'increasingly alienated and their relationship with authorities seriously damaged,' which, according to Liberty, 'makes tackling the terrorism threat in [the UK] more difficult' (7). Moreover, Liberty has also found that 'Of the more than 7,000 people detained in Britain under the Prevention of Terrorism Act, the vast majority were released without charge and only a small fraction have ever been charged...Almost without exception these people could have been arrested under the ordinary criminal law' ('Terrorism'). In the month after the 7 July 2005 London bombings that killed 52 people, as reported by Joe Friesen, hate crimes against Muslims rose by over 600 percent thereby increasing the sense of localized paranoia and insecurity. It is crucial to understand that both terrorist attacks and the legislative responses to them are heinous and work together to weaken and even suspend civic liberties, and create the climate for racialized responses to global conflict generally. The rhetoric by which the conflict is polarized in terms of attack and counter-attack produces insecurity, especially in complex multicultural spaces such as those to be found in the contemporary UK.

In India, the 2002 passage of the Prevention of Terrorism Act (POTA) permitted widespread abuses, including the targeting of the Adivasis (the original, tribal inhabitants of India), Dalits (so-called untouchables), women, and Muslim minority populations: 'In Gujarat after the 2002 state-assisted pogrom in which an estimated two thousand Muslims were killed and one hundred and fifty thousand driven from their homes, two hundred and eighty-seven people have been accused under POTA. Of these, two hundred and eighty-six are Muslim and one is a Sikh!' (Roy *An Ordinary Person's Guide* 99). Despite the repeal of POTA in September 2005, India's new government 'refused to drop charges against the 1,600 people charged under the act and eliminated safeguards against the interception of electronic and telephone communications' ('State of Fear' 19).

Both HRW and AI note that while the POTA was repealed, security legislation of various sorts continues to be used in India to 'shield security forces from accountability' (HRW 2005 Human Rights Overview 'India 2005') and 'to facilitate arbitrary arrests, torture, and other grave human rights violations, often against political opponents and marginalized groups' (AI 2005 Annual Report 'India 2005'). As is so often the case when one law is repealed, other laws kick in surreptitiously to do its work, a major problem in consistency of application that applies generally to legislation that affects rights. In India, for instance, amendments to the Unlawful Activities (Prevention) Act in 2005 included provisions similar to the POTA and some state authorities, which continue to apply these 'security' laws, made use of the lapsed Terrorist and Disruptive Activities Act for the detention and harassment of rights activists and political opponents. Moreover, other laws, like the National Security Act, the Disturbed Areas Act, and the Armed Forces Special Powers Act provided a variety of legislative tools that permitted abuses, deaths in custody, and led to widespread allegations of torture (HRW 2005 Human Rights Overview 'India 2005').

The Annual Report of the Indian National Human Rights Commission (NHRC) for 2003-04 emphatically stated that 'Anti-terrorist measures must be, and be seen to be, directed only against terrorists and not against innocent civilian populations' (23) and that 'any lasting peace and long term national security depend on proper respect for human rights' (23). In India, the imbalance between the use of security legislation for ongoing local acts of state repression and the laudable declarations of the NHRC underlines the post-9/11 situation where anti-terrorist security legislation is used against vulnerable civilian populations that have nothing to do with the kind of terrorism unleashed in the tragic events of 9/11. Sadly, India is not the only democracy in which this is the case.

In Canada, Bill C-36, the 2002 Anti-Terrorism Act, was found by the Executive Director of CAIR-CAN (Council on American-Islamic Relations-Canada), Riad Saloojee, to have institutionalized 'norms that violate the rule of law: secret evidence, secret proceedings, secret processes to list people and individuals as terrorists.' At the end of 2004, 'Five Muslim non-citizens have waited a combined total of more than 174 months—about 14 years—in Canadian jail cells under what might be the country's dirtiest little secret: security certificates' (Saloojee)—these men are being held without charge or bail based on evidence neither they nor their lawyers are permitted to see. The disastrous case of Maher Arar has further aggravated concerns that the desire for security is destroying basic rights. The Syrian-born Canadian citizen Arar was detained on 26 September 2002 by U.S. officials while in transit from Tunisia to Canada (with his wife and children returning from a vacation) in New York's JFK airport. Twelve days later, he was chained, shackled, and flown ('rendered') to Jordan aboard a private plane and from there transferred to a Syrian prison where he was imprisoned, interrogated, and tortured for 10 months.

Arar's case violated Article 3 of the UN Convention Against Torture, which addresses *non-refoulement*, the principle that under no circumstances should a person be transferred or returned to a country where he or she risks torture. The October 2005 report of Stephen J. Toope for the Canadian Commision of Inquiry into the Actions of Canadian Officials in Relation to Maher Arar concluded that Arar, whose transfer to Syria violated Article 3 of the UN Convention Against Torture, was 'subjected to torture in Syria.' Shockingly, memos written by the Canadian ambassador to Syria, Franco Pillarella, suggested that rather than defending the rights of a Canadian citizen, the ambassador and Canadian officials generally were, according to CBC News reports, 'extremely eager to obtain the fruits of the torture that was inflicted on Mr. Arar' ('Documents suggest Canadian involvement in Arar interrogation').[3] Because Arar was innocent, his case prompted a public inquiry in Canada but has done little for security purposes except raise suspicions that racial targeting and clandestine inter-governmental dealings threaten the security of Canadian citizens more than they do anything to stop actual terrorists.

The U.S. Patriot Act, also known as the Uniting and Strengthening America by Providing Appropriate Tools Required to Intercept and Obstruct Terrorism Act, was rapidly developed as a response to the 9/11 attacks. But the Patriot Act also turned into law items on the FBI and others' agendas that had previously not passed Congress. These items were now deemed passable because of the terrorist threat. The exceedingly complex law received little Congressional oversight and debate, much less a close reading by any of the Congressmen who passed it in its amended form (remember the scene in Michael Moore's documentary *Fahrenheit 9/11* where Congressman John Conyers, a Michigan Democrat and member of the House Judiciary Committee, ironically says of himself and his colleagues, 'we don't read most of the bills'), and was signed into law by President Bush 26 October 2001, a little over a month after the 9/11 attacks. Noam Chomsky notes how 'The Patriot Act, and the new, planned Patriot 2 Act...undermine...fundamental civil liberties to a remarkable extent...the current Justice Department has claimed the right to arrest people, including American citizens, put them in confinement indefinitely, without charge, without access to lawyers and families, until the president declares that the war on terror is over. They have even gone beyond that. The new plans include…actually tak[ing] away citizenship if the Attorney General decides to do so' (Chomsky 'Amsterdam Forum').

As with the other anti-terrorism acts we've already examined, the U.S. Patriot Act entailed extensive restrictions and changes to acquired civil liberties, as documented by groups like the American Civil Liberties Union (ACLU) and the Electronic Freedom Foundation (EFF). The latter notes how the Patriot Act 'threatens the basic rights of millions of Americans' because it permits, among other things, increased surveillance of citizens (with little restriction), increased government secrecy round its covert actions aimed at citizens, and has set in motion the creation of a Defense Advanced Research Projects Agency (DARPA) to develop a system known as 'Total Information Awareness' (TIA), to mine, collect, and analyze massive amounts of hitherto private information about individual Americans.

Worse, due to lack of transparency in the application of the law, none of these measures can be understood to have produced meaningful anti-terrorist results. The little evidence that does exist suggests—as in the case of the Guantánamo Bay detention and torture facility—that minimal useful information has come of these measures in proportion to the damages done to human rights codes and covenants. Louise Arbour, the United Nations Human Rights Commissioner, stated at the end of 2004 that the response to terrorism, which she described as 'confused,' is 'in danger of jeopardizing civil liberties' and that there is a 'constant threat to human rights in areas where there is armed conflict' (CBC News 'Fight against terrorism threatens human rights: UN'). Such a finding echoes other such findings, which state that a pro-interventionist stance in the securing of human rights via armed intervention 'functions as a continuous generator of increasingly frequent conflicts' (Babic 65). The urgent necessity of developing and deploying sophisticated responses to complex security situations must begin by recognizing this fundamental truth especially with regard to the use of military force and its contribution to the erosion of rights standards and sustainable notions of conflict resolution in which achievable ententes are produced.

Tortured Bodies/Tortured Logic: The Myth of Militarized Global Security

Article 3 of the UDHR—'Everyone has the right to life, liberty and security of person'—establishes a core principle that ties together the right to life in relation to liberty and security. Security as a concept is all-encompassing, not just a matter of security from violence. Vandana Shiva states that 'Ecological security is our most basic security' (*Earth Democracy* 5) and all securities move out from this basic formulation into security of person from violence, from injustice, from prejudice, and so forth. Hunger, lack of potable water, the threat of death from lack of sanitation or endemic diseases and how these are interrelated with militarized responses to security situations, let alone to forms of economic warfare (as in the UN-sanctioned blockade of Iraq that led to an estimated 500,000 deaths of children in that country),[4] must all be factored into the global security reality that has emerged as a function of the war on terror. Life's rights in their fullness are, in other words, concomitant with secure freedom, which has as its starting point ecological security but also includes security of sustenance and economic security. But, as with any simple, self-evident legal declaration, spin-masters of various types have confused and eroded an integrated interpretation of Article 3 such as we propose above. The result is that some 60 years later, security of person is being spuriously achieved through causing insecurity of person to those tortured or dealt with militarily, as a result of the all-encompassing war on terror, which has produced a dramatic increase in state-sanctioned global terror.

The global militarization of notions of 'security' (and here we include torture as part of that approach) has produced a rights climate that justifies unimaginable suffering, a crude 'eye for an eye' response that subverts basic life rights and values (Christian, Islamic, or otherwise) embedded in a global civil commons supposedly founded on the comprehensive respect for the dignity of all life at all times. The result: tortured bodies and tortured logics of ethical accommodation that have severely undermined global security, especially for those most vulnerable and defenseless, the civilians caught in the hail of bullets, 'smart' bombs, and illegal detentions of the last years. Rights outcomes that respect the logic of the UDHR's Article 3 will never be achieved through the myth of a comprehensive militarized global response to security issues, for that response propagates insecurity and the conditions for long-lasting threats to the global enactment of Article 3. Every body tortured or killed in this war for security exponentially increases the number of people affected negatively. Families, friends, and neighbors see their perilous 'security' reality and its devastating effects on local communities while the perpetrators of torture and civilian killings return to their own 'secure' environments, all the more dehumanized by their own actions, which in turn affect their own local communities. Ezat Mossallanejed, a counselor and policy analyst at the Canadian Centre for Victims of Torture (CCVT), argues, in his account of the victims of torture brought on by the war on terror, that 'The ongoing massacre of vulnerable civilians, women, children, and elders alike, and the destruction of houses, crops and livestock are justified by both sides as...the inevitable price that must be paid for "freedom." Humanity has lost ground in the process of dehumanization of Westerners (especially Americans) on the one hand, and Muslims on the other. Torture, war crimes, and various crimes against humanity are sanctioned and justified as necessary evils with almost no respect for customary international law' (21). Mossallanejed's findings are congruent with the AI report on torture and accountability on the war on terror, which begins by stating that 'The torture and ill-treatment of Iraqi detainees by U.S. agents in Abu Ghraib prison was—due to a failure of human rights leadership at the highest levels of government—sadly predictable' (AI 'United States of America: Human dignity denied' 3). The AI report continues by citing a senior UK judge, Lord Justice Steyn, to the effect that 'It is a recurring theme in history that in times of war, armed conflict, or perceived national danger, even liberal democracies adopt measures infringing human rights in ways that are wholly disproportionate to the crisis' (3).[5]

When disproportionate actions taken in the name of security wreak death, destruction, humiliation, and broken, scarred bodies, all in the name of a spurious logic that says such actions result in a greater global good, it is clear that meaningful rights outcomes are seriously compromised and subverted over a long term. While crude militarized responses to security threats leave long-lasting damage, they also sow the seeds of long-term insecurity, an ever-widening spiral of violence and counter-violence that undermines the dignity of all life and the very principles upon which the UDHR was founded. Recent conclusions by Human Rights Watch suggest that government policies that allow torture and militarized responses to terror are deliberate and are used to attack political opponents, as is the case in Uzbekistan, Russia, and China, to name a few. Of equally serious concern is how countries that identify themselves at the forefront of preserving democracy and human freedoms have made 'deliberate policy choice[s] embraced by the top leadership' that permit torture and that seek to resolve complex security issues through military initiatives (*Human Rights Watch World Report 2006*).[6]

Numerous issues complicate this scenario, including the contracting out of interrogation to private contractors trained by Lockheed Martin, the largest military company in the world, with human rights groups noting that contractors are less trained, less accountable, and less controlled than are their military counterparts. Other issues include the use of secret detention centers to imprison secret detainees, including what William Schulz of AI says is an 'archipelago of prisons around the world, many of them secret prisons, into which people are literally being disappeared, held in indefinite, incommunicado detention without access to lawyers or a judicial system or to their families' ('Rights group leader says U.S. has secret jails'). Add to that the not-so-secret detention centers at Guantánamo, Cuba, and the notorious Abu Ghraib prison 20 miles west of Baghdad, with all the documented abuses and torture meted out in these places, and the rights scenario related to achieving human security becomes even more fraught. In the case of secret detentions, the lawyers' group Human Rights First concluded its detailed report on this practice by stating, 'The United States is losing the critical moral high ground that is essential to achieving success against terror; we are now used as an example of unchecked government power by the most repressive regimes in the world' (Pearlstein 28).

What to do about this state of affairs? The 2003 *Human Security Now* report produced by the Commission on Human Security, co-chaired by Sadako Ogata and Amartya Sen, calls for a visionary 'people-centered' approach by policies and institutions and a global initiative for human security that protects and empowers at the local, regional, and national levels. Measures to achieve this initiative would include preventing local and global conflict and promoting human rights and development; addressing massive global economic inequalities that are often at the root of persistent conflicts; deepening democratic principles and practices and especially the development of responsible, empowered citizenship; protecting people from arms proliferation, whether small arms or weapons of mass destruction while at the same time carefully scrutinizing military spending in relation to other human security priorities like a safe environment and sustainable food and water supplies; supporting the human security of migrants, refugees, and displaced persons; the establishment of human security transition funds for post-conflict situations; encouraging fair trade and markets that benefit the extreme poor; providing globally minimum living standards; allowing universal access to basic health care; empowering all people with universal basic education through stronger global and national efforts; clarifying the need for a global human identity using education to 'promote understanding of people's multiple identities and of the interlinkages within the common global pool of learning' (141); affiliating the aforementioned initiatives in a global alliance (130-43). The report clearly recognizes the complex dimensions of security as a concept that exceeds reductive definitions of it solely to military terms. And it exposes the spurious logic, which associates militarized responses that produce tortured civilian bodies, with meaningful security outcomes. Human security, then, cannot be based on the myth of the effectiveness of militarized interventions where torture and collateral damage are permissible side effects. Rather, human security is based on a comprehensive, integrated vision of ecological, economic, cultural, and political well-being that begins and ends with the respect for the dignity of all life at all times.

State Terror and Convenient Non-Intervention

Clearly, when the common people's civil liberties including the right to security of person are under consistent, demonstrable threat from terrorist activities, proactive measures must be taken to protect them while at the same time balancing those protections against accrued freedoms—not to mention the threat of proliferating conflict. Dictatorships (Iraq) and fundamentalist religious states (Afghanistan under the Taliban) are affronts to the universal application of internationally agreed-upon human rights doctrines. But the selective application of definitions of terrorism to suit state self-interest, which conveniently ignores other forms of terrorism, is a major problem in the just, equitable, and universal application of rights standards globally.

The selective application of definitions of terrorism has been conflated with attacks on the poorest most disempowered peoples in the world, thus further compromising the just application of global rights agreements. Afghanistan, for instance, falls outside of rankings by the UN Human Development Report because it does not even have the national institutions necessary for the proper compilation of the required data. The logic that underlies though is that poverty and terror go hand-in-hand, that in the 'War Against Terror, poverty is being slyly conflated with terrorism' (Roy *An Ordinary Person's Guide to Empire* 86). The retributive acts of post-9/11 America focused on two hugely impoverished countries, Afghanistan and Iraq: remember, as mentioned earlier, that as a function of UN-approved, American-led sanctions against Iraq alone, some 500,000 children died as a result of preventable disease and hunger, a situation that Arundhati Roy has described as neo-genocide, where indirect actions lead to massive casualties and accountability is fudged in the name of imperial self-interest (ibid. 88).

But poverty and terror are married in other ways too. Consider the case of the terrorist actions that took place in Rwanda, ranked in 2003 as 158 out of 175 countries for its human development, culminating in genocidal acts that killed between 800,000 and a million people in about 100 days, from April through June 1994. A 30,000-strong unofficial Hutu militia group called the *Interahamwe* ('those who attack together') led the genocide in Rwanda and sponsored horrific acts of terror during the short time it took to kill so many people, most of whom were Tutsis. And the most vulnerable suffered, from women and children butchered in unspeakable ways (bullets were expensive so machetes were used), through to moderate Hutus, intellectuals, the elderly, and the poorest of the poor. Friends and neighbors were enlisted to kill each other as this ultra-poor country erupted into a tragic orgy of terror and violence.

What happened in Rwanda as a result of longstanding ethnic tensions between the Hutu-majority and the Tutsi-minority did not lead to a war on terror in Rwanda or in other parts of Africa, much less a war on genocide. And this in spite of what could only be described as state-sponsored terrorism manifested through paramilitary and unofficial militia forces. If anything, the Rwanda example made clear how those with true power apply selective self-interest on a global level. President George W. Bush, then Governor of Texas Bush, stated the principle of selectivity as clearly as it can be put when asked what the United States would do if faced with another Rwanda situation: 'Rwanda held absolutely no strategic interest or value for the United States whatsoever and therefore the United States would simply watch from the sidelines once again' (cited by Stephen Lewis, 'Politics, Resources' 2).

Selectivity in the application of rights principles on a global scale is a major obstacle. And it is compounded by how rights principles are almost always interpreted to suit particular interests. Thus, when disproportionate attention was given to the human rights violations of the Iraqi Kurds (involving the chemical massacre of some 5,000 residents of Halabja in 1988) as opposed to the Kurdish people in Turkey where some 30,000 people have died, most of them Kurds, as a result of state violence against them, one must ask who benefited from such an interpretation?[7]

And what about other sites of extraordinary violence? The Congo where, after the colonial genocide that took place between 1880 and 1920 when over 10 million people died, some 3.5 million now lie dead since 1998 with a similar number turned into refugees; in 1952, the struggle for independence that Kenya entered into with Britain, the so-called Mau Mau Rebellion, left possibly hundreds of thousands dead and led to detainment in camps for many more, as well as torture, starvation, rape and mass executions; the American-backed Indonesian military occupation of oil-rich East Timor in 1974, which claimed about 200,000 lives (about one-third of the entire East-Timorese population) and where ongoing violence continues to claim lives as in the Santa Cruz massacre of 1991 where Indonesian military fired on unarmed pro-independence demonstrators at the Santa Cruz cemetery in Dili; Kashmir, where since 1989 over 80,000 now lie dead, killed by security forces most simply for being Muslim; the massacre by police forces of hundreds of peacefully protesting students in Tlatelolco, Mexico City, in 1968, an action that was extensively supported by CIA analysis that went so far as to claim that Cuba was preparing to smuggle arms to the students (to this day estimates of the actual number killed range from two to three hundred dead to several thousand); the July 1995 gendercide in Srebrenica, where one of, if not the worst, mass murders in 20th century history since World War II took place, with over 7,800 Bosniak Muslim males of all ages murdered by Chetnik Serbs under the command of war criminal Ratko Mladic[8]; the 1997 Acteal (Chiapas) massacre by paramilitaries of 45 Tsotsil Mayan women, children, and men attending church, sanctioned by the Mexican military as part of a low-intensity ongoing war against indigenous peoples in Chiapas seeking land and other rights (and protesting neo-liberal economic policies that harm indigenous rights); the example of the Al-Aqsa *intifada* (the uprising begun in September 2000, as opposed to the first *intifada*, 1987-1993 prior to the signing of the disastrous Oslo accords) in Israel/Occupied Territories/Palestinian Authority, an intractable situation where rights violations are the norm—as reported by AI in its examination of extra-judicial state killings, attacks on residential areas, killings of children justified odiously as 'collateral damage,' use of torture, collective punishment and so forth (since the initiation of the second *intifada* in 2000, and as of April 2004, the Israeli army [IDF] had killed approximately 545 and imprisoned 348 Palestinian children, while simultaneously Palestinian suicide bombers and insurgents were targeting Israeli civilians and children, a campaign that has wrought immeasurable suffering on both the occupied Palestinians and the occupying Israelis)[9]; the genocide (cultural and otherwise), ecocide, and ethnic cleansing that are ongoing in Tibet as a function of Chinese totalitarian practices that have left at least 1.2 million people dead and produced egregious human rights abuses and violations involving torture, illegal detention, disappearances, and clampdowns on freedom of expression and religion[10]; the genocide of 1.5 million Bengali and Hindu East Pakistanis (Bangladeshis) in 1971; the targeting, killing, and displacement of Shan and Karen peoples in Burma/Myanmar under a brutal military dictatorship (with at least 100,000 people dead); and Chechnya where, as reported by James Meek in the *Guardian*, Tom de Waal of the Institute for War and Peace Reporting says that since 1994 the Russian army has killed 'between 50,000 and 100,000 civilians...in addition to 13,000-20,000 combatants—shocking numbers in a territory whose overall population is about a million.'

Add to these examples, among others, from a depressingly long list: Armenia (1915-1917), approximately 1.5 million dead, victims of genocidal ethnic cleansing; the Algerian war of independence (1954-1962) with well over a million dead; Vietnam (1961-1975), approximately three million dead; Indonesia (1965), approximately one million dead; the Cambodian civil war (1974/1975-1979), with some documentation suggesting a death toll as high as 3 million people[11]; Mozambique (1979-1989), approximately one million dead; the Iran-Iraq war (1980-88), the longest conventional war of the twentieth century that claimed over a million and a half lives and cost over a trillion U.S. dollars (in the latter stages of the war Iran was spending a scandalous 250 million dollars a month on the war effort); Angola (1986-1994), half a million dead; Guatemala (1962-1996), with approximately 200,000 dead, mostly indigenous peoples; and Iraq again (1991-present), approximately 1.2 million dead. We reiterate that the pattern in these massive killings is increasingly showing civilians to be the targets, despite supposed improvements in war technology like the odiously anthropomorphized 'smart' bombs: in World War I 15 percent of all casualties were civilians; in World War II, 50 percent of all casualties were civilians, and as of 2004, 90 percent of war casualties were civilians (Ellis 5).

These numbers and body counts are appallingly reductive, a travesty of statistical violence. They necessarily misrepresent the specificity of suffering associated with human after human after human who has endured globalized brutality and targeted aggression. And they mark the utter ease with which legal covenants—like the UDHR or the Fourth Geneva Convention (1949), which explicitly prohibits '(a) violence to life and person, in particular murder of all kinds, mutilation, cruel treatment and torture; (b) taking of hostages; (c) outrages upon personal dignity, in particular humiliating and degrading treatment; (d) the passing of sentences and the carrying out of executions without previous judgment pronounced by a regularly constituted court, affording all the judicial guarantees which are recognized as indispensable by civilized peoples'—are broken in the name of state and military expediencies.

The planet is pockmarked with grief and suffering that result from crude, militarized responses to ethnic difference, struggles for social justice, imperial self-interest, and gratuitous acts of violence to name only a few. In all the cases listed above (and they are, lamentably, an abbreviated listing), a groundwork of terror, predominantly state/military-sponsored, has caused incalculable grief and suffering. And leading nation states, the preeminent defenders of human rights, have stood by (or contributed to the violence) as these events have played out and large numbers of people of color and different ethnicities have died.

Mladic's first target was Srebrenica, whose fighters had waged an aggressive war against neighboring Serb villages early in the conflict. Their attacks often were followed by a wave of desperate, angry Muslim civilians—many of whom had been cleansed from their own communities—looting and burning homes and exacting vengeance on the Serbs they caught.

After an overwhelming Serb offensive in 1993, the enclave's defenders had agreed to a U.N.-monitored demilitarization,* and Srebrenica had become the first U.N. safe area.

Mladic launched his attack on Srebrenica in July 1995. His forces brushed aside the Dutch peacekeepers stationed there and took some of them hostage. The Dutch put up no resistance themselves but called for air support to halt the Serbs six times.

Finally, five days after the first request, two NATO planes made bombing runs. They were ineffective.

Their requests were turned down or postponed by top U.N. officers, including Janvier personally, even after the Dutch themselves came under attack.

The Serbs threatened to kill their Dutch hostages and shell panicked civilians if NATO attacked again.

In any case, it was too late. Bosnian soldiers, who had believed the U.N. would defend the safe area, put up an ineffectual defense.

The Serbs entered Srebrenica.

THERE WAS A VERY BIG PANIC.

Nermin

"I left Srebrenica with other soldiers. The civilians went to Potocari, the main base of U.N. forces..."

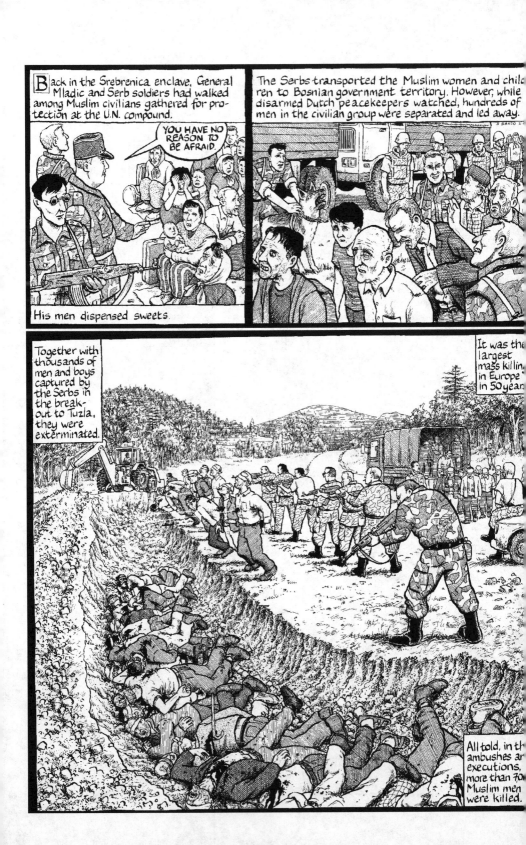

Back in the Srebrenica enclave, General Mladic and Serb soldiers had walked among Muslim civilians gathered for protection at the U.N. compound.

YOU HAVE NO REASON TO BE AFRAID.

His men dispensed sweets.

The Serbs transported the Muslim women and children to Bosnian government territory. However, while disarmed Dutch peacekeepers watched, hundreds of men in the civilian group were separated and led away.

Together with thousands of men and boys captured by the Serbs in the break-out to Tuzla, they were exterminated.

It was the largest mass killing in Europe in 50 years.

All told, in the ambushes and executions, more than 70,000 Muslim men were killed.

The Right to Security

The response to post-9/11 terrorism has produced two consequences: one, to consolidate anti-civil libertarian forces, the other to reinforce strategies of selective application of rights principles based on imperial self-interest that ignores global evidence of terrorist activity. Neither of these consequences is in fact new. AI's report on Colombia dating back to 1994 noted, 'The use of anti-terrorist legislation, with its greatly increased sentences, to deal with a wide range of offences such as damage to state property which are included in the ordinary penal code, appears intended to deter legitimate social and labour protests' (AI *Political Violence in Colombia* 35).

Rights activists, then, must be vigilant and identify the moment at which anti-state terrorism that threatens legitimate civil liberties crosses over into state-sponsored constraints that limit legitimate civil liberties—or that cross the line over into state-sponsored terrorism. And they must be especially vigilant about how selective principles of rights application are applied to global situations in which terror is a factor. In both cases, the innocent majority ends up being terrorized by both the threat of terror and threat of the response to terror. As Sanjana Hattotuwa argues, citing Michael Walzer, 'The ramifying evil of terrorism...is not just the killing of innocent people but also the intrusion of fear into everyday life, the violation of private purposes, the insecurity of public spaces and the endless coerciveness of precaution' (Hattotuwa 13).

Manufactured fear. Intrusive fear. Retributive fear. All compromise the rights of innocents and do so in ways that beg the question of how responses to rights abuses can themselves become abusive, how responses that further spiral into cycles of violence that altogether ignore root causes are themselves a severe threat to global rights. When William Schulz, the Executive Director of Amnesty International USA, argues, 'We are unalterably opposed to all those who would employ the violation of others people's rights as a means to accomplish their own ends,' let us not naively assume that this declaration applies only to terrorists (as it does in Schulz's book on rights and terrorism, *Tainted Legacy: 9/11 and the Ruin of Human Rights*).

The *Amnesty International Report 2005* unequivocally reports that in 2004 the 'U.S.-led "war on terror" continued to undermine human rights in the name of security, despite growing international outrage at evidence of U.S. war crimes, including torture, against detainees' ('Amnesty International Americas'). Further, in specific relation to national security and the 'war on terror,' AI found that the 'blatant disregard for international human rights and humanitarian law in the "war on terror" continued to make a mockery of President George Bush's claims that the USA was the global champion of human rights' (ibid.). The August 2004 Fay-Jones Report, which examined the conditions of prisoners at the Abu Ghraib prison in Iraq, summarized a lengthy list of abuses perpetrated by U.S. military personnel in defiance of the Geneva Conventions that apply to prisoners of war, including: physical abuse (from restricted breathing to dislocation of joints resulting from enforced restraint or 'stress' positioning of inmates); use of dogs (including forcing detainees to defecate in front of dogs); humiliating and degrading treatments; nakedness; degrading photographs; simulated sexual positions; improper use of isolation; failure to safeguard detainees; failure to report detainee abuses; and sleep adjustment techniques (Greenberg and Dratel 1070-1104). Over and above this list were further incidents that included possible rape, the withholding of medical care, bananas inserted into detainees' anuses, sodomy of inmates, and the striking of genitals.

Many of these 'techniques' that are violations of international law, let alone of natural justice, were applied in Guantánamo Bay, Cuba by American soldiers as well. Irene Khan, Secretary General of AI, reports that the U.S. government has, in the name of seeking security in its war on terror, 'gone to great lengths to restrict the application of the Geneva Conventions and to "re-define" torture. It has sought to justify the use of coercive interrogation techniques, the practice of holding "ghost detainees" (people in unacknowledged incommunicado detention) and the "rendering" or handing over of prisoners to third countries known to practice torture. The detention facility at Guantánamo Bay has become the gulag of our times, entrenching the practice of arbitrary and indefinite detention in violation of international law. Trials by military commission have made a mockery of justice and due process' (*Amnesty International Report 2005* 'Foreword').

BBC News and AI reports on the treatment of detainees at Guantánamo allege torture that included the threat of rape, beatings, physical abuse including being urinated on, forced feedings for hunger-striking prisoners, the lack of due process in open and transparent courts, exposure to extreme temperatures, noise and light, cultural and religious abuse, and repeated attempts at suicide among multiple prisoners (including mass suicide attempts), all compromised by lack of open access by international agencies and their lawyers to the prisoners. In all of these four basic principles of torture are at work: sensory deprivation and assault (through hooding or sensory overload), a brutally effective form of psychological torture that leads to breakdown[12]; self-inflicted pain (through, for instance, standing in held positions for extended periods); attacks on culturally sensitive areas involving religion, gender, and sexuality; and preying on individual phobias and fears. These degrading, venal, and highly damaging torture techniques violate established human rights norms, whether at the level of the UDHR or specific clauses of the Geneva Conventions. Further, they represent profound violations of principles of natural justice that underlie those norms.

The United Nations' 2006 joint report on the situation of Guantánamo detainees was explicit. Recommendation 96 of the report states that 'The United States Government should close the Guantánamo Bay detention facilities without further delay' and 'all special interrogation techniques authorized by the Department of Defense should immediately be revoked' ('Situation of detainees at Guantánamo Bay' 38-39). Like the use of so-called administrative detentions in the Occupied Territories, a practice condemned by AI in which '[Palestinian] detainees are held without charge or trial. No charges are filed, and there is no intention of bringing a detainee to trial' (AI 'Administrative Detention')—and like other illegal and undemocratic strategies used to 'disappear' people (whether in Latin America or any number of other places globally where these sorts of practices are or have been used), the abhorrent practices of rendition, torture, rights abuses, and dehumanization that Guantánamo represents are pressing and serious threats to democracy and the global rights scenario. They are so because they normalize the slippage from hard-won principle to unregulated expediency that threatens the rights of all peoples who are subject to state power of any kind.

How any of these practices actually contribute to meaningful global security based on fundamental precepts of justice, human dignity, and reciprocal understanding (let alone the much-trumpeted Christian values of the American state) is highly debatable. When arbitrary torture and detainment trump social justice values predicated on respect for life and intrinsic dignities of all people as a function of state policy, and when this occurs on the watch of the most globally powerful nation, then no one's security is enhanced. Security merely becomes a euphemism for bullying self-interest and a betrayal of the values embedded in the UDHR. Add to this the economic abuses documented by British parliamentarian George Galloway: the disappearance of $8.8 billion of Iraqi wealth during the first 14 months of the war; the wartime profiteering of Halliburton and other American corporations; the oil being shipped out of Iraq that was unmetered; and the $800 million given to American military commanders 'to hand around the country' (Keefer 12). A picture emerges of narrow state self-interest completely undermining the long-term security interests that would require building mutual respect in legal and economic, let alone human, terms.

Revelations about the former School of the Americas (SOA), located in Fort Benning, Columbus, Georgia, and used to train soldiers and police primarily for Latin America in counter-insurgency and combat skills, further exemplify how euphemistic language camouflages practices that deeply threaten human security at a global level.[13] Imagine a 'school' that produced 'some of the [Western] hemisphere's most notorious dictators, death squad operatives, and assassins' (Gill 137). In the case of the SOA, 10 graduates participated in the Salvadoran El Mozote massacre (primarily women and children murdered), two were accused in the murder of Archbishop Oscar Romero (the SOA-trained Salvadoran death squad leader Roberto D'Aubuisson), 124 of the 247 Colombian officers cited for gross human rights abuses in 1992 trained at the SOA, one of them, Haitian death squad leader and CIA operative General Raoul Cedras, led a coup against Jean Bertrand Aristide (1991), and so forth (Gill 137). Further, seven training manuals used at the SOA from 1982-1991 advocated torture; 'Critics drew a direct line between the SOA and the brutal practices of Latin American security forces, and they opened the door for thinking about the United States as a perpetrator of terrorism' (138). American anthropologist Lesley Gill's work on the SOA and human rights education concludes that its graduates, regardless of the lip service paid to human rights at the SOA, function in alignment with U.S. interests that seek one form of security (in the name of national self-interest) at the expense of other forms of security (for local populations). Gill cites the case of Bolivian Julio Miranda, an SOA graduate placed in charge of the Ecology Police whose aim was to wipe out coca cultivation in the Chapare region of Bolivia. Gill's study concludes that Miranda's SOA indoctrination and frame of reference for dealing with indigenous and peasant peoples in the Chapare played a role in decisions that 'certainly provoked peasant antipathy to the state' (162) in 2001.

Since then, Bolivia, a country with a majority population of indigenous peoples and the poorest, least developed country in Latin America, has experienced extraordinary turbulence. Despite its poverty and largely agricultural status, profound struggles are underway in Bolivia to break free from transnational corporations that control its natural gas and oil reserves (Bolivia, after Venezuela, has the second largest gas and oil reserves in South America) and from restrictions on water usage that led to the now famous Cochabamba incident: 'In 1999, following World Bank advice, Bolivia granted a 40 year privatization lease to a subsidiary of the Bechtel Corporation, giving it control over the water on which more than half a million people survive. Immediately the company doubled and tripled water rates for some of South America's poorest families' (Schultz). All of these issues represent profound localized security concerns for those Bolivians who wish to prosper equitably from their resources, even as global businesses and political interests seek contrary outcomes that suit their own purposes.

Moreover, Bolivia represents a classic example of how the imposition via World Bank or SOA-associated directives on a local civilian population of external interests that violate social and economic justice norms clearly stated in the UDHR, has led to an increasingly volatile political situation in which the struggle for localized security is pitted against a global system of 'security' pursued in the name of imperial economic and military self-interest. The bottom line is that what 'security' means very much depends on whose interests are at stake. The use of 'security' as a goal of the 'war on terror' cannot be read uncritically in light of our arguments here: for no one's security is improved via actions that demean international standards of justice in which respect for life and human dignity are paramount.

If global military and economic dominance are being pursued at one end of the spectrum while perverse acts of localized terror are occurring at the other, maybe it is time to see the relations between both more clearly. The ever-expanding gyre of violence, fueled by political, ideological and economic self-interest, presents the most significant threat to global aspirations for a constructive, healthy rights environment, in which respect for life and security of person are essential. The right to meaningful security must be advocated as a right to end multiple forms of terror. The selective defense of security rights in the name of a war on terror related to the cynical pursuit of strategic interests undermines universal security rights, thus contributing to the cycles of extraordinary violence characteristic of the last century. That this 'defense' entails acts of war in which large civilian populations are themselves terrorized is scandalous.

'Whether terrorism can be "defeated" by military means,' as the Worldwatch Institute notes, 'is questionable since extremist groups do not represent easily identifiable targets. Terrorism is a path chosen by protagonists who tend to be politically desperate and militarily weak. Acts of terror are not going to disappear as long as the roots of extremist violence are not tackled' (*State of the World 2005* 13). The terror associated with the fight on terror will do little to dissipate the global foundations of insecurity, promulgating instead an ever-expanding circle of retribution and injustice in which, it must be remembered, the most likely (and most numerous) victims are the innocent and the disempowered.

Notes

1. The perplexing problem of why so many leading nation states have stood by as human rights violations are taking place is explored at length by Stanley Cohen's study, *States of Denial: Knowing about Atrocities and Suffering*, which documents denial of knowledge, denial of responsibility, denial of injury, denial of the victim, condemnation of the condemners, appeal to higher loyalties, moral indifference, and so forth as elements in the composite picture of nation states' reneging of involvement in human rights abuses and violations. Examples of this sort of denial are legion, including a recent case in Canada that involved the 'rendering' of a Canadian citizen, Maher Arar, to Syria for a year during which time he was tortured in the Palestine Branch detention camp on suspicion of having terrorist links, this despite his innocence. The former Canadian ambassador to Syria, Franco Pillarella, in the subsequent public inquiry, astonishingly denied knowledge of torture in Syria. This denial occurred in spite of the voluminous evidence accumulated by AI, HRW, and even the U.S. State Department. The key question we pose is the extent to which this sophisticated rhetoric of denial is always in some way an expression of sovereign self-interest, one that ignores the basic rights precepts of the inter-connectedness of all expressions of life elaborated by Mahatma Gandhi and Martin Luther King, Jr. in the epigraphs to the Introduction of this book.

2. At midnight, Friday, 11 March 2005, a new Prevention of Terrorism Law Bill in Britain was passed and used to 'restrict and monitor the activities of 10 terrorism suspects, many of whom were freed from prison earlier [that day], because the old law that held them behind bars had been ruled unconstitutional' (Saunders). The debate over the new bill was the longest in modern parliamentary history.

3. In Pillarella's June 15 2005 testimony at the Arar inquiry, he stated, contrary to vast documentation from independent sources like AI and HRW that proves otherwise, 'I did not have any indication that there were serious human rights abuses committed [in Syria], that I could verify' ('Sharp rebuke for ambassador over Arar comments'). Pillarella, ironically, was a former Head of the Human Rights Division at the Canadian Foreign Affairs office in Ottawa.

4. Joy Gordon reports that sanctions imposed on Iraq since 1991 'have been comprehensive, meaning that virtually every aspect of the country's imports and exports is controlled, which is particularly damaging to a country recovering from war. Since the program began, an estimated 500,000 Iraqi children under the age of five have died as a result of the sanctions—almost three times as many as the number of Japanese killed during the U.S. atomic bomb attacks.'

5. The AI report makes numerous recommendations to U.S. authorities, including the condemnation of torture, ensuring access to prisoners, the abolition of secret detentions, the provision of safeguards during detention and interrogation, the prohibition of torture in law, the investigation and prosecution of abuses and violations related to torture, the abolition of the use of statements extracted under torture, the effective training of all officials with regard to torture as a criminal act, the provision of reparation to victims of torture, the ratification of international treaties, and the exercise of international responsibility. The fact that in 2004 such a lengthy list of recommendations should have had to be

brought to the attention of a country that proclaims itself at the forefront of the defense against human rights abuses is telling.

6. 'Evidence of that deliberate policy included the threat by President George W. Bush to veto a bill opposing "cruel, inhuman and degrading treatment,"…and Vice President Dick Cheney's attempt to exempt the Central Intelligence Agency from the law. In addition, Attorney General Alberto Gonzales claimed that the United States can mistreat detainees so long as they are non-Americans held abroad, while CIA Director Porter Goss asserted that "waterboarding," a torture method dating back to the Spanish Inquisition, was simply a "professional interrogation technique" ' (*Human Rights Watch World Report 2006*).

7. HRW reports that 'the overwhelming number of these 30,000 deaths, not to mention widespread mutilation and rape, are the responsibility of the Turkish military' (Shah 'Kurds and Human Rights'). The Kurds are the world's largest ethnic minority without a territory, with 19 million people living effectively in four countries, Turkey, Syria, Iran, and Iraq. Turkish Kurds have been the subject of 'a policy of virtual cultural annihilation…giving them few rights to use their language and express their identity' (*New Internationalist World Guide 2001/2002* 536). Turkey has the distinction of having committed the twentieth century's first genocide/Holocaust with the deaths of an estimated 1,500,000 Christian Armenians from 1915-1917 through direct killing, starvation, or deportation—ironically the Kurds themselves directly participated in the Armenian genocide. Stanley Cohen argues that the Armenian genocide and its denial by Turkish authorities represent the 'most consistent, strident and elaborate state-organized attempt to conceal a record of past atrocities' (134).

8. This brutal event occurred in the larger context of Serbian ethnic cleansing in Bosnia and Herzegovina from 1992-1995, with 2 million people displaced, 200,000 killed, and tens of thousands raped, tortured, abused, and subjected to continuous shelling and sniper attacks. The vast majority of the people who suffered were civilians.

9. AI reports that since the outbreak of the second *intifada* 'Palestinian and Israeli children have been targeted in an unprecedented manner. In the period from 29 September 2000 to the end of August 2002, some 1,700 Palestinians, including more than 250 children, were killed, and more than 580 Israelis, most of them civilians and including 72 children, were killed' (AI 'Killing the Future: Children in the Line of Fire').

10. The approximate breakdown of how people have died as a result of the Chinese invasion and occupation of Tibet that began in 1949 is as follows: prisons and labor camps—173,221; torture—97,731; execution—156,758; uprising—432,705; starvation—342,970; suicide—9002.

11. See Etcheson's study funded by the Dutch and U.S. governments, which argues the following: 'If as little as 31% of the death toll was the result of executions, then a total of 3.3 million deaths would imply slightly more than one million executions, and the Documentation Center data suggest they have already found more victims of execution than that [during the Khmer Rouge régime]. If we apply Heder's top estimate of 50 percent for base people to the entire population, and find upon the completion of the mass grave surveys that the number of suspected victims of execution is around 1.5 million, then we again end up with a figure in the vicinity of three million total dead in the Pol Pot time. In either

case, we would be driven to the conclusion that not one million, not two million, but rather three million Cambodians died untimely deaths during the Khmer Rouge regime.'

12. Alfred McCoy, who has investigated torture techniques deployed at Guantánamo and elsewhere, notes that the source of this technique was 'Dr. Donald O. Hebb [1904-85] of McGill University, a brilliant psychologist, who had a contract from the Canadian Defense Research Board, which was a partner with the CIA in this research [on torture]. Hebb found that he could induce a state of psychosis in an individual within 48 hours. It didn't take electroshock, truth serum, beating or pain. All he did was had student volunteers sit in a cubicle with goggles, gloves and headphones, earmuffs, so that they were cut off from their senses, and within 48 hours, denied sensory stimulation, they would suffer, first hallucinations, then ultimately breakdown' ('Professor McCoy Exposes the History of CIA Interrogation…').

13. The School of the Americas was formally closed in December 2000 and the Western Hemisphere Institute for Security Cooperation (WHISC) was opened in its stead in January 2001. Army Secretary Louis Caldera announced in 2000 that the new Institute would teach military personnel, law enforcement officers, and civilians and would be a 'place where human rights courses are prevalent' ('School of the Americas Closes'). In spite of this assertion, a 2003 graduate, Salvadoran Colonel Francisco del Cid Diaz, 'was cited by the 1993 U.N. Truth Commission for commanding a unit that dragged people from their homes and shot them at point-blank range' (Hodge and Cooper 226). And it is clear that the change in name was largely PR-driven and motivated by the increasing knowledge about the war crimes and terrorist activities of SOA graduates. The home site of the WHISC, under the heading Democracy and Human Rights, makes the following claims: 'The Democracy and Human Rights Program in the Institute fulfills the congressionally-mandated mission of promoting understanding and respect for democratic values and institutions, human rights, the rule of law and civilian control of a nation's armed forces. *A comprehensive three-hour class provides an overview of U.S. democracy and the traditions, customs and practices common to most U.S. citizens. A minimum of eight hours of training in the Human Rights Class creates a culture of respect for human rights.* Offered at the beginning of each course, these classes demonstrate how deeply embedded U.S. values, respect for the rule of law and our constitutional structure have maintained a strong democracy and uninterrupted civilian control of the military throughout our history' (our emphasis; 'Democracy and Human Rights at WHINSEC'). In total, then, the WHISC allows for a minimum of 11 hours of human rights training to its graduates, some of whom are facing some of the most complex human rights situations imaginable—hardly a sufficient or meaningful schooling. Moreover, these courses are congruent with 'embedded U.S. values' themselves under attack by U.S. actual practices around the world (with Guantánamo Bay and Abu Ghraib being only the most recent, notorious instances). The debatable claim at the end of the web material that the U.S. has 'maintained a strong democracy and uninterrupted civilian control of the military throughout our history' elides the degree to which military-industrial interests have managed American democracy, with narrow elites composed of overlapped military and business interests largely controlling access to and dissemination of power.

The famed comics artist Joe Sacco has reported from Iraq on the U.S. Military in action.

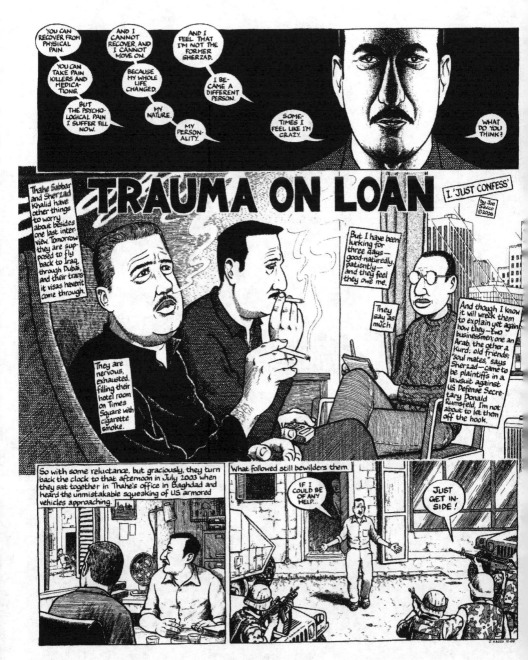

Now he's met former Iraqi prisoners who are accusing the troops of torture. Here he tells their tale.

YOU KNOW WHEN YOU WATCH MOVIES AND YOU HEAR THE WORD 'FIRE!'

IT WAS THE SAME.

THEY SAID, 'FIRE!' AND THEY FIRED.

"I fell down to the ground. And then I heard the soldiers' laughter. So I started looking at my body, trying to find a trace of blood. I realized it was just a mock execution..."

According to Thahe and Sherzad, by then a number of detainees had pissed on themselves.

They spent the night shackled to a tennis court fence, and the next day they were taken to the prison at Baghdad's international airport, where they were made to run a gauntlet of baton-wielding soldiers before reaching their cells.

II. 'THE LION THING'

In America, another sort of gauntlet awaited them:

Cameramen!

Photographers!

Reporters!

By the time I met them in Washington, D.C., their lawyers, who include members of the American Civil Liberties Union and Human Rights First, fretted that all the interviews had pushed their clients to the edge.

ATTORNEY HINA SHAMSI, HUMAN RIGHTS FIRST

SOMETIMES WE DON'T KNOW WHEN THEY'VE HAD ENOUGH, AND SOMETIMES THEY DON'T KNOW THEMSELVES UNTIL AFTERWARDS.

Thahe and Sherzad's visit to the States is meant to draw attention to their legal complaint, which alleges "torture or other cruel, inhuman or degrading punishment" while they were in U.S. military custody.

They "are representative of so many hundreds or thousands of others whose shockingly brutal mistreatment" is ultimately Mr. Rumsfeld's responsibility, according to Emily Whitfield, the ACLU's media relations director.

In effect, Thahe and Sherzad are standing in for all the hooded and beaten. For this case, they are sacrificial detainees.

J. SACCO 17

* THEY ARE JOINED BY SIX OTHER PLAINTIFFS: FOUR AFGHANS AND TWO IRAQIS

So when their lawyers expressed misgivings about Thahe and Sherzad reopening their wounds for one last journalist—me!—when they hinted my interview might be cancelled, I wanted to snap back—

"Come on!"

"You brought them here to reopen their wounds."

"No point worrying about their feelings now."

Besides, the media blitz has had an impact. Even the chief defendant has taken notice.

THE LION THING WAS MENTIONED AT THE RUMSFELD BRIEFING.

Yes, it's "the lion thing" that is raising eyebrows. Much else of what Thahe and Sherzad allege — the shackling in extreme temperatures, the electric shocks, the desecration of the Koran — might seem ho-hum to an American public that has long digested the enormities of Abu Ghraib.

And at his press conference, Mr. Rumsfeld called Thahe and Sherzad's lion story "farfetched" and referred to Al-Qaeda documents that—

— TRAIN PEOPLE, TERRORISTS, TO LIE ABOUT THEIR TREATMENT.

Thahe and Sherzad might take exception to Mr. Rumsfeld's implication that they have studied Al-Qaeda manuals or that they are "terrorists."

Neither of them was ever charged with anything by the Americans.

III. "WHAT IS YOUR FAVORITE SPORT?"

WHEN I WAS FIRST TAKEN FOR INTERROGATION, I WAS HAPPY.

I THOUGHT, NOW I CAN EXPLAIN MYSELF.

"But the first question was—

WHERE IS SADDAM?*"

"I laughed, and he hit me."

After perfunctory questions about weapons of mass destruction, Al-Qaeda, etc., the interrogator asked—

WHAT IS YOUR FAVORITE BREAKFAST?

WHAT IS YOUR FAVORITE SPORT?

WHAT TIME DO YOU GO TO SLEEP?

WHY WAS HE ASKING YOU THOSE LAST THINGS?

I DON'T KNOW.

But then, does Sherzad know why he was subjected to "simulated] anal rape" with a water bottle? Does Thahe know why "one or more soldiers in the presence of male and female soldiers inserted their fingers" into his anus?

* SADDAM HUSSEIN WAS STILL IN HIDING WHEN THIS INTERROGATION TOOK PLACE.

I've quoted Thahe's and Sherzad's sexual assault allegations from the lawsuit. Their attorneys ask me not to bring up the subject with the men. When CNN broke that ground rule and badgered Thahe about his ordeal, he was retraumatized, I'm told.

IV. 'I HAVE NO DESIRE TO TELL A SAD STORY'

In the morning an interview with 'Time' magazine; in the afternoon, a meeting with earnest Senate staffers who promise to relay Thahe and Sherzad's story to their bosses.

And now one of the attorneys suggests a quick get-together with her colleagues in an office nearby.

IT'S UP TO YOU.

But Thahe is only being diplomatic. He boards the van rented for the day's activities and waits for his handlers to follow.

WE WANT TO GO SEE THE WHITE HOUSE.

The lawyers are sensitive to the moods of their clients. The rest of the day will be given over to sight-seeing.

For an hour or two, Thahe and Sherzad smile in front of America's monuments to liberty.

But the cell phones are ringing again. A senator has agreed to meet with Thahe and Sherzad personally.

When? Now!

Thahe is almost despondent.

He has to remind himself why he's here.

WE DIDN'T COME AS TOURISTS.

Sherzad, on the other hand won't have it.

AFTER SEEING THIS BEAUTIFUL VIEW, I HAVE NO DESIRE TO TELL A SAD STORY.

The attorneys turn down the senator. And they tell Thahe and Sherzad they will get to see the White House in the morning.

V. THE AIRPORT

AT THE AIRPORT, THERE WERE 75 TO 150 DETAINEES IN EACH TENT.

"There was a place for people to sit, but not to sleep. The ground was earth. We were given one blanket. My pillow was my shoes.

"I had a beard. I had long hair just like a beast.

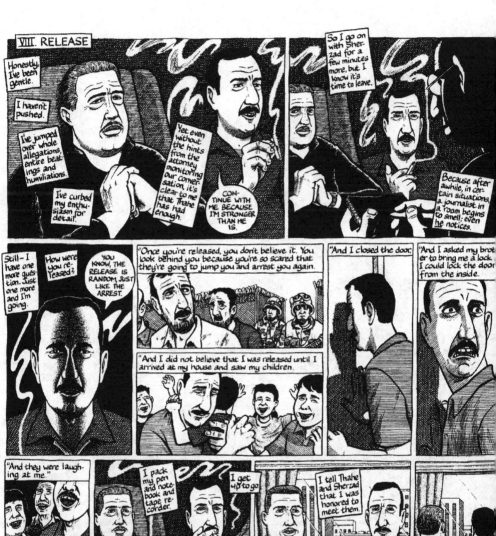

Chapter 5

Communicating Rights: Media, Rights Organizations, Education, And The Arts

Whether in a pop song, a classroom debate, a skewed television report, a poem, or a formal report from a major rights organization like Amnesty International, how we communicate rights plays a critical role in the rights we think we have. Since rights are a crucial form of marrying information to feeling, we must consider how rights are communicated via the media, different educational contexts, rights organizations, and diverse forms of human expression linked to the arts.

Seeing Isn't Believing: Media Disinformation in a Human Rights Context

> The French Revolution would not have taken place if the *philosophes* had not laid waste to the concept of aristocratic privilege, the civil rights revolution of the 1950s and '60s would never have happened if innumerable writers, journalists, and others had not taken similar aim at an entire body of racist ideology. —Daniel Lazare

The mainstream media have been converted into weapons of mass distraction, anesthetizing critical thinking, spreading misinformation, and reinforcing visual clichés about so-called reality. Instead of being associated with the public's right to communication, media is profit-driven and overlaps ideologically with state and corporate agendas, and works towards creating a compliant, misinformed citizenry. The primary forces driving mass media are profit and entertainment (both invariably linked to specific ideologies), and they have been effectively diverted from the careful, independent, investigative analysis and critical dissemination of a broad range of information.[1]

And where alternative media exist, offering important interventions in rights situations, they are under extraordinary pressures and subject to censorship, exile, or extra-judicial killing, as was the case with Haitian radio journalist, Jean L. Dominique, assassinated (along with a groundskeeper) in front of his radio station, Radio Haiti Internationale, on 3 April 2000. Dominique had worked for 40 years promoting democracy and human rights in Haiti, one of the poorest countries in the world, broadcasting in Haitian Creole and giving voice to exploited farmers and disempowered populations. For his efforts he was twice exiled, suffered imprisonment and torture, and was subject to almost constant intimidation by state authorities and paramilitaries (Tonton Macoutes). The gap between mainstream media and the work of someone like Dominique is enormous and a sad comment on the ways in which privately owned mainstream media using publicly owned airspace shirk their responsibilities to civil, democratic societies.[2] Moreover, where other forms of alternative media exist, as is the case with Cuba's ubiquitous, state-controlled *Granma*, other forms of distortion can be seen at work, especially in terms of the media's lack of independence from the state and its access to diverse, transparent, and accurate forms of information.

Limits to freedom of speech, whether self-imposed or enforced, affect every aspect of our lives, from our knowledge of what is happening on the other side of the world and why we should care, to simple labeling on the food we eat. Our right to know is systematically curtailed by courts, corporations, governments, education, and the media. The lawsuit by McDonald's against activists David Morris and Helen Steel, popularly known as the McLibel case, brings to our attention a severe constraint under which journalists, activists, and even the general public have to work to promote rights and disseminate information. British libel laws are widely regarded as the most repressive in the West, and are the envy of the rich and powerful around the world (Searls and Lloyd 1-2).[3] The 'McLibel-two,' as they have come to be known, provoked the wrath and legal might of the fast-food chain by distributing a six-page fact sheet produced by London Greenpeace, entitled 'What's wrong with McDonald's? Everything they don't want you to know,' which detailed the agricultural, labor, and slaughterhouse practices associated with the corporation and health concerns that would be of interest to the consumers of McDonald's and other fast-food products. Instead of answering the criticisms contained in the fact sheet, McDonald's sued five activists—three of whom apologized and fled —leaving the remaining two with 40,000 pounds in libel damages awarded by the British court. Morris and Helen, who could never have paid such an amount, refused to do so, claimed that the libel trial was unfair, and took it to The European Court of Human Rights where they won their case against the British government. Observers hope that their victory will change UK libel law, but for the time being, it remains a threat to anyone whose published material is sold in limited copies or even made available on the Internet in the UK.

Unfortunately, the effects of this form of censorship are not limited to the country whose legal system threatens to punish those it can't silence through litigious intimidation. Vandana Shiva was to appear on a prerecorded BBC program to talk about transnational corporations, and even though she had agreed not to name names, her interview was canceled abruptly on the advice of BBC lawyers who worried about her inadvertently libeling someone. In another case, a stage play about the fast-food industry (which also named no names) 'closed after McDonald's demanded changes in the script and a public apology' (Monbiot 'Publish and Be Damned' 1). Both Shiva's talk and the play could have circulated to other countries, but British self-censorship aborted them from ever taking place. Seemingly inspired by such impunity, a coalition of cattle ranchers in the U.S. used food disparagement laws to sue Oprah Winfrey and her TV guest Howard Lyman for $10.3 million for discussing the connections between the feeding practices of American beef ranchers and BSE or Mad Cow disease. The Texas Beef Group lost the case ruled over by Judge Mary Lou Robinson who concluded, 'It would be difficult to conceive of any topic of dissension that could be of greater concern and interest to all Americans that the safety of the food that they eat' (Nomai 1).

Despite being unconstitutional because they limit free speech, food disparagement laws or 'veggie libel' have been enacted in 13 states. According to legal scholars 'these laws seem to have one purpose: to put individual rights on hold in favor of the economic prerogatives of corporations' (ibid. 1). Absurdly, laws protecting perishable food products from damaging speech give food the same defamation rights as a person. These laws have combined to severely limit labeling on foods and the consumer's right to know: 'The industry says that people have a right to NOT know how their food is produced, or what is in or on it, and that labeling irradiated food will lead to "irrational" behavior on the part of the consumer (i.e. people will not purchase the food)' (ibid. 3). Maybe Americans and others should be as concerned about war and torture as they are about their food, but in this arena too, the law of defamation can be used by public bodies to suppress and punish public criticism: 'A good example is COPEX, the company that organizes the Covert Operations Procurement Exhibition, where the world's police chiefs and spy-masters come to buy the latest in hi-tech repression and surveillance. COPEX has sued (among others) a pensioner and a schoolgirl who wrote to the manager of the exhibition's venue, questioning what they believed was the sale of dangerous goods to despotic governments' (Searls and Lloyd 3).

'Sophisticated technology,' as Stanley Cohen persuasively argues, 'can spread images of live atrocities around the world in minutes. But self-evident truth will not be self-evidently accepted' (185). Access to media has accelerated, but at the same time that access has not always produced meaningful effects. Dissemination does not equal meaningful reception in a corporate context defined by the appeal to the lowest common denominator, parameters of profitability, and media value obsessed with celebrity. Thus, as Cohen argues, 'In an electronic age dominated by visual, rather than written, communication technologies for observing, recording and presenting information have opened extraordinary new opportunities' (185). But at the same time, 'The increased international awareness of atrocities and suffering, the spread of new information technologies, and the globalization of the mass media indeed mean that sovereign states (or some of them) are being "watched" as never before. But representing this information is more difficult than ever. There is a profusion of similar images; lines are blurred between fiction and fact (reconstructions, factoids and documentary dramas); "reality" is always in inverted commas, and multi-culturalism encourages many truths to bloom' (187).

We walk the line between media saturation and the potential for civic disengagement, and canny, critical reading of the mediascape, a necessary pre-condition for civic engagement. Rights activists' use of various media must account for the gap between simplistic dissemination and the meaningful reception of relevant information. This is especially true when the dominant corporate thinking with regard to media function is profit-driven entertainment as opposed to, say, civic responsibility.

Corporate do-gooders: public image and/or civic responsibility?

'Reebok is very dedicated to supporting young human rights activists…It's great to see a large corporation take social responsibility to heart' says a recent Fletcher graduate who, after admiring the giant banners displaying articles from the Universal Declaration of Human Rights prominently situated in a huge glass lobby at Reebok world headquarters in Canton, Massachusetts, concluded: 'It strongly suggested that a genuine commitment to human rights principles was important for the entire company' (Lindenbaum 1). Meanwhile, on the other side of the globe in Jakarta, 1,000 Indonesian employees of Reebok gathered outside the U.S. Embassy shouting ' "Reebok the oppressor! Reebok the killer!" and set fire to huge cardboard replicas of Reebok sports shoes' ('Workers kick back at Reebok' 1). Who are we to believe? Is it even a matter of truth or deception, or is corporate do-gooding a paradox, a double bind that promotes human rights activism on the one hand, while disregarding labor rights on the other?

Some large corporations are enlisting the high-profile services of political figures, musicians, and actors to promote their human rights reputations. Reebok established a $50,000 Human Rights Award in 1988 to support the work of young activists all over the world. Its board members include Jimmy Carter and Kerry Kennedy Cuomo; its awards celebrations are presided over by an odd mix of celebrities from Desmond Tutu to Robert Redford to Cameron Diaz. It is not clear why the recipients must be under 30 years of age; or is it? Do they appeal more to young shoppers who have not necessarily committed to brand loyalty yet? While the Reebok website states that over 60 activists in over 35 countries have received the award, a more detailed breakdown published by the *Thai Labour Campaign* reveals that '16 of the 50 awards presented between 1992 and 1998 went to individuals from the largest Reebok market, the U.S. People in Latin America and Mexico received 11 of the awards. Thus, more than half of the awards went to the Americas' ('Can There Be Labor Rights without Labor Unions?' 1). 'Says Jeff Ballinger, an anti-sweatshop organizer who's organized with shoe workers in Indonesia the past 13 years, "With this kind of ceremony, Reebok gets its name into respectable company. When they give a prize to someone like Julie Su, a lawyer for immigrant workers in California, people who wouldn't be seen dead in Nikes are impressed" ' (Cockburn 1).

One of the 2005 Reebok Human Rights Awards is helping Shan-Burmese refugee Charm Tong to publicize the plight of hundreds of women belonging to ethnic minorities who are routinely gang-raped and tortured by the Burmese military. Despite being only 23 years old, Tong is a veteran activist who started to defend women's rights at the age of 16 (Llewelyn Leach 1). She established a network to support Shan women escaping violence in Burma/Myanmar, as well as a school which accommodates 24 students who learn to become teachers, human rights defenders, health workers, and community radio broadcasters (Marshall 2). The Reebok Human Rights Award will help to fund both the Shan Women's Action Network (SWAN) and the School for Shan State Nationalities Youth, besides leading to speaking engagements and contacts enabling Tong to disseminate information about the situation in Burma/Myanmar not deemed newsworthy enough by mainstream media to warrant sustained reporting.

A former 2002 nominee and labor activist, Dita Sari decided that accepting the Reebok Human Rights Award would compromise her integrity and present a serious conflict of interest: 'The decision I have made is not merely based on data, report, statistics or assumptions. In 1995, I was arrested and tortured by the police, after leading a strike of 5000 workers of Indoshoes Inti Industry. They demanded an increase of their wages (they were paid only U.S.$1 for working 8 hours a day), and maternity leave as well. This company operated in West Java, and produced shoes of Reebok and Adidas. I have seen for myself how the company treat the workers, and used the police to repress the strikers [sic]' (Sari 30). Having turned down the $50,000 award, Sari hopes that the stand she takes will contribute to changing the labor conditions in Reebok-produced companies.

Reebok, like Nike, has been the object of labor scrutiny, and continues to sub-contract to companies that pay their workers between $1.00 and $1.50 a day, thereby forcing them to live in slums with all the stresses and dangers resulting from surviving on lower-than-subsistence wages. The angered Indonesian workers protested Reebok's move to slash orders and cut their salaries while threatening to move the operations from West Java to Vietnam. It is not clear why Reebok behaved this way given that in its second quarter of the same year (2002), while 'international sales had fallen 2% to $250.9 million from $256 million in the corresponding year in 2001…U.S. sales rose to $334 million from $315.4 million over the same period' according to their own announcement ('Workers kick back at Reebok' 2). According to Ballinger's Press for Change, 'the labor cost of a $70 pair of sneakers made in China, Vietnam or Indonesia is $1 or less' (Cockburn 2-3).

The underlying question to this dilemma of promoting and funding human rights work by corporations who are complicit with corrupt and repressive governments like former President Suharto's (1967-1998) in Indonesia, which was much favored by multinationals, seems to be: are labor rights separable from human rights? As we have noted in the U.S. government's position on several UN resolutions and U.S. and EU pressures on WTO negotiations, the rich and powerful part ways from the majority world when it comes to evaluating business practices in light of human dignity and rights.

Even the entertainment aspect of corporate media is 'filler,' just the hook to get audiences to watch in order to sell them to advertisers. The CEO of Westinghouse (which also owns CBS) openly proclaimed: 'We are here to serve advertisers. That is our *raison d'être*' (Shah 'Media Conglomerates'). And that *raison d'être* is more than backed up by the studies done on corporate interference with the media, making the claim of objective reporting for the most part a laughable fiction. A 1992 survey of 147 editors of dailies conducted by Marquette University's Department of Journalism produced the following results, among others: '93.2 percent said sponsors had "threatened to withdraw advertising from [the] paper because of the content of the stories" (89 percent replied that the advertisers followed through on this threat)' and '89.9 percent responded that advertisers had "tried to influence the content of a news story or feature" ' (Kick 116). More recently the King of Spain, Juan Carlos, gave a Spanish award for the best in international journalism to a Venezuelan film with footage supposedly shot in April 2002, 'showing vicious *chavistas* [supporters of President Hugo Chavez] firing on an innocent protest by unarmed oppositionists. The footage was a sham. The demonstration did not take place, as has since been irrefutably proven. But such details are obviously of no importance, since the prize was not withdrawn' (Galeano 'Nothingland—or Venezuela?').

The effects of scenarios like these on rights realities cannot be underestimated. These examples underline how state and corporate interest effectively shape the content of mass media while at the same time corrupting the civic, democratic purposes the media were originally intended to serve. As Edward Herman and Noam Chomsky observe, 'Neoliberal ideology has provided the intellectual rationale for policies that have opened up the ownership of broadcasting stations and cable and satellite systems to private transnational investors. The culture and ideology fostered in this globalization process relate largely to "lifestyle" themes and goods and their acquisition; and they tend to weaken any sense of community helpful to civic life' (*Manufacturing Consent* xiv).

Not a great deal has changed since these authors first identified five filters that function to 'sanitize' the 'news fit to print' back in 1988: (1) the size, concentrated ownership, owner wealth, and profit orientation of the dominant mass-media firms; (2) advertising as the primary income source of the mass media; (3) the reliance of the media on information provided by government, business, and 'experts' funded and approved by these primary sources and agents of power; (4) 'flak' as a means of disciplining the media; and (5) 'anticommunism' as a national religion and control mechanism (ibid. 2). With the disintegration of the Eastern Bloc and its former support of revolutionary

172/   THE CONCISE GUIDE TO GLOBAL HUMAN RIGHTS

movements in the majority world, we can probably change 'anti-communism' to 'anti-terrorism' (usually but not exclusively expressive of 'anti-Islam').

The trend toward concentrated ownership, which means that media outlets are being bought up by mega-corporations, continues: in 1983, 50 corporations dominated most of every mass media...in 1987, the 50 companies had shrunk to 29...in 1990, the 29 had shrunk to 23...in 1997, the biggest firms numbered 10 (from Ben Bagdikian's *The Media Monopoly*, cited in Shah, 'Media Conglomerates'). Even Ted Turner, who launched CNN (which is seen in 212 countries and has a daily audience of 1 billion globally), gripes about 'how government protects big media—and shuts out upstarts like me,' and reports that 'in 1990, the major broadcast networks—ABC, CBS, NBC, and Fox—fully or partially owned just 12.5% of the new series they aired. By 2000, it was 56.3%. Just two years later, it had surged to 77.5%' (Turner). And in 2002 the U.S. was ranked 17th, below Costa Rica and Slovenia, on a global index of press freedom created by Reporters Without Borders, a major cause for concern in a country whose Supreme Court in 1945 established a constitutional requirement that 'the widest possible dissemination of information from diverse and antagonistic sources is essential to the welfare of the people' (Ivins).

It may not be immediately apparent what the problem is with media concentration since, from a narrow business perspective, the growth of corporations is for them, a good thing. From the theoretical perspective of capitalism, competition profits everyone including consumers. More companies means more diversity of products including points of view accessible through various media. This basic principle of capitalism seems to have been completely abandoned, though lip service is still paid to it on occasion. Instead it has been replaced with the rather obvious, but socio-pathological, idea that competition does *not* profit companies. Monopoly profits companies (the few that survive at the top, of course) because it allows them to limit the quality of products, fix prices, and engage in all the rights violations we have been considering in this book, without worrying about social-conscience competition from companies who would be prepared to do business more democratically. Ted Turner points out that the big media companies are not antagonistic; 'they do billions of dollars in business with each other. They don't compete; they cooperate to inhibit competition' (Turner). This powerful CEO agrees with grassroots recommendations to 'bust up the big conglomerates' (ibid.).

The concentration of power in fewer and fewer hands leads to obvious biases in news reporting and in the general worldview promoted by corporate media. A recent scandal reported in the *Guardian Weekly* and other newspapers centers around the disclosure that journalists are paid directly by departments and agencies of the U.S. government to promote their agendas. This, while journalists and news executives who dare to express dissenting views have been fired.[4] The result of such censorship, which is also generally internalized by journalists so that they don't even need to be told what is permissible to print, drastically reduces the range of opinion, which consequently becomes narrow enough to be almost homogenous (despite the so-called 'liberal bias'). The restricted view of the world disseminated by corporate media seems therefore natural, incontestable, and true.

In response to this curtailing of perspectives, the Media Carta movement wants 'to enshrine the Right to Communicate as a fundamental human right in the constitutions of all free nations and in the Universal Declaration of Human Rights.' '[W]e, the people, must win control of society's most powerful means of expression. Without the ability to share ideas and opinions, we cannot debate issues or make informed decisions. We cannot raise healthy children, create good public policy or hold elections that matter. We lose the power to shape our own consciousness, our own future. We lose even the power to imagine what that future might look like' (Lasn and Walker). And in India, the world's largest democracy, citizen groups are organizing to fight for the RTI (Right To Information), exemplified in the 2004 national convention held in New Delhi. Grassroots activists in Rajasthan started the RTI movement as a result of trying to get transparency on local development expenditures and finding 'time and again...glaring discrepancies in official records' (Mehrotra).

Proponents of democratizing media and society like Herman argue that 'the civic sector is the locus of the truly democratic media and that genuine democratization in Western societies will be contingent on its great enlargement. Those actively seeking the democratization of the media should seek first to enlarge the civic sphere by every possible avenue, to strengthen the public sector by increasing its autonomy and funding, and lastly to contain or shrink the commercial sector and work to tap its revenue for the civic sector' (Herman *The Myth of the Liberal Media* 313). Democratization of media is a global issue. Even the most marginalized people in poor countries struggle to have access to media in order to represent themselves, to communicate with each other, and to create solidarity networks across borders—all of which have a major role in influencing rights outcomes at local and global levels.

One of the countless examples of such efforts is the clandestine radio station in Oaxaca, Mexico: Radio Guetza which broadcasts traditional and populist music, cultural programs, and news in several indigenous languages spoken by the 24 communities who are members of the Popular Indigenous Council of Oaxaca 'Ricardo Flores Magón' (CIPO-RFM). Herman writes that 'it is urgently important that the Third World...try to maintain and encourage an indigenous media and Third World press networks that can reflect local and Third World interests. This is in fact essential to the preservation of any kind of national and cultural independence and integrity' ('Freedom of Expression' 178-79). Despite this sane recommendation, Radio Guetza is illegal and persecuted by the Mexican government because it promotes solidarity and awareness among diverse indigenous communities whose access to communication facilitates united efforts to pressure the government to respect their human rights.

Media is important for the dissemination and interpretation of human rights issues but we must be aware of the biases within rights reporting itself. James Ron, a former investigator for HRW and now a Canada Research Chair in Conflict and Human Rights at McGill University, has produced eye-opening work on the biases in rights reporting. Ron's research has shown that between 1981 and 2000, 'reference to "human rights" in two leading newsmagazines jumped by more than 130 percent.' In a multi-year study of *The Economist* and *Newsweek* (1986-2000), Ron found that human rights coverage focused on 'China, Russia (including the USSR), Indonesia (including East Timor), the United States, Chile, Turkey, Serbia, Colombia, Britain (including Northern Ireland), Cuba and Nigeria. There were some glaring omissions: The list includes none of the world's most deadly civil wars, including those in Sudan, Rwanda and Afghanistan, and makes no mention of the world's poorest countries. And many of the world's most autocratic regimes, including Saudi Arabia and North Korea, did not earn "most reported on" status.'

The effects of this imbalance are, in Ron's estimation, significant, especially with regard to how AI, for instance, produces its advocacy work via the media: 'An analysis of Amnesty's press releases from 1986 to 2000 found that it was more likely to devote written advocacy efforts to abuses in countries with media-friendly profiles.' Further, 'while journalists increasingly seek out Amnesty's views, they tend to ask questions about a small group of countries, putting Amnesty's press officers in a bind. Although they are committed to exposing abuses wherever they occur, their press releases on low-profile countries evoke little reaction.' The size of a particular country's economy or even the number of NGOs it has in place can lead to an undue impact on overall media representation, as Ron's study shows.

Libel suits are becoming a serious concern for presses, newspapers, and human rights organizations. Greg Palast reveals that while an AI report was the first source for his story on the murder of Tanzanian miners, the story resulted in a lawsuit against *The Guardian* by Canadian gold mining company Barrick. When Palast called Amnesty headquarters in London, they refused to help: 'The organization whose motto is "Silence is complicity" announced that, on advice of lawyers, they would be silent' (2). Barrick used AI's self-censorship to report that, after conducting an investigation into the case, AI concluded that 'no one was killed in the course of the peaceful removal of miners' (ibid. 2). Yet there is no evidence of such clearance from AI, who even said that Tanzania had barred them from investigating. Palast's assessment of the situation is a stark warning about the limits of communication and the resulting human rights violations that can be more easily perpetrated with impunity once bearing witness becomes too dangerous (i.e., costly) for journalists and human rights advocates: 'The withering, costly pounding of an enraged corporate power with too much money to spend has chilled reporters' and British newspapers' will to take on the tougher investigative matters. Amnesty is "silent on the advice of lawyers." And so, the witness statements of those who watched the bodies exhumed, and one who dug his way from the mass grave, will now also remain entombed in legal silence' (DiMauro 4).

Thus, seeming globalized access to media and affirmations about their dissemination effect with regard to rights issues must be balanced by knowledge of the degree to which an international class system of media privilege and celebrity is in place. And further, the place of alternative reporting via alternative media must be figured into the scenario Ron describes, itself an indictment of conservative mass media editorial practices that are being challenged through alternative media found on the Internet and in both local and international communities of concern. The international class system that naturalizes such terms as 'First' and 'Third World,' causes distortions that do not lead to empowerment, change, or even mild interest. But that version of the media and human rights is not the whole story.

Access to media ideally empowers people by enabling the crucial exchange of views on how to work collectively toward more democratic social formations, in which the full range of human rights are protected. The right to communication is the fundamental vehicle to opening up a truly inclusive discussion on this and all other rights.

Rights Bureaucracies: A Critical Perspective

One of the stunning accomplishments of rights advocates in the last half-century has been the formation of global organizations devoted to the promotion of rights.[5] The significant increase of rights discourses across a wide variety of local and global platforms occurs largely thanks to well-organized and informed groups like AI and HRW, which generally strive to be autonomous, non-partisan, and politically neutral. Therefore, they play an enormously vital role in the reportage and denunciation of rights violations and abuses worldwide.

This said impartiality is not always easily achievable, especially in complicated rights scenarios where competing interests are at stake. For instance, a number of reports accuse Human Rights Watch 'Americas Director' José Miguel Vivanco of being anything but neutral. The way in which he voiced his opposition to Telesur the Latin American-wide TV station that received start-up funds from the governments of Argentina, Venezuela, Uruguay and Cuba leads many to suspect that Vivanco is very much engaged politically in maintaining the status quo in Latin America, which, after years of U.S. domination, has begun to shift toward new political and economic alliances: 'If the shareholders of this company belong to a government like Cuba where they have no basic concept of free speech and zero tolerance for independent views, God help us' said Vivanco (reported in *Chicago Tribune* and cited by Giordano in 'Vivanco Attacks Telesur' 1). The relationship between Vivanco and Alberto Federico Ravell (owner of the privately owned Venezuelan TV network Globovision) clearly shows how the media and human rights organizations sometimes intersect in ways that seriously compromise human rights work. '...that...Vivanco is attacking Telesur network [which] he has never even seen on the air, in light of his three-year silence about the anti-democracy coup participation by Commercial media barons like Ravell, is yet another nail in the coffin of Human Rights Watch's dwindling credibility in Latin America' (Giordano 'Vivanco Attacks Telesur' 2). Vivanco's simplistic association of Telesur with Cuba, a country that does indeed have media and free speech problems within a complex geopolitical context, does little to advance the issue of how Latin American countries, so influenced by global corporate media, can develop independent alternatives to those media, which in turn will require scrutiny of whether they address rights issues with integrity.

Collaborative journalism relating to human rights issues is greatly facilitated by the Internet. One such news organization and the School of Authentic Journalism as it calls itself is the Narcosphere 'a participatory, online, forum, where readers and journalists come together to discuss, correct, add new information and relevant links, and debate the work of the journalists who publish on NarcoNews.com...[T]he readers in this forum become co-publishers who besides expanding on reports, asking questions, and suggesting new leads, 'often do investigative reporting themselves' since as editor Giordano observes, 'It is time for the readers to start driving the coverage of news' ('Welcome to the Narcosphere').

The Narco News team attending a Senate Hearing on Venezuela's referendum reported that 'the State Department is trying to keep pressure on Chavez through the OAS, and non-governmental organizations like the Carter Center and the Americas Division of Human Rights Watch...' (Giordano 'State Dept works "through" HRW'). Such allegations cannot be dismissed lightly and should alert us to the fact that no one institutional source on rights can be trusted unquestioningly, regardless of that source's status and prestige; that situations are complex and require careful comparative readings of multiple sources in order to bring us closer to understanding.

In this section, we briefly examine human rights organizations, their accomplishments, and the challenges they face. First some basic facts related to the U.S., again, only because it presents itself as a 'leading advocate' of human rights worldwide and is indicative of some of the major issues that must be addressed in any discussion of rights organizations. The rhetoric around this leadership in rights advocacy is exemplified in Under Secretary of State Paula Dobriansky's comments on U.S. human rights policy to the Senate Foreign Relations Committee in 2001: 'We shall continue to be the world's leading advocate for democracy and human rights. We shall continue to meet foreign government officials, and insist that our views on human rights be known. We shall speak up for the dissidents, the victims of persecution, the tortured and the dispossessed. We shall continue to tell the truth when we submit our Country Reports on Human Rights Practices to Congress and to the millions who now access them via the Internet.'

But in 2001, Stephen Rickard, Director of the Robert F. Kennedy Memorial Center for Human Rights (a character we met earlier in the book), presented testimony entitled, 'Bricks Without Straw: Taking Action on the Annual Country Reports on Human Rights Practices,' that places Dobriansky's assertions in a clearer light. Rickard was assessing the Bureau of Democracy, Human Rights and Labor (DRL)—the primary agency charged with supporting U.S. human rights policy through, among others, producing the Country Reports mentioned by Dobriansky. These Country Reports serve, ostensibly, as a basis for policy decisions. Rickard says there is a 'staggering gap between the amount of money now being spent on democracy promotion—about $750 million—and the amount currently spent on the entire human rights bureaucracy at the [U.S.] State Department (less than two percent of that sum)' (5) —an amount, by the way, that is less than the amount spent on recent U.S. presidential inaugurations. So what appears to be a significant bureaucracy in the nation that supposedly leads in the advocacy of human rights is, in fact, *not*. Moreover, based on work done in Venezuela by U.S. attorney Eva Golinger, it is clear that in that country the U.S. supports subversive groups 'under the guise of promoting democracy' (Herrera), again suggesting that the way in which resources are seemingly spent on rights outcomes needs to be very carefully evaluated. Diligent critical scrutiny of organizations working toward rights outcomes, then, is as necessary as are the organizations themselves.

Rickard's report is telling in other ways. He notes that the DRL has one of the smallest budgets within the overall State Department ('one-third of one penny out of every dollar the congress provides to the State Department'); its budget is 'less than half the budget of the U.S. section of Amnesty International'; there are 'country desk officers in DRL responsible for covering as many as 33 countries'; and 'the annual travel budget is...in the range of about $250,000' (4). These amounts, within the context of annual military spending, for instance, are laughable—and an indictment of the kind of window-dressing that goes on when governments do not dedicate sufficient resources in a meaningful way to rights outcomes. Examination of funding reports from the UN Office of the High Commissioner for Human Rights (OHCHR) is also indicative: in the 2003 Annual Report the OHCHR details how it receives only '1.8% [approximately U.S.$50.4 million] of the full U.S.$2.9 billion United Nations regular budget for the biennium' (9).

Even more tellingly, the report shows that voluntary contributions to OHCHR, which account for over half of its budget, on a country by country basis has a major developed country like Canada contributing less than Ireland, Denmark, Sweden, Finland, Belgium, and even Libya (11). Such small amounts seriously compromise the ability of the resources to keep up with the enormity of the tasks facing the High Commission, whatever one's position on the use-value of the UN as a whole.

When placed in perspective of hyper-developed countries like Canada and the U.S.'s international aid numbers for 2003, which for Canada amount to 0.24 percent of Gross National Income and for the U.S. 0.15 percent of GNI, the lowest percentage in the developed world, the lack of resources going into human rights funding is part of a much larger pattern of inequitable and unethical allocation of resources globally ('Rich countries pilloried'). Moreover, when the total 'amount of money spent by Western industrialized nations on weapons and soldiers every year' is in the area of U.S.$422 billion (Steger 43), the allocation of resources is shown to be a fundamental, brutal, politely ignored part of the global human rights scenario. Until this substantial inequity is addressed by developed nations, their leadership in the global advocacy of rights will remain largely rhetorical.

The importance of rights bureaucracies is not to be underestimated, so long as those instruments are adequately resourced and reclaim their mandates apart from institutional mandates pushed upon them by specific political agendas that empty rights institutions of utility or meaning.

Rights Organizations

Rights advocacy functions in multiple contexts and would have to include the following types of organizations:

* local grassroots groups focused on single-issue advocacy, from abused women through to homelessness through to children's rights, disability rights, education rights, landless rights, the abolition of the death penalty, and so forth;

* non-governmental groups like AI, HRW, and the International Helsinki Federation for Human Rights (a self-governing group of non-governmental, not-for-profit organizations that act to protect human rights throughout Europe, North America and Central Asia), that have broad mandates and presence in multiple national sites and that are at the forefront of documenting, researching, and activating political pressure targeted at specific rights outcomes often with significant results—as in the case of Augusto Pinochet, the former Chilean dictator responsible for numerous crimes against humanity, where AI's relentless pressure turned Pinochet's evasion of justice into an international *cause célèbre*; AI is the largest human rights NGO with 1.8 million members in 150 counties;

* specific national, governmental agencies, like the state commissions in Mexico or like Montreal-based Rights & Democracy (International Centre for Human Rights and Democratic Development), a non-partisan organization with an international mandate created by Canada's Parliament in 1988 to 'encourage and support the universal values of human rights and the promotion of democratic institutions and practices around the world';

- non-governmental national organizations devoted to specific issues, such as HaMoked and B'Tselem, Israeli human rights organizations that address human rights violations in the Occupied Territories and assist Palestinians whose rights are violated due to Israeli policies, and the Palestinian Centre for Human Rights (PCHR), an independent legal body based in Gaza City dedicated to protecting human rights, promoting the rule of law, and upholding democratic principles in the Occupied Palestinian Territories;

- non-governmental organizations located in a specific national site but with global or regional outreach, like Helen Bamber's Medical Foundation for the Care of Victims of Torture (England), which, in 2003 alone, had some 3,415 men, women, and children referred to it for help from nearly 100 countries, including Turkey, Iran, the Democratic Republic of Congo, Eritrea, Iraq, Ethiopia, Kosovo, Uganda, Somalia and Congo (Brazzaville); the Canadian Centre for Victims of Torture (CCVT), which on average sees 700 people a year from 60 different countries through its doors; and the New Delhi-based South Asia Human Rights Documentation Centre (SAHRDC), which 'seeks to investigate, document and disseminate information about human rights treaties and conventions, human rights education, refugees, media freedom, prison reforms, political imprisonment, torture, summary executions, disappearances and other cruel, inhuman or degrading treatment';

- global rights organizations like the UN Office of the High Commissioner for Human Rights; and continental organizations like the African Commission on Human and Peoples' Rights, headquartered in Banjul, Gambia, that was established by the African Charter on Human and Peoples' Rights (1986) to ensure the promotion and protection of Human and Peoples' Rights throughout the African continent;

- academic/institutional centers for the research on and dissemination of information on rights, like the University of Minnesota Human Rights Center, the Human Rights Centre at the University of Essex, England, the Human Rights Research and Education Centre at the University of Ottawa, the Carr Center for Human Rights Policy at Harvard University, and the Center for the Study of Human Rights at Columbia University. The proposed Canadian Museum for Human Rights represents an unusual addition to this scenario as it is intended to perform the traditional museum work of collection and the dissemination of research more traditionally associated with centers and NGOs like AI.

We note that an emergent global institution like the International Criminal Court represents a major new direction for rights organizations. The breakdown we give above among the numerous types of organizations lists none with a global reach that has the power to implement legal solutions to rights abuses. The imbalance between the number of groups devoted to documentation and advocacy as opposed to implementation is a serious problem facing the rights community.

Stephen Marks, in his assessment of the fifty years after the UDHR and in asking how we gauge progress made on global rights issues, concludes positively that 'every major government has a significant department of human rights' and states 'From its beginnings as a small division in the forties, the Office of the High Commissioner for Human Rights now employs hundreds and oversees numerous field operations around the world. The regional institutions (OAS, OAU and Council of Europe) have advanced even further. NGOs have proliferated in all parts of the world and their access to and influence on governmental and intergovernmental decision makers has been extraordinary. The voice of people's suffering from repression and oppression is now heard through organized civil society movements that have had a dramatic impact on the transformation of Central and Eastern Europe, Latin America and South Africa, and they are gaining strength in the rest of Africa and in Asia.'

The enduring paradox that underlies all this progress, both real and imagined, is that despite the proliferation of rights organizations since the 1948 UDHR, the proliferation of abuses continues. More real resources from the most economically powerful nations in the world must be shifted into effective human rights advocacy and aid for meaningful change to occur. Beyond that, legislators, policymakers and politicians of every stripe must increasingly sensitize themselves across non-partisan lines to the work done by non-governmental, neutral organizations like AI and HRW, whose combined existence and work at a global level (remember, independent of any and all government funding) provides for ample examples of where and how to direct resources toward solving specific rights issues.

The December 2005 passage of a law by the Russian State Duma that severely restricts the operations of NGOs in that country represents another kind of threat to NGOs. Authoritarian states critiqued by human rights organizations that demand real, as opposed to managed, democracy are increasingly vulnerable to the global influence wielded by credible NGOs. In the case of Russia, NGOs 'can be refused registration' if their names 'offend citizens' moral, national or religious feelings' (Alimov and Kudrik) or if an NGO threatens 'national uniqueness [*samobytnost*]' or the 'cultural inheritance and national interests of the Russian Federation' (ibid.). These provisions are clearly so vague as to be risible and written so as to cater potentially to the worst aspects of nationalist paranoia. The executive director of the leading human rights organization in Russia, Memorial, stated that the law will 'mean the destruction of civil society in Russia' ('Duma approves NGO Bill'). Igor Yakovenko, head of the Russian Union of Journalists, claimed, 'The passing of the bill may be considered as an official declaration of war by the state against those sproutings of civil society that still exist. Passing the bill is evidence of Russia's transition from authoritarianism to totalitarianism.' And Alexander Nikitin, chairman of the Bellona Environmental Rights Centre in St. Petersburg, argued, 'It is impossible to openly prohibit all independent NGOs. The Kremlin is building up a mechanism to make them die' (Alimov and Kudrik). Shortly after the law had been signed by President Vladimir Putin (but prior to the law's having come into force), the Russian justice ministry moved to close the Russian Human Rights Research Centre (Human Rights House) in Moscow, one of the oldest rights groups in the country yet founded in only 1992.

Rights NGOs, then, will have to address increased competition for access to resources in conjunction with the proper allocation of these resources. But they will have to also address the counter-measures mounted against them as the targets of their campaigns react to the globalization of rights values. Lastly, they will have to confront the internal pressures of self-interest and the external factors, political, legal, and otherwise, that compromise their effectiveness. Ultimately, rights organizations represent a major (potential) cultural shift in how the world organizes and evaluates itself, one that extends beyond the interests of any one of these organizations. The principles that underlie these organizations, and here we are thinking of AI and HRW specifically (but also of many other like-minded groups worldwide), must be disseminated across a much wider spectrum of all societies at a basic level of feeling and thinking critically about the world—one that takes us to our next topic, human rights education.

Your Ignorance Is Their Power: Education and Human Rights

Education is the most powerful weapon which you can use to change the world. —Nelson Mandela

We want to have access to education, but our concern is what kind of education. Do we want education that destroys our culture, our traditions, and our language and knowledge? —Stella Tamang

Dear Teacher: I am a survivor of a concentration camp. My eyes saw what no man should witness: Gas chambers built by learned engineers. Children poisoned by educated physicians...So I am suspicious of education. My request is: Help your students become human. —Haim Ginott

The World Conference on Human Rights stated that human rights education, training, and public information were essential for the promotion and achievement of stable and harmonious relations among communities and for fostering mutual understanding, tolerance and peace. Traditionally, rights education is seen to fall rather reductively between what Stanley Cohen summarizes as the positive focus on human rights values (largely inspired by the UDHR) and the negative focus on atrocities and human suffering (267). But clearly, education in many parts of the world, especially for women, children, and the impoverished, must include basic literacy, before issues of content can even be addressed.

There are 100 million children (60 million girls and 40 million boys) in the world that cannot attend primary school for financial reasons. While at first glance this number may suggest an insurmountable problem, comparing education aid spending to military spending puts things into sharp perspective: 'for only $5.4bn more per year, we could provide a quality, free education to every child, and unlock the full power of education to beat poverty. This amounts to less than two and a half days' global military spending. For the price of just one of the Cruise missiles dropped on Baghdad, 100 schools could be built in Africa' ('Missing the Mark' 1). The required funding over and above the 2000 levels would amount to a 500 percent increase, showing just how far behind rich countries are lagging in their commitments to global education.

There is arguably no better investment in aid than education for long-term benefits to individuals, communities, and countries. The Millennium Development Goals set by heads of state in 2000 recognize that education gives poor people the tools to solve their own problems: 'Evidence gathered over 30 years shows that educating women is the single most powerful weapon against malnutrition—even more effective than improving food supply' (ibid. 1). Yet an Oxfam report shows that most rich countries are falling well short of the financing targets they set themselves, with the two richest —the U.S. and Japan—providing less than 10 percent of their fair share, while Norway, the Netherlands, Sweden, and Denmark are the best donors (ibid. 2). While Americans consider themselves the most affluent people in the world, in 2003 each U.S. citizen contributed only 55 cents to education in the developing world, compared to the 66 dollars contributed by each Norwegian citizen.

Another important issue in development through education is how funding is allocated. Basic primary education produces the most tangible and far-reaching effects, while specialized technical training produces the least impact. Even though extensive research shows this to be a fact, most donor countries like Canada 'allocate the lion's share of aid to "optional extras" such as seminars, consultancies, and expensive small-scale pilot projects' (ibid. 4). Only about 17 percent of Canada's total aid goes to education and 7 percent to basic education. This is because education is a real donation and not a money making enterprise for donor corporations like most of the projects that self-interested First World countries prefer to fund. Even within education, the more cynical donors (11 of the richest countries in the world) contribute to the 'optional extras' because 'a good deal of this ends up generating lucrative contracts for foreign experts' (ibid. 16). We may even ask whether it is in the First World's business interests to aid education in poor countries, since the outcome of literacy tends to encourage people to stand up for their rights and to reject exploitation.

The story of Chico Mendes shows both the process of self-awareness that leads to desiring knowledge, and the brutal backlash from those who think that education should be a luxury reserved for the ruling class. Chico Mendes was a poor Brazilian who as a child worked tapping rubber trees, and didn't learn to read until he was 18 years old. His story is a case study in an excellent book published by AI to teach elementary school children about rights and responsibilities: *Our World, Our Rights: Teaching about Rights and Responsibilities in the Elementary School*. Mendes became an environmental activist, because once literate 'he learned that the rainforest was being destroyed by rich landowners to make money and that this affected the people who lived and worked in the forest and also the climate of the world' (Schmidt, Manson, Windschitl 115). His education clearly helped him see beyond the local effects of deforestation to some of its economic causes and global impact. Mendes worked to set up schools funded by Oxfam and Christian Aid, since 'the Brazilian government only gave a little money; they feared that education would make people dissatisfied' (ibid. 115). Mendes showed how education can empower people to stand up for human and environmental rights. His story, however, ends tragically, since power that disregards rights persecutes knowledge that challenges power: gunmen hired by landowners assassinated Chico Mendes in 1988. Mendes left an important legacy. What he said about activism links it to education and the process of learning and growing beyond one's self-interest: 'the struggle teaches us many things, everyday we learn something new. Our roots are too deep for us to think of giving up the struggle' (ibid. 116).

Indigenous groups around the world have been critical of Western approaches to education that often teach Western values and downplay or denigrate students' own cultural knowledge. Education should enhance one's life and not take anything away from people, as was so often the case in colonial administrations in Africa and residential schools in North America, where indigenous culture was supplanted by colonial culture. When education is imposed from outside and above, it can create negative self-images and estrange people from their communities, their language, their customs and culture. Often development programs are promoted as educational; farmers are taught to adopt modern methods, which are ultimately in the interest of agribusiness. The results of a bad education in pesticide use and monoculture can be a devastating lesson in first world hypocrisy and ignorance.

'Miseducation' is not limited to poor countries, but is also widely practiced in the West due to the many governmental and corporate pressures whose effects we have already observed in the gagging and outright appropriation of the media. Chomsky makes the point that it is especially important to indoctrinate the 20 percent of the population belonging to the political class destined to become what he calls the 'cultural managers.' This is a very particular kind of knowledge that tends to be highly specialized, trained not to make connections or to spread roots in community. Diametrically opposed to this narrow knowledge of the 'expert' is the concept of 'making conscious' of the political dimension of community promoted by educators like Paulo Freire. As Joyce Nelson observes, 'When the word is used at all, conscience is understood in our society to be a thoroughly private matter. And yet, the word's Latin root, *com+scire*, means "to know together"—an indication that the ability to make moral distinctions between right and wrong has something to do with community' (Brooks and Verdecchia 8).

Majority world people have also made valuable observations about how to interpret a wide range of experiences that are educational, though they may not be restricted to a classroom, separated from work and other community activities. Oral storytelling, music and dance, apprenticeship, and working in an integrated way with members of the community all teach life skills together with cultural memory and knowledge. The traditional stories of most communities around the world have teachings on human and environmental rights built right into them. Deer hunting for the Pueblo involves an important ritual that connects animal, human, and the earth: 'They went to the deer and lifted the jacket. They knelt down and took pinches of cornmeal from Josiah's leather pouch. They sprinkled the cornmeal on the nose and fed the deer's spirit. They had to show their love and respect, their appreciation; otherwise, the deer would be offended, and they would not come to die for them the following year...They said the deer gave itself to them because it loved them, and he could feel the love as the fading heat of the deer's body warmed his hands' (Marmon Silko 51-2).

A Mayan story, retold by Subcomandante Insurgente Marcos, reflects upon the importance of recognizing diversity in equality, a crucial precept of human rights as we have seen at length in our chapter on minority rights. It tells how the gods accidentally left their box of paints open and fell asleep after an exhausting day of gathering colors with which to paint the world (which originally had been black at night, and white by day). Very different from the representation of the Judeo-Christian Genesis in which God creates and names in an orderly way, '...it was a mess the way the gods threw the colors because they didn't care where the colors landed. Some colors splattered on the men and women, and that is why there are peoples of different colors and different ways of thinking...because they didn't want to forget the colors or lose them, [the gods] looked for a way to keep them safe...they saw the macaw' (which at this point was still grey with stunted feathers like a wet chicken) 'they grabbed it and started to pour all the colors on it and they stretched its feathers so that the colors could all fit. And that was how the macaw took hold of the colors, and so it goes strutting about just in case men and women forget how many colors there are and how many ways of thinking, and that the world will be happy if all the colors and ways of thinking have their place' (Marcos). All world religions are also founded on the principles of respect for life and intrinsic, shared human dignity, and only deviate from this commonality when self-interested leaders and their followers choose to read scriptures in highly selective and perversely 'specialized' ways.

Despite the important cultural differences that need to be respected in the realm of education as in any other, human rights education must be universal and incorporated into the curricula in all countries. An especially constructive approach to teaching social justice is to take a global approach, thereby not only informing students about their rights and freedoms, but getting them to think about how and why they should stand up for all peoples' rights and freedoms.

An impressive example of progressive educational publications dealing with fundamental rights issues is a book geared to elementary and secondary school children, but also useful in colleges, universities, and in non-institutional settings: *Rethinking Globalization: Teaching for Justice in An Unjust World*, edited by Bill Bigelow and Bob Peterson. This text combines creative literature, essays, games, and testimonies from children and adults around the world to explore various forms of injustice, rooting this knowledge in an introductory section on colonial history. The book serves as a blueprint for other such initiatives in that it promotes a holistic approach to analyzing problems with a view to finding long-term, sustainable solutions through student commitment and solidarity movements. How different is this way of telling the story of the global economy —its causes and consequences—from textbooks currently used in economics courses, which tend to devote a few pages to the majority world, as if this were an afterthought with no real connection to 'Free Market' economics and First World interests!

Stories dealing with cultural survival and community-based knowledge revolve around respect for life and dignity. Thanks to the kind of global communication geared to ensuring universal human rights, contemporary education can draw inspiration from the wisdom inherent in communities around the world, thus avoiding the constraints on knowledge production that align with political opportunism and self-interest. Teaching *for* peace and human rights should be at the core of *all* levels of education globally (respective of culturally specific contexts) because, as AI notes, 'schools have a responsibility to enable children to make sense of the world around them' (Schmidt et al. 5). We now turn to the arts as another mode of communication that also has an important role to play in raising awareness of social justice through enacting freedom of expression.

'You Have to Be Careful with the Stories You Tell' (Thomas King)

Human rights documents like the UDHR narrate a particular vision of the world—they tell stories every bit as much as do other textual forms (like poems or novels) and these stories demand interpretation. Who has the power to interpret these narratives is a crucial aspect of how inequality gets apportioned on a global scale. Eurocentric stories about human rights widely disseminated as a function of economic power vary widely from majority world narratives of rights. For that reason, it is crucial that close attention be paid to how 'we' narrate what human rights or social justice means. How we shape the stories we tell, in other words, *does* have consequences for human rights.

The UDHR, as noted earlier in this book, makes no mention of the environment except very secondarily in terms of property and ownership. Only urban dwellers whose livelihood is completely alienated from the land, and from such activities as agriculture and fishing, can dissociate human life and rights from the environment. Come to think of it, if urban-dwellers' livelihoods depend on clear-cut forestry, genetic engineering of crops, industrialized agriculture, dragnet fishing, strip-mining, and all other forms of exploiting the environment without regard for sustainability, urban-dwellers might be especially eager to dissociate human life and rights from the environment. This dissociation reveals a striking parallel between the stories told by the UDHR and the aspects of the Bible that support human dominion over the planet, especially Genesis (9.3), which states, 'Everything that lives and moves will be food for you. Just as I gave you the green plants, I now give you everything.'

Native writer Thomas King compares Biblical Genesis to a native creation story to illustrate how 'you have to be careful with the stories you tell' (10). 'In Genesis, we begin with a perfect world, but after the Fall, while we gain knowledge, we lose the harmony and safety of the garden and are forced into a chaotic world of harsh landscapes and dangerous shadows. In our Native story, we begin with water and mud, and, through the good offices of Charm (the female protagonist), her twins, and the animals, move by degrees and adjustments from a formless, featureless world to a world that is rich in its diversity, a world that is complex and complete' (24). The first human in this story is a woman who completely depends on animals for survival: animals create for *her* benefit the land on which she dwells. The earth is created collaboratively and involves ongoing negotiations to maintain it as the fount of human existence. Genesis, on the other hand, ends sadly for the expulsed humans, and while many interpretations over the centuries have tried to infuse this with the positive implications of human freedom, it is a dead-end story in terms of humans' relation to the earth.

Author and historian Ronald Wright reminds us that 'President Reagan's secretary of the interior told Congress not to bother with the environment because, in his words, "I don't know how many future generations we can count on until the Lord returns." ' As a result, George W. Bush, according to Wright, 'surrounded himself with similar minds and pulled out of the Kyoto Accord on climate change.' Wright interprets this ludicrous use of the Revelation story saying that 'mainstream Christianity is an altruistic faith, yet this offshoot is actively hostile to the public good' (130).

Here, too, a comparison of Revelation and the related native concepts of Koyaanisqatsi (a state of life that calls for another way of living) and the Seventh Fire or Pachakuti (the World Turned Upside Down) shows how the stories we tell determine or greatly influence how we perceive reality and how we respond to it. The Christian apocalypse leaves the Earth behind. The righteous are dispatched to the New Jerusalem which, despite being described by John in concrete terms involving all sorts of precious stones and metals, is located on the other side of death, somewhere in heaven. Hence the absurd, apocalyptic, death-driven logic of President Reagan's Secretary of the Interior: why care for the earth when the end is near? Entertaining the idea of colonizing space as a way out of the mess we have created is a more recent, but equally symptomatic, outcome of John's story in Revelation. And all these stories are used to justify rights violations and abuses in the name of a profoundly skewed form of storytelling that has precise ideological consequences.

There are, thankfully, alternatives. Native stories of the end of the world *as we know it* do not forsake the earth. They are predicated on the idea that the earth is our mother and is a sacred place, the *only* place for her human offspring to live and die and regenerate like all her other creations. It is the system, the current state of affairs, that is out of balance, thanks to bad choices made by humans, growing out of the bad stories they tell. According to these native prophecies, the fundamental reason for life's being out of balance is the exploitation of the earth by those who see her as a commodity, as an indefinite resource for human consumption, as a launching pad for abandoning her after she has been poisoned and pillaged to death.

The 'World Turned Upside Down' emerged as a concept during the Conquest of the Americas. It relates to the revolutionary impulse of wanting to oust invaders who have proven themselves unworthy of the earth through their greed and deceitful ways. It is not a story simply about wanting to regain cultural hegemony, and it is not even human-centered. Rather, the story is open-ended, leaving hope for the seventh fire to light the eighth fire on condition that the 'misguided' descendents of Europeans (though we can broaden that category with the advent of global capitalism) see the light, the writing on the wall, smell the roses, and realize that apocalypse is not the pre-ordained end to (hi)story. The ending can actually be changed through our actions as we live out the story (history).

A brief example of how this works is in order. In her novel *Ceremony*, Pueblo author Leslie Marmon Silko narrates the ordeals of a young mestizo man called Tayo. After having been taken prisoner by the Japanese in World War II, he is diagnosed with battle fatigue by white doctors who can't understand why Tayo confuses his Pueblo community with the Japanese on the other side of the planet. Tayo comes to understand the relationship only once he realizes that the uranium used in the nuclear bombs dropped on Japan was mined just outside of his community in New Mexico—the bombs created at the Los Alamos National Laboratory and tested at the Trinity Site.

The connection between Tayo's Pueblo community and the Japanese community evokes the following cosmological vision, another story told about why such connections matter: 'The Hopi's cosmology perceives this [here and now] to be the Fourth World. There were seven worlds created at the beginning. The first three were each destroyed in turn because the humans inhabiting them had diverged too far from their original sacred path of connectedness with and love and respect for all life on Mother Earth.' Hopi prophecies describe the possibility of such a destruction of the Fourth World in poetically precise terms, evoking the very uranium and bombs that are part of Tayo's story:

> *If we dig precious things from the land, we will invite disaster.*
> *Near the Day of Purification, there will be cobwebs*
> *spun back and forth in the sky.*
>
> *A container of ashes might one day be thrown from the sky,*
> *which could burn the land and boil the oceans. ('Koyaanisqatsi')*

Marmon Silko doesn't mention this Hopi prophecy explicitly in Ceremony. Instead, the reader must work to make the connections, enacting the very process that leads Tayo to realize that his actions will determine the outcome of the story—not just his personal story, but the story of the world, of our inter-connected humanity. This search for connections and truthfulness in the stories we tell is a clear, alternative vision of what it means to be a global citizen. Further, Marmon Silko's story underlines how the self-serving, fatuous end-time stories told by politicians, military officials, corporate executives, and the mass media must be rejected in order to live out this phase of the story in a way that does not buy into simplistic apocalyptic myths that reject life on earth. Inequality of voice and vision as disseminated through access to mass media is a crucial determinant of the rights stories that shape rights realities.

The first indigenous president of Bolivia was inaugurated in January of 2006, in a country with a majority indigenous population. In his speech, Evo Morales announced: '[W]e are taking over now for the next 500 years. The campaign of 500 years of resistance has not been in vain.' According to a kind of thinking that historian Ronald Wright calls 'prophecy-history,' this collective indigenous 'take-over' would seem to be a *pachakuti*, a shift of cosmic significance that nevertheless is ratified in the election of a leader in accordance with the conventions of representational democracy. Nervous and unsure of the implications of a discourse that is alien to European ears, in that it doesn't divorce history from myth/prophecy, metaphysics from political action, non-Natives might wonder where such a vision relegates us. Are we to pack our bags after centuries of co-habitation on American soil, and head back to a distant memory of origins on a continent that is now alien to us? Morales, like many indigenous leaders, made it clear 'that his people would not seek vengeance for centuries of oppression, but he called on other nations, including the United States, to treat Bolivia and its resources with respect' (Harper). It will be difficult for non-Natives not to judge indigenous forms of governance in terms of being Marxist, leftist, or any other Western conception of political possibilities, and in some cases it is clear that these designations are meant to tarnish the image of leaders like Morales, and to raise the red alert against practices like limiting private ownership of land and resources through nationalization and other approaches. It will be interesting to see what visions such leaders bring to the discussions about human rights, given that indigenous peoples think water and other resources should be communally shared since they are the very basis of all other rights. The ways in which indigenous leaders and their followers reframe these stories and tell them from a perspective rooted in collective memory will be a powerful antidote to the fragmentary and short-sighted arguments based on profit for an elite.

IN THE BEGINNING...

THE GODS BROUGHT FORTH THE UNIVERSE, AND IT WAS GOOD.

THEY FILLED IT WITH SPARKLING SHARDS, GEMSTONES ON AN EBON BLANKET.

THEY WERE ESPECIALLY PLEASED WITH ONE TURQUOISE BEAD, THE EARTH.

THEY HAD THE HERO TWINS SCULPT THIS WORLD WITH MOUNTAINS AND RIVERS, AND SPIDER GRANDMOTHER POPULATE IT WITH LIFE. THIS THEY DID.

THE GODS INSTRUCTED THEIR CHARGES TO LIVE IN HARMONY. BUT THE PEOPLE DISOBEYED, FLAUNTING THEIR IRREVERENCE AND SIN. SO ANGRY DID THE GODS BECOME--

--THAT THEY DESTROYED THE EARTH NOT ONCE, NOT TWICE, BUT THREE TIMES.

THE FIRST WORLD DIED IN FIRE, THE SECOND IN ICE. THE THIRD IN RAGING FLOODS.

ONLY A FEW WORTHY SOULS SURVIVED THE ALL-ENCOMPASSING WATER--BY CLIMBING A SPRUCE TREE, OR A HOLLOW REED.

THEY EMERGED FROM THE SIPAPU INTO THE FOURTH WORLD. SOME SAY THIS OPENING WAS IN THE GRAND CANYON; OTHERS AT THE BOTTOM OF A LAKE.

Speaking Truth to Power: The Arts, Freedom of Expression, and Human Rights Activism

For far too long, as we argue throughout this book, rights discourses have found their seat in legal, juridical, and governmental offices, part of the inevitable process of entrenching rights in the law and in legal covenants and constitutions. The process has largely excluded or marginalized multiple voices, ranging from the most disenfranchised to those deemed 'inexpert.' Art, as a fundamental expression of creative human potential that relates to freedom of expression, is a basic human right—a universal, essential aspect of all human society. In this section we examine how different voices from the worlds of artistic expression have played an inspirational role in imagining the world aright and how those voices continue to offer major contributions to global rights movements.

On 10 November 1995, Nigerian author and activist Ken Saro-Wiwa was executed along with eight other members of the Movement for the Survival of the Ogoni People (MOSOP). The group had been founded by Saro-Wiwa in 1990 to fight for ethnic Ogoni rights in oil-rich lands being exploited by Shell, a target of MOSOP's ongoing campaign. The trial and the attack on the MOSOP were, in part, caused by the publication of Saro-Wiwa's books, *Nigeria: The Brink of Disaster* (1991), and *Genocide in Nigeria: The Ogoni Tragedy* (1992). Saro-Wiwa was buried in an unmarked grave in Port Harcourt where the trial took place. Shell's response to the execution was silence, whereas AI condemned the executions as 'politically motivated' after a travesty of a trial in which there was no impartiality and independence, and basic rights, such as the right of appeal to a higher independent court, were denied.

The state-sponsored killings (effectively judicial murders) revolted people the world over and reinforced at once the power and the vulnerability of writers and artists when targeting and being targeted by state and multinational corporate self-interest. As reported by Karen McGregor in *The Independent* (September 19, 2000), 'Allegations that the oil multinational Shell aided and abetted the torture and murder of Nigerian activists including the executed writer Ken Saro-Wiwa will be tested by a full jury trial in New York, after the oil company's attempts to have the case thrown out were rejected [by the U.S. Supreme Court]. Shell will also stand accused of orchestrating a series of raids by the Nigerian military on villages in the Ogoni region that left more than 1,000 people dead and 20,000 homeless.' As of this writing, the trial into Shell's activities in Nigeria and its alleged complicity in the death of Saro-Wiwa is ongoing.

Ken Saro-Wiwa's Final Words to the Nigerian Military Tribunal That Authorized His Execution:

> I repeat that we all stand before history. I and my colleagues are not the only ones on trial. Shell is here on trial and it is as well that it is represented by counsel said to be holding a watching brief. The Company has, indeed, ducked this particular trial, but its day will surely come and the lessons learnt here may prove useful to it for there is no doubt in my mind that the ecological war that the Company has waged in the Delta will be called to question sooner than later and the crimes of that war be duly punished. The crime of the Company's dirty wars against the Ogoni people will also be punished. In my innocence of the false charges I face here, in my utter conviction, I call upon the Ogoni people, the peoples of the Niger delta, and the oppressed ethnic minorities of Nigeria to stand up now and fight fearlessly and peacefully for their rights. History is on their side. God is on their side. For the Holy Qur'an says in Sura 42, verse 41: "All those that fight when oppressed incur no guilt, but Allah shall punish the oppressor. Come the day."

Saro-Wiwa's example of speaking truth to power is pressing, if not emblematic of the position of the artist in relation to struggles for rights. Bearing witness and giving testimony are two of the most powerful rights tools that artists have, especially when married to critical thought and resistant thinking. Saro-Wiwa's life and death exemplify the convergence of human rights issues with the power of artists to activate meaningful forms of resistance to those that place national and corporate self-interest over the interests of the 'common people' addressed so eloquently by the UDHR in its preamble: 'Whereas disregard and contempt for human rights have resulted in barbarous acts which have outraged the conscience of mankind, and the advent of a world in which human beings shall enjoy freedom of speech and belief and freedom from fear and want has been proclaimed as the highest aspiration of the common people...'

Multiple examples exist of ways in which artists through their art articulate rights issues that outrage human conscience, at once informing a wide public and activating what musician Frank Zappa called 'unwanted mass behavior':

- from Nigerian musician and activist Fela Kuti's musical assault on corruption in African politics, through to Elena Poniatowska's poignant documentation of testimonials about the massacre of students at Tlatelolco, the Budhan Theatre Group's struggle to transform racist laws in India directed against Chharas, an indigenous tribe relocated just outside of Ahmedabad by the British, and La FOMMA (Fortaleza de la Mujer Maya or Strength of the Mayan Woman), a women's playwright collective in Chiapas formed in 1994 to address women's rights, domestic and cultural issues, and reproductive health;

- from Tupac Shakur's indictment of the conditions that leave most Blacks in America disadvantaged, exemplified in the philosophy of 'Thug Life,' through to Michael Franti's appeal to 'Stay Human' in a concept album attacking the death penalty, through to Zapatista leader Subcomandante Marcos' forensically humorous short stories and essays about indigenous values and the challenge they represent to modernity;

- from author Leslie Marmon Silko's indigenist tellings of pan-American injustices, through to Guillermo Gómez-Peña's multidisciplinary performance artworks that challenge purist notions of identity, through to Spanish filmmaker Pedro Almodóvar's witty work on gender and transgender rights and Senegalese filmmaker and author Ousmane Sembene whose work *Moolaadé* (2005) critically examines Female Genital Mutilation and women's resistance to traditionalist male societies in Africa;

- from brutal images of war atrocities like Picasso's 'Guernica' and Sebastião Salgado's heart-rending photos of majority world dignity in the face of exploitation, to visual artist Claudia Bernardi, whose work is informed by both Argentina's Dirty War (1976-1983) in which at least 30,000 people were disappeared and her own role in exhuming a mass grave at El Mozote, El Salvador, where 767 civilians, many of them children, were slaughtered in cold blood by members of the U.S.-trained Atlacatl Brigade in 1981[6] through to graphic novelist and journalist Joe Sacco's brilliant and moving works on Palestine and the Bosnian conflict;

- from Bangladeshi writer Taslima Nasrin's critiques of fundamentalist Islam that culminated in several *fatwas* being issued against her by Islamic fundamentalist groups from 1993 on and the banning of her book *Lajja* (*Shame*) about Muslim atrocities committed against Hindu minorities, through to

Ugandan playwright George Seremba whose play *Come Good Rain* (1993) re-stages his attempted execution (Seremba was shot and left for dead) at the hands of Milton Obote's soldiers during Obote's bid for the presidency of Uganda in 1980 after Idi Amin's fall from power; Obote was reinstated as president and from 100,000 to 300,000 people died as a result of fighting between Obote's Uganda National Liberation Army (UNLA) and other military groups vying for power.

All of these examples, and the many more they must necessarily stand in for, point to the crucial role artists have in shaping discourses of rights globally and the challenges artists face in creating and disseminating their art.

As listed by PEN, a worldwide association of writers founded in 1921, many authors find themselves threatened or imprisoned as a result of their writings—from Russian journalist Anna Politkovskaya (for her writings on Chechnya) through to Tohti Tunyaz, the ethnic Uighur historian and writer currently serving an 11-year prison term that expires in 2009 for allegedly 'inciting national disunity' in China. The Tibetan music scholar, Ngawang Choephel, object of a vigorous international campaign by AI, was released in 2002 after serving six and a half years of an 18-year sentence dished out by the Chinese, merely for seeking to make a video documentary on Tibetan music and dance.

Every case of artistic repression and censorship documents the perceived threat and the power of that expression to act upon the world. In 2004, for instance, 61 Cuban writers and scholars were denied visas by the U.S. to attend the Latin American Studies Association convention in, of all places, Las Vegas—and a similar visa restriction was imposed on famed Cuban musicians Ibrahim Ferrer and Gonzalo Rubalcaba who were deemed security threats and barred entry to the U.S. to attend the Grammy Awards in 2004. These examples reinforce the very real, not to mention symbolic, power that artists possess in a rights context.

Art's capacity to invigorate the public and private spheres with activist critique that produces 'affect,' that connects a wide audience with an activated emotional response, is a crucial element in the evolving global dynamic related to activating rights generally. And we argue that one of the most noticeable emergent trends in late twentieth and early twenty-first century art has been the movement toward the production of transdisciplinary art that is closely tied to examining the human condition in relation to both the assertion and violation of rights. This trend is not negligible and will have major consequences in shaping rights discourses of the future.

Artists poised at the intersections of multiple local and global communities have a special role to play in the dissemination of rights discourses, the education of people in diverse communities that they can speak to, in the articulation of freedoms of expression and the creation of alternative social spaces, and in the networking of rights communities with each other, all crucial pre-conditions to activating rights across the globe. It is perplexing that, despite the enormous amount of creative and economic activity generated by progressive artists globally, no worldwide organization exists to promote their objectives in a comprehensive fashion. Despite this, examples of localized and more global arts organizations do exist. These would include, among many others, artists in the Durban-based Artists for Human Rights Trust, organizers of the International Human Rights Documentary Film Festival (whose seventh annual gathering occurred in Prague in 2005), the living artists from over 50 countries who participated in 'The Right to Hope' exhibition first mounted in Johannesburg in 1995, the Lost Carnival Theatre group in Toronto, whose activities prompted Artists Against War and the One Big No Peace Festival in 2003 (with over 90 acts and exhibitors, it was the largest political arts festival in Toronto since the 1980s).

Further, a number of progressive writers and artists have their work supported through foundations like the Lannan Foundation (and its Cultural Freedom Prize), which 'recognizes the profound and often unquantifiable value of the creative process and is willing to take risks and make substantial investments in ambitious and experimental thinking. Understanding that globalization threatens all cultures and ecosystems, the foundation is particularly interested in projects that encourage freedom of inquiry, imagination, and expression' ('Welcome to Lannan Online').

The need for artists to join forces across different forms of rights organizations has been taken on most notably by Amnesty International, which has promoted and supported numerous kinds of artistic expression, from 'The Secret Policeman's Ball' events in England through to huge, global-scale events like the 1998 AI celebration of the fiftieth anniversary of the signing of the Universal Declaration of Human Rights (featuring artists like Peter Gabriel, Youssou N'Dour and the Asian Dub Foundation) and in 1999 the publication of *A Map of Hope: Women's Writing on Human Rights—An International Literary An-*

thology, in which a 'global community of women writers' is shown to have 'created a literature of consciousness and of social justice' (Agosin xx). The challenge for artists will be to organize in a way that increases the global flow of artistic activity devoted to enhancing and promoting human rights and social justice outcomes. And to do so without succumbing to the market forces that compromise either their artistic expression or the social justice goals they support.

Finally, artists will have to work to find a seat at the tables where policy decisions are made, forging alliances beyond their traditional spheres of influence. The many examples of grassroots artists who take their work directly into local communities in order to affect change is inspiring and part of a larger strategy that will increasingly require artists to link their expressive, creative powers and the cultural capital they accumulate with specific rights undertakings. Underlying all these, then, will be the struggle artists face to preserve the integrity of freedom of expression as a basic human right across all cultural and national boundaries in the name of the fundamental human right to create and to be creative.

Notes

1. Eminent Middle East war correspondent Robert Fisk tells a relevant parable about distortional media in his detailed account of his experiences reporting on the tragic downing of Iran Air Flight IR655 on 3 July 1988 flying from Bandar Abbas to Dubai. The civilian flight, with 290 people aboard, was shot down by the *USS Vincennes* captained by Will Rogers III as a result of inefficiency, incompetence, and a consistent pattern of 'the U.S. Navy's constant misidentification of civil aircraft over the Gulf' (*The Great War* 263). Fisk was on-site shortly after the crash and assembled a comprehensive account of what had happened, confirmed later by independent investigations. His report on the crash was heavily censored and edited by *The Times* of London (which had been acquired by Rupert Murdoch) leading to Fisk's conclusion, 'Readers of *The Times* had been solemnly presented with a fraudulent version of the truth' (ibid. 271). The incident led to Fisk's leaving *The Times* to take up a position with *The Independent* (see *The Great War* 259-71, for a more complete account of what happened).

2. American director Jonathan Demme's 2004 film *The Agronomist* is an eloquent testimony to Dominique's life and work, and an excellent example of the use of media and art to convey social justice ends.

3. 'Unlike in criminal cases, in a libel trial the burden of proof falls largely on the defendant. The plaintiff only has to demonstrate to the court that the words are capable of lowering their reputation. They do not even have to prove that actual damage has been suffered.

The defendant on the other hand has to prove that all the statements made are true in substance and in fact. Much of the evidence needed to prove these facts is often in the hands of the plaintiffs, and it is up to them whether they release this information or not. If the defendants fail to prove the truth of their statements to the court's satisfaction, they lose even if every word they said was true. Little wonder then that the plaintiff wins the overwhelming majority of cases which come to court' (Searls and Lloyd 2-3). We note the striking similarities between the plaintiff's privilege in these libel cases and the privilege of corporations to sue national governments for expropriation under Chapter 11 of NAFTA.

4. As George Monbiot reports '60 Minutes ran an investigation into how George Bush avoided the Vietnam draft' and produced memos disclosing how Bush's service records had been doctored. After an inquiry into the program, 'the producer (Mary Mapes) was sacked and three CBS executives were forced to resign.' One of the most problematic effects of such measures was that after CBS was denounced by the rightwing pundits, during the pre-election period 'hardly any broadcaster dared to criticize George Bush,' a fact that would obviously influence voter perception of the issues and the candidates ('A Televisual Fairyland' 6). Among the several journalists paid to promote government programs, 'Maggie Gallagher, a conservative columnist and president of her own marriage institute, divulged that she had been paid $21,500 (U.S.) by the Health and Human Services Administration to promote Mr. Bush's $300-million marriage initiative. The marriage initiative is a program designed to encourage traditional marriage as a way of helping low-income families' (Freeman 'Won't Pay Columnists'). Clearly, the marriage initiative would have provoked some criticism from those who would question placing the burden of social welfare exclusively on the shoulders of heterosexual couples, and leaving same-sex couples and single parents entirely out of the picture.

5. See the chapter entitled 'International Human Rights Regimes' in Jack Donnelly's *Universal Human Rights in Theory and Practice* for an alternative summary of rights organizations to the one we present in this chapter. Our survey argues toward a more inclusive, diverse, and flexible notion of the kinds of organizations, bureaucracies, and regimes producing rights work at both local and global levels.

6. Stanley Cohen notes how the 'essential facts of the massacre [El Mozote] were known and disclosed almost immediately' via the *New York Times*, but that the *Times* journalist who broke the story was 'pulled out of Central America under State Department pressure' and that 'U.S. government officials came up with elaborate linguistic tricks and prevarications to deny the whole story...The denial was patently constructed to avoid opposition to renewing aid to the El Salvador regime' (135). Bernardi's work is exemplary of the ways in which artists not only can speak truth to power's distortions and self-interest but also do so in a way that performs an important, restorative historical function.

Chapter 6

The Future Of Human Rights: Reclaiming Hope And The Commons

Liberal democracies are poised between advancing and corrupting the principles on which they were founded. Evidence abounds of this struggle, from the silent coup being affected by the transnational economic system that puts shareholder interests above wider civic and global responsibilities and duties, through to the displacement of citizen participation with mechanisms of governance that are unelected and unaccountable to the electorate. Human rights, as a result, are put in a more and more difficult position: at once a marker of a terrible decline and failure, and a beacon of hope for a future in which current directions can dramatically change for the better, if...

The battle over what a democracy actually is has *not* been lost—the plain truth is that publishing a book such as this would be inconceivable in multiple sites globally where repression and human rights violations have truly taken hold. Vast numbers of citizens are mobilizing, actively pursuing more salutary models on which to base a political system founded on basic principles of equity and justice. And the instruments for freedom of expression, however challenged, are nonetheless still in place and in use.

That said, the current versions of liberal democracies so tightly wedded to corporate models are not the only models on which to base a pervasive human culture of rights in which respect for the integrity and dignity of life is enacted. The struggle for democratic values in developed countries is exemplified by the Ukrainian 2004 electoral fraud, remedied through an extraordinary sequence of events shortly thereafter in a manifestation of 'people power' via the 'Orange Revolution.' Further evidence of the struggle includes the increasingly worrisome allegiances between state apparatuses and fundamentalist religious doctrines (in the West, the East, the Middle East), and the number of states worldwide in which one-party political systems are still operative or in which two- or three-party states show virtually no difference in baseline ideology among the parties. Add to that the grievous irregularities surrounding the 2000 presidential vote in the U.S., especially with regard to the disenfranchisement of African American voters in Florida, the documented exit poll irregularities in the 2004 election, and the increased reliance in the U.S. on electronic voting technology operated by less than politically neutral corporations like ES&S and Diebold,[1] and the threat to global democratic rights becomes serious indeed. The extent to which alternative models of governance are generally barely acknowledged by let alone incorporated into mainstream politics in developed nations, the glacial pace of political change, and the cynical management of democracy in the name of economic and media interests that violate people's rights all suggest that democracy needs more critical scrutiny. Reinvigoration and constructive change in the name of social justice and the underlying respect for life, that grounds all rights doctrines, must be our most fundamental and urgent goals.

Rights culture, then, must continue to press forward on two major fronts: the first, where the most egregious forms of violation and abuse are taking place; the second, where political systems claim to have internalized rights culture but nonetheless continue to compromise its principles. The two vectors of concern are integrated, connected parts of a much larger global system of rights relationships that needs significant improvement.

Rights need constant self-critique and re-invention. And this challenge will be one aspect of the potential that remains to be enacted in relation to the future of rights globally. Thus, the ways in which rights NGOs have the potential to imitate the very structures they seek to change, preferring their own self-interest and survival to those they seek to help, has to be watched very carefully. Upendra Baxi, following on a study by Katarina Tomasevski, notes how 'much discourse of the UNHCR has been focused on the right of intergovernmental agencies to victims of wars or hunger, rather than of the human rights of access by the violated to ameliorative agencies' (118). Baxi further explains how AI is often criticized by activist networks for over-emphasis on civil and political rights rather than on economic, social, and cultural rights and how rights organizations succumb to specializations that ignore all sorts of other abuses, violations, and needs. And Baxi eloquently articulates the case for how market forces affect rights discourses through the controls they exert on access to resources: 'the NGO movement remains exposed to the new grammar of market rationality' (122), thus producing a situation where the 'flow of South-South resources for promotion and protection of human rights is minuscule compared to the flow of North-South resources' (121).

Further, Baxi notes how human rights markets articulate suffering as a commodity in which 'compassion fatigue' and 'bystanderism' (125-26) have to be managed in order to access rights resources. How to develop 'exemplary arenas of human solidarity' via the mass media, thus going 'beyond [the] commodification of suffering' (126), is a critical challenge faced by rights movements everywhere. And how the 'de-commodification of human suffering' can be used to convert the 'politics of denial' into the 'politics of acknowledgement,' thus promoting sustained and enacted empathy, is a related challenge that any critical assessment of human rights markets must confront. Such critiques map out an especially important terrain of rights responsibility, sustainability, and enactment: especially if many of these critiques point to the need for sophisticated, globally co-ordinated mechanisms for addressing multiple, complex rights issues in critically informed, balanced, and integrated ways.

Just as globalized forms of self-interested economic organization that destroy, distort, or exploit rights organizations have to be stopped dead in their tracks, so must similar forces that attack local, vulnerable communities with differential economies and values. For instance, the battle over land and development rights in the Choco district of Colombia, which has one of the largest untouched rain forests in the world, has resulted in profound human rights consequences for the indigenous peoples who have lived in the area for centuries: 'the Embera people have been heavily impacted by human rights violations. 30 cases of human rights violations were reported by November 2003 with a total of 762 victims. 84 of these violations were categorized as homicides, disappearances, massacres or personal harm' ('The Human Rights of Indigenous People: In the Red'). For the people of the Choco, threatened by hydroelectric dams, logging, the completion of the Pan American Highway, and so forth, their rights to security, to health, to control over their ancestral lands are all deeply compromised by distorted, globalized economic imperatives. This kind of globalization must be replaced with viable alternatives that enable equitable, sustainable development with respect to the dignity, integrity, and diversity of all life.

The system of global apartheid we have described earlier in this book threatens the basic, underlying principle of all rights cultures with respect to the integrity, equality, and respect for all life, and it must be dismantled by the rights movement: 'Global apartheid...is an international system of minority rule whose attributes include: differential access to basic human rights; wealth and power structured by race and place; structural racism, embedded in global economic processes, political institutions and cultural assumptions; and the international practice of double standards that assume inferior rights to be appropriate for certain "others," defined by location, origin, race or gender' (Booker and Minter).

Building rights solidarity networks and understandings across multiple constituencies will remain a crucial aspect of any rights future that does away with global apartheid. This profound change will be enhanced by increased accessibility to different cultures, whether through digital media, international development, or new forms of political organization in media-space (and other transnational locales) such as the Zapatista uprising that spread from the Lacandon jungle in Mexico to international Zapatismo.

The pressure to increase meaningful access to rights instruments will require intensifying, especially in the reallocation of resources currently devoted to militarization and the arms trade. Alternatives to the trillion-dollar global expenditure on arms exist, including a budget co-developed by the Stockholm International Peace Research Institute, the World Policy Forum, and the World Game Institute. That budget, in which pressing human needs are addressed over spurious military needs, includes global line items for shelter, the elimination of starvation and malnutrition, safe water, the elimination of nuclear weapons and land mines, refugee relief, literacy, the prevention of soil erosion, and the like. Total cost: $105.5 billion or about one-tenth the cost of total global military spending ('Mom Says: Clean Your Room').

The cost effectiveness of such a reallocation would be immeasurable in terms of global quality of life, sustainability, and equity. Imagine the complete elimination of structural debt for the poorest citizens of the global economy —often, as we have shown, the result of cumulative colonial practices rooted in exploitation, racism, and inequitable distributions of political and military power that advantage narrow elites. Alternatives to the current mismanaged system of global distributions of wealth *do* exist with the power to significantly alter the course of majority world futures.

Furthermore, other forms of inequitable distribution of resources that translate into disempowering the Majority World need to be resolved. The inequitable access to the courts that favor wealthy empowered corporate interests against impoverished, disempowered individual or community interests must be addressed. Too often, as we have argued throughout this book, meaningful rights outcomes are perverted or diluted by the lack of true access to legal help when basic rights are at stake.

If, for instance, carcinogenic PCBs that can be traced to a single industrial source contaminate a major water supply, why should it require years of expensive litigation to get a judgment that can then be appealed *ad nauseam* by a wealthy corporation, the *only* possible source of the contamination? If, as another example, communities are threatened by the proliferation of cell masts in their midst, whose biological side effects via different kinds of radiation are still largely unknown, why should it be next to impossible to enact the precautionary principle (PP), which advocates the right of people to protect themselves from potentially threatening new technologies or situations, pending clarification of the effect of those technologies or situations on their well-being? Improved access to new legal instruments, whether the International Criminal Court (ICC) or instruments that give the precautionary principle the force of law, are crucial for rights progress.

The PP, to cite but one example, will need to be fought for as a legal and ethical tool in achieving rights outcomes where issues of environmental safety are paramount. The principle is a key adjunct to rights doctrines and a major innovation in how rights talk conceives of itself, especially that form of rights discourse that has been perverted by 'patterns of state-industry collaboration [that] *normalized* risk-analysis to the point of industry-oriented, rather than *human rights-oriented* risk and management' (Baxi 157-8). The PP arises from the speed at which, for instance, transnational industries introduce new technologies globally (whether from genetically modified organisms [GMOs] through to industrial chemicals, nuclear power sources, and communications devices) and is based on the notion that people have the fundamental right to take anticipatory, precautionary action to prevent potential harm caused by indiscriminate use of those technologies.[2] This right is especially important when industry with vested interests produces the studies that claim a new technology as safe, when long-term effects that are incremental over time and require careful measurement are part of the larger knowledge economy associated with safe usage, and when purported social values such as speed and progress are associated with new technologies whose long-term effects are demonstrably unknown.

The PP has been 'adopted as official policy by a range of governments, from the city and county of San Francisco to the European Union' and has been 'invoked in treaties addressing North Sea pollution, ozone-depleting chemicals, fisheries, climate change, and sustainable development' (Gardner 30). Its sensible premise is based on the ethical notion 'First, do no harm,' one that constrains various forms of macro-organization (corporations, governments, large institutions) to consider the global implications of their actions before that of more localized participants, like shareholders or citizens. And, powerfully, it articulates a basic ethical resolve with enormous rights implications: the long-term imprint —environmental, human, global—of any new product or means of production must be carefully evaluated for safety before implementation. As Gary Gardner, Director of Research for the Worldwatch Institute, argues, 'A precautionary approach that restricted coal and oil burning in the 19th and 20th centuries might have prevented our current climate predicament, perhaps the greatest environmental threat the human community has ever faced' (31).

In globalized economies, as we have shown in several examples throughout this book, technology—whether military, genetic, communications, industrial, agricultural, transportation, and so forth—is frequently at the centre of rights problems, a situation we anticipate accelerating in the near term. Access to technologies that improve human life will become crucial in rights terms: think of how many lives might have been saved if the early warning technologies that already exist had been shared more effectively for the 2004 Indian Ocean tsunami catastrophe; think of the stunning proliferation of alternative sources of media that exist via the Internet and associated technologies; think of an organization like *Witness*, which uses video, satellite phone, email, Internet websites, and imaging and editing software to pursue social justice and grassroots advocacy goals with over 150 partner groups in 50 different countries.[3]

By the same token, the use of technology to clamp down on expressive rights is also a major concern, as is the use of technology that infringes on basic rights like security of person via threats to the environment. The adoption of restrictive encryption technology policies (like the outlawing of export from the U.S. of software like Pretty Good Privacy [PGP]) poses a threat to human rights activists and dissidents who can protect the free flow of sensitive information via such technologies. The use of technology for repressive purposes, then, is a problem: whether in the case of information technology like IBM's Hollerith punch-card machines, which gave the Nazis an unprecedented tool for streamlining their genocidal techniques[4] or in Microsoft's delivery of technology to the Chinese government for purposes of censoring the Internet, as reported by AI: 'China is the world's most aggressive censor of the Internet. Websites are banned for using words such as "Taiwan," "Tibet," "democracy," "dissident" and "human rights" ' (Mathiason). Investigative reporter Rebecca Mackinnon, in describing how a Chinese researcher for *The New York Times*, Zhao Jing (also known by the name Michael Anti), had his blog removed from MSN servers hosted in the U.S., commented that 'The behaviour of companies like Microsoft, Yahoo and others—and their eager willingness to comply with Chinese government demands—shows a fundamental lack of respect for users and our fundamental human rights. Microsoft, Yahoo and others are helping to institutionalize and legitimise the integration of censorship into the global IT business model' (Donoghue).[5]

China, which 'already has the highest number of imprisoned journalists in the world—at least 42, according to the New York-based Committee to Protect Journalists' (Pocha 13), has also made use of technologies developed by companies like Cisco Systems to 'bar access to more than 250,000 Web sites (including pages hosted by AI and the BBC) and scans e-mail, online chat forums, and blogs for offending information' (ibid. 14). Harvard Law School's Berkman Center for Internet and Privacy, echoing AI's finding outlined above, concludes that such repressive techniques, including the use of 30,000 human Internet monitors, make China 'more successful than any other country' in its censorship of the Web (ibid.). The perverse but familiar situation of global corporate Western culture making money from sales of technology to local human rights abusers again begs the question of responsible corporate citizenship in which the overall global rights good is shirked or undermined in the name of localized profits that improve shareholder returns.

HRW notes, 'The Internet dramatically empowers persons in the exercise of their right to seek, receive, and impart information and ideas regardless of frontiers. Online communication must therefore be fully protected by international guarantees of the right to freedom of expression' (HRW *The Internet in the Mideast and North Africa* 1). As the Digital Divide between developed and developing nations narrows and the technology expands into other media (like cell phone use), free access to the Internet will play a crucial role in rights advocacy and implementation. Yet major companies like Microsoft that exercise control over freedom of expression via the use of proprietary technologies developed for the monitoring and censorship of freedom of expression will need to be closely watched. HRW's study makes the following instructive assessment: 'The Middle East and North Africa is one of the most under-represented areas of the world in terms of per capita Internet connectivity. In a region where nearly every government censors or punishes speech critical of the authorities, there can be little doubt that Internet growth has been slowed by the fear among those in power that democratizing Internet access will undermine state control over information (ibid.).

The evolution of the Internet and the battles being fought over how it gets used are telling. The Internet is a technology that was sponsored by military research with initial work funded by the Pentagon's Advanced Research Projects Agency (ARPA) in 1968 leading to the creation of the Internet's precursor the ARPANET in 1969. It has since evolved into an astonishingly different array of potential uses pertinent to freedom of expression and the rights and responsibilities associated with that freedom. A few clicks of the mouse can bring people from across the globe into virtual proximity, sharing information that has been archived and disseminated via digital technologies. In short, a whole new area of expressive rights situations relative to new technologies must be addressed insofar as state controls are being exerted on the free flow of information precipitated by these new technologies.

But it must be recognized, too, that the free flow of critical information about the effects of globalized technologies themselves is crucial to taking action on the wide variety of environmental situations that threaten rights worldwide. One example is illustrative: between 1993 and 2003, 928 peer-reviewed scientific articles about global warming were published with 0 per cent casting any doubt on 'human-caused' global warming; between 1988 and 2002 a total of 3,543 news stories about the phenomenon were published by *The New York Times, Washington Post, Los Angeles Times,* and *Wall Street Journal,* 53 per cent of which cast doubt on it ('Emerging Ideas'). The cynical manipulation of information by mass media and the resulting distortion of public discourse must be countered by critical alternatives linked to forms of global dissemination that provide for an informed global civil commons. The struggle for the right to information, both as a transparent and an accessible resource, is crucial to the advancement of global rights scenarios. Coincident with these expressive and information rights, so profoundly linked to the hyper-acceleration of new technologies and their effects on sustainability, global environmental rights must also be aggressively pursued.

Human rights will be utterly redundant if species survival has been irrevocably compromised. Environmental degradation resulting from technology is linked to the degradation of human rights on a global scale and needs immediate action. Wangari Maathai's prophetic call for a collective vision and responsibility that link peace to the need to protect the environment must be acted on across multiple fronts, including via the kind of information flows made possible, paradoxically, by technology. A baseline target for rights advocates will be the principle that consumers and producers must pay the full cost of any item sold on any market in terms of its impact on the environment. That is, goods and services will need to be made and offered with a zero-sum environmental impact if the sustainability and long-term meaningful development that we see as congruent with rights are to be achieved.

The challenge of linking environmental sustainability with rights activism is urgent. The UN Millennium Ecosystem Assessment, begun in 2001 as the most comprehensive review of planetary ecosystem health ever (more than 1,360 experts from 95 countries produced the report), issued a 'stark warning. Human activity is putting such strain on the natural functions of Earth that the ability of the planet's ecosystems to sustain future generations can no longer be taken for granted' (3). The loss to diversity of life alone, itself a key component of any bottom line rights scenario, has been staggering: 'Human activity has caused between 50 and 1,000 times more extinctions in the last 100 years than would have happened due to natural processes' ('Scientific Facts on Ecosystem Change'). The rights implications on a global level of such environmental changes are overwhelming and urgently require action.

The planet has *never* been as militarized as it is now, as threatened by the staggering number of arms in circulation. The drive to militarize is (and has been) located in the so-called developed world, where militarization and economic self-interest are profoundly aligned. The paradox of democratic countries contributing to rights violations and abuses through their production of a surfeit of weaponry distributed worldwide must be addressed (not to mention the environmental, social, and cultural harm produced by the use of this weaponry). That the arms produced in self-titled democracies largely end up killing civilians, as witnessed in the stunning numbers of people who have died in the last 50 years as a result of the use of these weapons, is a fundamental point of hypocrisy that the rights movement must address vis-à-vis the developed world.[6]

The staggering disproportion between military spending and spending on rights-based resources will thus remain a key struggle for rights activists, recalling Martin Luther King, Jr.'s comment that 'A nation that continues year after year to spend more money on military defense than on programs of social uplift is approaching spiritual death...' (Bigelow and Peterson 326). Events like the 2003 First Hemispheric Forum Against Militarization that took place in San Cristóbal de Las Casas, Chiapas, Mexico, and organizations like the Center for Arms Control and Non-Proliferation ('that seeks the reduction and eventual elimination of nuclear weapons as a significant tool of U.S. national security policy'), the Council for a Livable World (a major American organization and lobby group devoted to arms control) and the Coalition to Oppose the Arms Trade (COAT), a national network in Canada that began in late 1988 to organize opposition to ARMX, the country's largest weapons bazaar, all need to sustain and intensify their efforts against militarization.[7]

As we have said elsewhere in this book, rights talk is cheap when the actual resources being allocated to the support of social justice in all its myriad forms is a minuscule percentage of the military spending that has produced unspeakable harm globally.

The crucial battle over resource allocation, then, is a pressing concern for rights advocacy groups. A related concern has to do with the unrestricted flow of massive amounts of capital across borders via the so-called free market. When global capital and equity have more rights than human beings,[8] and when stringent legal and rights structures exist as an armature to capital in a manner that imbalances the responsible inter-connectedness of different forms of economic, cultural, and political human creation, changes to correct that imbalance need to be effected. One example of such a change would be to restrict or tax global flows of capital in such a way as to benefit stakeholders in the struggle for rights. Progressive taxes like the Tobin Tax, proposed in 1978 by James Tobin, a Nobel prize-winning American economist, deploys a small tax on foreign exchange transactions to deter short-term currency speculation. Such a tax, if implemented meaningfully, must be directed at rights outcomes that redress global inequities. And a related struggle must go forward against the ways in which corporations are given equivalent rights to humans—legal personhood as a way of legally defining corporate entities and their limited liability (thus eviscerating the sense of reciprocal and responsible citizenship) cannot be allowed to continue as a model for truly responsible corporate citizenship at a global level.

Debt relief for impoverished countries, as we have repeatedly argued, will need to be pressed for, as will a more progressive form of taxing the wealthiest citizens of the planet: 'Just a 4% tax on that wealth [of about 225 individuals] would finance the entire UNDP programme to ensure that all the world's people had enough food, clean water, sewerage, shelter, basic health services, and education' (Barrat Brown). The enactment of these strategies will produce enormous rights consequences for those most exploited by currency speculation, irresponsible transnational corporations, and inequitable structures of wealth allocation.

Moreover, we would argue that the ideal percentage of GNP devoted to development (0.7 per cent) should be matched in relation to support for human rights. And, importantly, the monitoring of development and rights funding must be made utterly transparent so as to expose corrupt practices. These practices extend from aid monies being funneled through complex deal-making practices back into the country doing the giving, to development monies being spent on elites in the corrupt regimes of receiving countries, as has been so often the case in Africa and Latin America.

Human rights will be vigorously defended by the Fourth World and the multiple social justice movements mobilizing across the globe, one of the most extraordinary phenomena of the last decades: 'No institution of global governance—the World Trade Organization, the World Bank, the International Monetary Fund—has been able to meet in recent years without being accompanied by protest' (Ainger 343). By a felicitous convergence of meanings and histories, the term 'Fourth World' brings together actors and ideas that share marginalization along with the will to end it by globalizing human rights. We have already noted earlier in the book that from the perspective of Hopi cosmology, we are all currently inhabiting the Fourth World, but this term also refers to peoples who live in extreme poverty and to the indigenous peoples who make up a third of the world's population—the 5,000 to 6,000 nations within states that did not consent to having their land and sovereignty appropriated by the modern state.

According to performance artist Guillermo Gómez-Peña, the Fourth World is 'a conceptual place where the indigenous inhabitants of the Americas meet with the deterritorialized peoples, the immigrants, and the exiles; it occupies portions of all the previous worlds.' (244). Gómez-Peña situates this transcultural convergence in the Americas, because he draws much of his inspiration from the U.S./Mexico border zone, but according to his work, the 'border' is now everywhere, and either people will learn to negotiate it in peaceful ways based on mutual respect and equality, or they will embattle themselves in a futile attempt to protect their privileges.

The Fourth World War, a fragmented and globally dispersed battle being waged by the powerful, primarily against civilians, is the global expression of the elites' attempts to put privilege before universal rights.[9] The Fourth World Movement is based on the belief that poverty is a violation of human rights. The NGO that goes by the name 'The Fourth World Movement' is active in 22 countries, and its mandate is to learn from those living in poverty about the root causes of their marginalization, and their ideas about how to create a true democracy ('Volunteer Solutions').

Another high-profile global effort to promote human rights, dignity, and social justice is the World Social Forum, whose slogan 'Another world is possible' brings together groups that favor bottom-up organizing and participatory democracy. The fact that anyone can sign up to convene a session at the WSF is an indication of the open process and participation on which this movement is based. There are typically over 2,000 sessions involved in this mega-event. While populist national leaders like Lula da Silva and Hugo Chavez participate and give speeches, they are not highlighted as plenary speakers, and are treated as equal to any other participant in the Forum's program. Another striking feature of the WSF is the atmosphere of joy and empowerment, characterized by an American reviewer as 'a six-day bazaar of workshops, debates, panels, performances and parties,' an event that gives 'the most jaded New Yorker a genuine sense of hope…the palpable energy for change that pervades the atmosphere, the sheer number of practical projects to learn about and from, the smarts, the sense of humor—it all simply overwhelms any impulse to snipe from the sidelines or to wallow in self-righteous powerlessness' (Solomon).

The WSF was traditionally held in Porto Alegre, Brazil, due to this city's exemplary inclusion of its residents in the running of municipal affairs, and their generous support of the Forum. In 2004 it was decided that the Forum be moved to Asia where half the world's population lives, amongst them the poorest people on the planet. Nearly 120,000 people attended the WSF on the outskirts of Mumbai, where Nobel Peace Prize winner and Iranian feminist lawyer Shirin Ebadi spoke of the WSF as a symbol of hope and related this movement to changing the negative impact of corporate globalization: 'I hope that, one day, there will be a world where globalization will not be synonymous with inequality, a globalization where the human being is in [the] centre.' ('World Social Forum: A symbol of hope'). 'Next year's WSF [2005], which will be a "multi-forum" held simultaneously in Africa, the Americas, Asia and Europe, will be an "excellent opportunity for the four continents to spread to the four winds the Forum's message" said spokeswoman Meena Menon of India' (de Queiroz).

Yet another important global movement is the Via Campesina, an international peasant organization that brings together the landless, farmers, rural groups including women, indigenous groups, and so forth from across the globe. The 1996 Tlaxcala Declaration made by Via Campesina articulates a clear vision of global solidarity among exploited Fourth World groups and calls for a 'rejection of the economic and political conditions that destroy our livelihoods, our communities, our cultures and our natural environment.' The Via Campesina has a 'combined membership of millions' and 'represents probably the largest single mass of people opposed to the World Trade Organization. This movement includes farmers of Thailand, India, Bangladesh, the indigenous of Ecuador, Aotearoa/New Zealand, Mexico, the U'wa of Colombia, the Ogoni of Nigeria, the dam protestors of the Narmada Valley in India' and the Landless Workers Movement of Brazil (*Movimento dos Trabalhadores Rurais Sem Terra*; MST) and the 'Karnataka State Farmers' Association (India), who burned Monsanto's genetically modified cotton crops' in a widespread campaign called 'Cremate Monsanto' (Ainger 344).

Add to this countless other groups in which some form of rights alternative is being proposed: from the labor activism of Argentina's *piqueteros*, the direct humanitarian actions taken by Action Medical, the culture jamming of Tactical Frivolity, multiple forms of indymedia based on the premise 'don't hate the media, be the media,' the No Borders movement advocating for migrants and asylum seekers and against refugee detention centers like the infamous Australian camp Woomera (now closed), through to many independent citizens from all over the world who are taking action to address rights inequities locally and globally. The efforts of active citizens committed to reinventing democracy across borders lift the Fourth World out of the old geopolitical divisions of the previous three worlds. The Fourth World Movement envisions global equality where the majority is no longer subjected to First World interests and where reclaiming hope in the name of social justice is accomplished through concrete actions. The challenge for the movement will be to sustain itself via networking across transnational boundaries as well as across institutional, organizational boundaries. And the potential for massive, incremental, positive change to the global rights situation via the networked, mobilized empowerment of these Fourth World groups is enormous.

Contrary to the tedious argument that rights and social justice only involve unilateral, utopian thinking driven by political correctness, itself a hopelessly reductive way of seeing complex debates, there is a great deal of room for expressions of difference within rights talk, as is evidenced in WSF and Via

Campesina discussions and strategies. And the absurd attacks on human rights as idealistic (and therefore unrealistic) have no more potent rebuttal than the equally absurd imperial, utopian drive to eliminate 'evil' from the planet through the violent pursuit of cynical economic and political interests. Rather, the challenges that rights present are an opening into the endless potential of human creativity as a vital, real expression of respect for diverse forms of life, diverse forms of difference, diverse forms of knowledge.

In this latter regard, the development and introduction of multiple educational resources, platforms, and learning opportunities devoted to rights at every level of social interaction present a major challenge and hope for the future. Human rights education(s) and pedagogies must become ubiquitous at a globalized level, and not just in the narrow context of localized civics classes that serve narrow national interests and state cultures. Domestic, localized, regional, and national civic rights must be taught in the larger context of global human rights and responsibilities, the densely interwoven global civil commons that is co-dependent on both the environment we all share and the institutions that give expression to human social organization and creativity. Domestic and civic duties must be taught as a function of global contexts that make the local indissociable from the global.

The UN's special envoy for HIV/AIDS in Africa, Stephen Lewis, frames the educational dilemma facing African orphans in pressing terms: 'Africa faces at least two generations of children whose life of the mind, if it was given breath at all, will cease abruptly just as they enter their teens' (*Race Against Time* 107). The fact that generations of refugees from disease and war (let alone the unthinkable toll taken on children by HIV/AIDS in Africa) have lost the enacted right to education is a calamity of global proportions that diminishes the global civic commons immeasurably. Contrast this loss with the toxic brand of extreme religious fundamentalism taught in Pakistani *madrassas* (schools for boys who undertake orthodox Islamic [Sunni] instruction, otherwise known as mosque schools), or the widespread diffusion throughout Latin America of torture methods via the former 'School' of the Americas, and the stakes around educational empowerment as pertains to positive rights outcomes become clear indeed.

The case of Afghani children's education as relates to rights scenarios is instructive. After two decades of civil war (including the Soviet and American invasions) and ongoing insurgency, Afghanistan has an extremely low literacy rate (with women's literacy estimated to be as low as 4 percent) and has had hundreds of thousands of its children killed 'in indiscriminate bombing and shelling of their homes, schools or playing fields.' AI reports, 'Amidst the devastation, children's educational and developmental needs have been forgotten. Access to education has been reduced as schools have been destroyed and teachers forced to flee. In recent years [the late nineties] the actions of various armed groups who have banned education for girls has further limited opportunities for learning' (AI 'Afghanistan children devastated by war'). A 1999 AI report noted that in the UN gender development index, Afghanistan is ranked at the global bottom of the heap, meaning that its girls and women are the least likely to have gender rights by comparison with any other place in the world. The difficulties these conditions impose on potential progress for the civil commons of Afghanistan in succeeding generations are daunting, even as they remind us of the surpassing importance of rights pedagogies.

Not surprisingly, in another of the globe's poorest countries another educational tragedy is taking place. Following what independent observers and the legally elected president of the country Jean-Bertrand Aristide called a coup that deposed the democratically elected Haitian government in 2004, the imposed government of Gérard Latortue moved to shut down a medical school to train doctors for needy areas and closed a government literacy program, while also eradicating subsidies for schoolchildren and schoolbooks (Engler and Fenton 86).[10] The Lavalas/Aristide government from 1994-2004 had built more schools than 'in the first 190 years of Haitian history, reversing a shockingly poor educational system where up until 1985 there was only one secondary school for every thirty-five prisons. Lavalas' literacy programs helped thousands of adults, driving illiteracy down from around 80 percent to 50 percent across the country. Despite sustained popularity among the poor, most of these programs were abolished after February 29, 2004. The coup attempted to sweep away the small steps in the direction of an empowered majority' (Engler and Fenton 100-1). Under the guise of establishing human rights in Haiti, then, and as a function of an illegal coup supported by human rights groups funded by the very governments that had backed the coup's aftermath (Canada, France, the U.S.), the new government eliminated educational opportunities that were making a difference.[11] Thus, a profound betrayal of the UDHR's Article 26 was enacted by both the Haitian régime and the nations backing it. That Article plainly states, 'Everyone has the right to education' and 'Educa-

tion shall be directed to the full development of the human personality and to
the strengthening of respect for human rights and fundamental freedoms. It
shall promote understanding, tolerance and friendship among all nations, racial or religious groups, and shall further the activities of the United Nations
for the maintenance of peace.'

It has been suggested that the interest shown in privatizing educational
services in Haiti, thus giving the 'business' associated with that 'service' to
first world companies, was behind these rights abuses, a reminder that *who*
shapes the context and content that informs a particular educational outreach
is a crucial battle to be fought from the perspectives of rights equity and justice. The conversion of education from a 'right' into a 'service' is an important
shift in meaning that aligns educational outcomes with trade and profit rather
than an integrated civic commons within a comprehensive rights framework.
WTO talks on GATS (General Agreement on Trade in Services) at the end of
2005 targeted education and, according to one observer, 'Many industrialized
countries clearly see education exports as a key offensive interest' ('Education
targeted'). Problems clearly arise when these sorts of 'offensive interests' override the uses of education to enhance quality of life via the creation of new
knowledge, via the creation of an effective, critical, and informed citizenry, and
via the creation of effective structures of governance that accommodate and
enact rights structures. The future of rights, especially for the poorest and most
fragile states globally, will depend not on the transmission of education as a
service but as a crucial right, an integral aspect in the formation of human beings with a critical capacity for justice and respect for the integrity of all life.

Globally, then, educators at all levels of knowledge making and knowledge
transmission (from parents on up) must be given the resources and means to introduce critical rights learning into social and curricular structures. All knowledge is essentially futile if the fundamentals of justice, equity, and respect for
sustainable life principles do not underpin 'learning' as a key co-creative, social
attribute of 'being' human and 'having' meaningful human agency.

Ultimately, the future of rights will very much depend on issues of personal
duty, responsibility, and agency. Unchecked personal, corporate, and national
self-interest is globally unsustainable and morally indefensible despite the soph-
istry so often used to argue in favor of it. Unthought privilege—whether economic, educational, cultural, or political, among others—based on reductive
utilitarian life philosophies and devoid of how human agency is co-dependent

and co-creative via various forms of community will have to be challenged as a form of ethical collapse and disengagement. More than ever, those with privilege will have to reconsider the ethical consequences of that privilege—where it comes from, how it is used, why it is abused. The abstract rhetoric of rights, diminished by the sheer amount of deceptive verbiage divorced from actual action that empties the concept of rights of its rich possible meanings, must be taken on via the agency of personal responsibility transmuted into action.

Much greater effort has to be expended on extending the community of potential rights actants especially in the places where privilege lies fallow and inert, stupefied by its own wealth, mesmerized by the baubles it buys in avoidance of the responsibilities that come with privilege. Globalization has meant that First World capital is more mobile than ever: a keystroke can send money hurtling from a wealthy suburb in Toronto to an impoverished town in West Africa.[12] And one of globalization's perhaps unintended side effects has been to condense space and time thus increasing awareness of the multiplicity of life on the planet, not to mention the fragile inter-connectedness of the human ecosystem. The same keystroke that sends money can send letters of support across vast divides pressuring policy makers to change oppressive laws, can establish relations between people of privilege and oppressed groups the world over. What this means for the ethics of individual agency is largely unconsidered amid the hapless flow of statistics, flowcharts of misery, death, inequity, and of course, profit. We would argue that those who have vanquished poverty in their own lives and communities only to become distracted by the need to increase their distance from that poverty *have* to reconsider the use of their privilege. To not do so is morally indefensible, a betrayal of one's own and others' humanity.

How much is enough? At what point does the pursuit of more become dysfunctional in terms of how that pursuit affects the global good? At what point is it morally indefensible for a person of privilege to renege on his or her duties to the disenfranchised, impoverished global majority? These questions are meaningful in the so-called real world: at what point, for instance, do the technologies of killing developed for military use suffice? At what point is our right to be mobile constrained by the environmental damage that mobility causes? Where is the line between sufficient profit and egregious greed? Why have discourses of ethical conduct that are so easily sermonized not been converted (or have been with the greatest of difficulty) into truly effective action at the macro-institutional level? The golden rule of 'do unto others as you would have others do unto you' and controversial Australian philosopher Peter Singer's axiom to that rule—'if it is in our power to prevent something very bad from happening, without thereby sacrificing anything else morally significant, we ought, morally, to do it'—provide an ethically engaged way of addressing systemic inequalities and oppression. But rights discourses that provide exemplars of these principles in action will need to become more omnipresent, more pressing, and more acted upon by both individuals and larger communities of concern.

In this latter regard, we see two immediate actions possible within the context of the questions we raise. One involves individual direct action, what we would call rights volunteerism, based on purposeful, intentional decisions to help produce rights outcomes in a specific, localized context. Many examples of this sort of work exist: youth who decide to help a particular village in Africa by funding and building a well or a school; retired doctors who gather medical supplies through their networks of affiliation to supply to majority world countries desperately in need of medical supplies; musicians who develop intercultural relations with aggrieved communities that involve different forms of aid (and reciprocal learning); pensioners who write letters on behalf of political prisoners; and school children who pressure for policy changes regarding the environment. Relatively minor effort—say involving from 1 percent to 10 percent of a person's net income—that is incremental across communities of privilege and widely diffused through communities that lack that privilege must become increasingly the norm as a reflection of one's ethical engagement with global citizenship.

The other form of action involves larger communities of concern, whether at the state, NGO, or local levels, in which group action translates individual responsibility into a measurable effect on a larger disadvantaged group or a larger rights problem, from localized homelessness and poverty, to the HIV/AIDS crisis in Africa, to global child labor abuses. Both streams of action open possibilities for ethical engagement. And sometimes, as in the case of 12-year-old Canadian Craig Kielburger, these possibilities for ethical engagement lead from one form of action to the next, one form of organization to the next. In Kielburger's case, the murder of 12-year-old Iqbal Masih, a Pakistani child-laborer in a rug factory from the age of four, who had become an internationally renowned advocate for child labor reforms (winner of a Reebok Human Rights in Action Award), prompted him to form a small group of school friends in 1995 to perform similar work. Ten years later what Kielburger and his friends began has morphed into Free the Children. The NGO is the 'largest network of children helping children through education in the world, with [today] more than one million youth involved' (Free the Children). Free the Children's goal is to liberate the approximately 250 million child laborers globally from abuse and exploitation and to empower children globally through education. Kielburger's example—and that of many others who operate well below the level of public scrutiny his organization has received—demonstrates how to begin to bridge the gaps between privilege and poverty, disengagement and empathetic action, self-interest and ethical responsibility, contempt for life and an enacted respect for it.

How to be fully human in the context of a basic respect for life? How to resist the most pressing challenges to that respect for life, especially the recourse to the toxic ethos of war, which eminent war correspondent Robert Fisk bleakly calls 'the total failure of the human spirit' (*The Great War* xviii)? How to translate ethical empathy and a sense of globalized duty into direct, effective action? These fundamental, creative challenges to humanity are posed by the underlying values of rights discourses and the alternatives they represent.

How to resolve differences that cut across local and global borders? In Guinea, the Malinke people created a dance and rhythm with vast variations and intricacies called the *doundounba*. Originally a way of expressing and resolving aggression between men only (where death might occasionally occur), the dance has evolved into a peaceful expression of Guinean community danced by both men and women. What was used to express difference and conflict has become evocative of community, and a realistic reminder of the challenges and potential of difference within community, which is founded on the capacity to allow diverse forms of expression synchronous articulation. The evolution of the *doundounba* along creative principles that respect difference as a sign of collective richness is exemplary of the kind of direction that rights and social justice activism need to take.

Incalculable suffering binds us to each other as does our potential to alleviate that suffering: one by one; community by community; nation state by nation state. No human is detached from that suffering or that potential, however uninformed, ghettoized, or unwilling to see. In spite of the advances in 'making conscious' of these problems on a global scale, that suffering must be taken as an aspect of our shared humanity. We are all caught up in a perverse, global system that normalizes indifference, inequity, disempowerment, and the progressive immiseration of others.

But we also exist in a world system in which creative alternatives are possible. Rights activities that translate effectively into direct actions provide the only viable, constructive response to this global dead-end. They ask that 'we' take on the 'why' of injustice, inequality, disrespect for life, and act out of the informed desire for social justice through the creative compassion that is the wellspring of civil societies in their most achieved forms.

Notes

1. Walden O'Dell, chief executive officer of Diebold Inc. a maker of electronic voting machines and associated software 'told Republicans in a...fund-raising letter [in August 2003] that he is "committed to helping Ohio deliver its electoral votes to the president [George W. Bush] next year" ' (Smyth). For extensive independent, nonpartisan, investigative analysis of electoral irregularities in the U.S., see BlackBoxVoting.org, a site that features Bev Harris's work on electoral tampering. See also investigative analysis by Greg Palast and Michael Keefer.

2. The PP is more formally defined, 'Where an activity raises threats of harm to the environment or human health, precautionary measures should be taken even if some cause-and-effect relationships are not fully established scientifically' (Gardner 30). A good example of the kind of threat the PP is intended to address is to be found in the issue of chemical production. While between 500 and 1,000 new chemicals enter commerce each year, the U.S. federal government's National Toxicology Program tests only about 10 to 20 of them a year for carcinogenicity, and not for any other possible adverse effects. As Herman and Chomsky note, 'this system works well for industry, however, as it wants to sell without interference, and leaving virtually all the research and testing for safety in its hands, with its members to decide when the results are worthy of transmission to the EPA (Environmental Protection Agency), is a classic "fox guarding the chickens" arrangement' (xlvi).

3. *Witness*, founded in 1992 by musician and activist Peter Gabriel and the Reebok Foundation for Human Rights (we discuss the latter earlier in an insert in the chapter 'Communicating Rights'), is a crucial example of how globalized, intercultural rights organizations can produce effective results. As stated on the *Witness* website, 'WITNESS uses the power of video to open the eyes of the world to human rights abuses. By partnering with local organizations around the globe, WITNESS empowers human rights defenders to use video to shine a light on those most affected by human rights violations, and to transform personal stories of abuse into powerful tools of justice. Over the past decade, WITNESS has partnered with groups in more than 60 countries, bringing often unseen images, untold stories and seldom heard voices to the attention of key decision makers, the media, and the general public—catalyzing grassroots activism, political engagement, and lasting change.' Witness documents the effects of its campaign to supplement other instruments

of testimony that document and attack human rights abuses worldwide. As instances of its many successes, it cites the following examples:

'* In the U.S.: In January 2005, the State Senate Majority Leader in California announced sweeping legislation to overhaul the State's juvenile prison system 5 days after a video by partner Ella Baker Center for Human Rights revealing rampant abuses in the system was screened at the Capitol.

* In Senegal: In January 2005, the Minister of Women's and Family Affairs pledged on the spot to fund a new development project for women landmine victims after viewing a video by partner RADDHO revealing the devastating effects of these weapons of war—marking the first time any governmental funding in Senegal has ever been earmarked for landmine survivors.

* In Paraguay: In February 2005, the Paraguayan government signed an historic agreement with partner Mental Disability Rights International (MDRI) and the Center for Justice and International Law (CEJIL) to reform the country's mental health system. This groundbreaking achievement follows the submission of two legal petitions and accompanying videos by MDRI to the Inter-American Commission on Human Rights documenting egregious conditions at a state-run psychiatric hospital, and has the potential to impact the lives of thousands of people with mental illness throughout Latin America.'

4. Author and researcher Edwin Black's *IBM and the Holocaust* (2001) describes in great detail the relationship between IBM and the Nazis. After the book was published, Black discovered further information including the fact that 'IBM equipment was on-site at the Auschwitz concentration camp' and that the 'Hollerith numbers assigned to inmates evolved into the horrific tattooed numbers so symbolic of the Nazi era' (Kick 38-9).

5. China has also banned access to Wikipedia, the rapidly growing on-line encyclopedia that has over 2.2 million articles (225 million words) in over 100 languages. In 2004 the site was blocked twice to Chinese users for its references, among others, to Taiwan independence, Tibet, and the Tiananmen Square student protests of 1989. On 19 October 2005, China initiated a long-term block of the site as part of its more generalized move to censor web access to its citizens (York). In early 2006 Google launched a self-censored search engine tailored to China's demands that information about democracy and human rights, among other topics, not be made accessible, a move condemned by Reporters Without Borders. Previously, China had blocked Google access to Chinese citizens and Google's new China site was launched within a week of the company's having resisted the U.S. Department of Justice's attempts to make it disclose data on what people search for on the Internet. The free flow of information is crucial to global human rights movements if only because censorship and control over information flows are historically tied to the repression of basic rights. In the case of China alone, approximately 100 million people had access to the Internet in 2006 with that number projected to rise to almost twice that by 2008.

6. Whereas soldiers used to make up the majority of casualties suffered in battle prior to the first two world wars, currently eight civilians are killed for every soldier, because civilians are routinely targeted.

7. 'COAT initiated a successful campaign that resulted in all military trade shows being forced off City of Ottawa property. ARMX eventually left Canada altogether thanks in large part to COAT's efforts' (Sanders). The importance of work done by groups like COAT cannot be underestimated relative to the disproportionate levels of investment in military as opposed to rights spending. A good example of the stakes occurs in the U.S.'s 'missile defense' initiative, which will lead to the militarization of space and significant investment (between an estimated 800 billion and one trillion U.S. dollars) in a technology that has been proven not to work.

8. For a brilliant summary and analysis of the precise ways in which capital rights supplant human rights, see Baxi 132-66. Baxi argues that 'the emergent collective human rights of global capital present a formidable challenge to the paradigm inaugurated by the UDHR' (70). He also traces how the entrenchment of property rights in the UDHR (Article 17) has been distorted into 'a paradigm of trade-related, market-friendly human rights (beginning its career with the WTO, maturing in an obscene progression in the draft OECD Multilateral Agreement on Investment)' (88).

9. *The Fourth World War* is also the title of a film that documents stories of resistance movements around the globe, made by independent filmmaker and journalist Rick Rowley, one of the founders of Big Noise Tactical Media. In an interview with Amy Goodman, Rowley talks about how the façade of dominant history has multiple cracks through which popular resistance constantly erupts. How this notion of Fourth World War relates to the Fourth World Movement is that these ruptures shatter the illusion of dominant history, promoted by those in power and their propaganda machine: corporate media. By contrast, the independent journalists who report on these ruptures are part of a global movement committed to documenting and bearing witness as participants and not mere observers ('The Fourth World War').

10. For a more complete account of the circumstances of Aristide's removal (what he called a 'new coup d'état,' or 'modern kidnapping,' see Amy Goodman's interview with Aristide and his personal security adviser, Franz Gabriel, regarding the circumstances of their being forced to leave Haiti for, at the time, an unknown destination in Africa (Goodman).

11. For a detailed description of what is currently known about how Canadian federal government monies were used to 'buy' support for the coup from 'supposedly progressive Canadian institutions and individuals,' see Engler and Fenton 50-60. In Australia, 'Publicly funded, community-based organizations such as immigrant and refugee rights groups have been told that they will not get funding if they criticize government policy, at the very time when such policy is reducing state action on behalf of human rights and social justice' (Yeatman). The influence of those who allocate rights resources on those who receive the allocations is highly problematic, especially in terms of perceptions around how support is literally 'bought,' thus compromising the independence and integrity of such organizations.

12. Or, as Peter Singer puts it in his famous essay on morality and poverty (dating from 1972), 'Expert observers and supervisors, sent out by famine relief organizations or permanently stationed in famine-prone areas, can direct our aid to a refugee in Bengal [Bangladesh] almost as effectively as we could get it to someone in our own block.'

Chapter 7

Timeline:
A Brief History of Human Rights

We note how this timeline of key moments in human rights history worldwide is heavily skewed to literate, Western cultures. The role of oral and marginalized cultures worldwide cannot be discounted, though much further work needs to be done in this area in order to address the gaps on this list, not to mention what has evolved into a Eurocentric historical perspective on rights histories. For a brief summary of early notions of human rights across a global range of thinking, see Micheline Ishay's chapter 'Early Ethical Contributions' in The History of Human Rights: From Ancient Times to the Globalization Era.

Codes associated with early historical rulers such as Menes, Draco, Solon and Manu outline standards of conduct for their societies, which existed within limited territorial jurisdictions.

c. 1750 B.C.E. —Code of Hammurabi, Babylonia: written on clay tablet, outlines punishment based on the talion principle of 'eye for eye, tooth for tooth'—the death penalty, though, is a frequent punishment and recourse.

c. 1200–300 B.C.E. —The scriptures of the ancient Israelites also form the basis of Christian and Muslim thinking. The Ten Commandments (*Decalogue*) outline respect for life and for the property of others. The principle that a person is innocent until proven guilty and the tradition of granting asylum originate in Jewish law. In Greek city-states, political rights and duties are conferred upon free male citizens.

c. 900 B.C.E. —The *Isho Upanishad*, a key sacred text in India and part of the Hindu Shruti scriptures, states, among others, that 'Each individual life form must…learn to enjoy its benefits by forming a part of the system in close relation with other species. Let not any one species encroach upon other rights' and 'A selfish man over-utilizing the resources of nature to satisfy his own ever increasing needs is nothing but a thief, because using resources beyond one's needs would result in the utilization of resources over which others have a right.' Both ideas lay the foundation for reciprocal and sustainable community sharing of resources as a fundamental human right.

c. 551–479 B.C.E. —Confucian teaching develops based on 'jen' or benevolence and respect for other people. Confucius 'believed that all individuals, even commoners, possessed rational, aesthetic, political, social, historical and transcendental qualities that could be cultivated through education' (Ishay, *History of Human Rights* 22). The *Tao Te Ching* by Lao-tzu, a possible older contemporary of Confucius, articulates a number of crucial rights ideas, including forerunner notions of the right to peace and human security. Chapter 31 famously states: 'Weapons are the tools of violence; / all decent men detest them…a decent man will avoid them / except in the direst necessity / and, if compelled, will use them / only with the utmost restraint. / Peace is his highest value.'

c. 300 B.C.E. —Kautilya's *Arthashastra*, 'Like Hammurabi's Code and the Hebrew Bible…provided an almanac of just rulings for kings' (Ishay *History of Human Rights* 29), though Brahmins are spared the death penalty and class distinctions shape the degree of punishment.

27 BCE–476 C.E. —Roman Empire develops natural law (a theory of morality derived from the nature of the world and of humans) and the rights of citizens.

40–100 C.E. —The Christian New Testament teaches equality before God as in Paul's famous dictum: 'In Christ there is neither Jew nor Greek, slave nor free, male nor female.' Followers were urged to feed the hungry, clothe the naked, and forgive their enemies.

476–1453 C.E. —Medieval Christian theology holds that infidels and barbarians are not entitled to humanistic considerations.

644–656 C.E. —*Qur'an* (original text): 'Abdurrahman Wahid mentions 14 points concerning human rights stated in the Koran, which on the whole support the aim of developing and forming a morally perfect being. These human rights are: (1) the right to life, (2) the right to justice, (3) the right to receive equal treatment, (4) the duty to uphold the truth and the right to refuse an illegal proposition, (5) the right to take part in social and state life, (6) the right to freedom, (7) the right to freedom from pursuit and prosecution, (8) the right to speech, (9) the right to protection against prosecution based on religion, (10) the right to privacy, (11) economic rights, including the right to work and the right to proper payment, (12) the right to protection of honor and reputation, (13) the right to own property, and (14) the right to proper repayment and fair compensation. The last is especially directed against governmental institutions that make decisions without consideration of the possible detrimental effects of a certain decision on the individual' (Muzadi and Rhoviq).

1215 —Britain's King John is forced by his lords to sign the Magna Carta acknowledging that free men are entitled to judgment by their peers and that even a sovereign is not above the law.

1400 —The Code of Nezahualcoyotl, Aztec law based on regulating anti-social behavior through the formation of a Supreme Legal Council of twelve judges.

c. 1450–1525 —The Iroquois Confederacy unites the Tuscarora, Mohawks, Senecas, Cayugas, Oneidas, and Onandagas under the Ne Gayaneshagowa (or Gayanashagowa) or Great Binding Law, an oral history about the relationship among these peoples, and a constitution to promote peace and harmony within the League. The constitution gives women rights, protects religious rites and festivals, and allows for correction and criticism of irregularities and improprieties in the exercise of the Binding Law.

1492–1537 —Colonization of Western Hemisphere culminates in massacre of the Incas by the Spanish Conquistadors, causing some Christian theologians like Bartolomé de Las Casas to challenge the means employed to enforce God's laws.

1583–1645 —Hugo Grotius, Dutch jurist credited with the birth of international law, speaks of brotherhood of humankind and the need to treat all people fairly.

1628 —British Petition of Rights is adopted describing the rights and liberties of the subject as opposed to the prerogatives of the Crown (Charles I). The Petition places the 'common man's' rights, as represented through Parliament, over the rights of the Crown and was championed by Sir Edward Coke (1552-1634). Article X is of particular importance, stating 'that no man hereafter be compelled to make or yield any gift, loan, benevolence, tax, or such like charge, without common consent by act of parliament; and that none be called to make answer, or take such oath, or to give attendance, or be confined, or otherwise molested or disquieted concerning the same or for refusal thereof; and that no freeman, in any such manner as is before mentioned, be imprisoned or detained; and that your Majesty would be pleased to remove the said soldiers and mariners, and that your people may not be so burdened in time to come; and that the aforesaid commissions, for proceeding by martial law, may be revoked and annulled; and that hereafter no commissions of like nature may issue forth to any person or persons whatsoever to be executed as aforesaid, lest by color of them any of your Majesty's subjects be destroyed or put to death contrary to the laws and franchise of the land.'

1634 —Maryland founded as a Catholic colony with religious tolerance.

1647 —Rhode Island assembly drafts a constitution establishing freedom of conscience, and separating church and state.

1648 —Treaty of Westphalia ends Thirty Years' War, which splits Germany into hostile religious camps. Europe reorganizes into a society of nation states.

1689 —British Bill of Rights is adopted which ensures that royalty cannot override laws created by a freely elected Parliament; John Locke sets forth the notion of natural rights of life, liberty, and property.

1776 —U.S. Declaration of Independence proclaims that 'all men are created equal' and endowed with certain inalienable rights. Thomas Jefferson was strongly influenced by Locke and French philosophers such as Montesquieu, Voltaire, and Rousseau. Some revisionist historians believe that the Gayanashagowa (Great Binding Law) of the Iroquois Conferederation has similarities with the U.S. Constitution, and may have influenced the Founding Fathers.

1783 —The Massachusetts Supreme Court outlaws slavery in that state, citing the state's bill of rights that 'all men are born free and equal.'

1789 —French Declaration of the Rights of Man and the Citizen is adopted.

1791–1803 —Haitian revolution ends slavery and defeats European occupation. Haiti is, at the time, France's wealthiest colony.

1791 —U.S. Bill of Rights incorporates notions of freedom of speech, press, and fair trial into the new U.S. Constitution.

1793 —Henri Gregoire, Bishop of Blois, proposes a code of immutable principles whereby 'the private interest of one nation would be subordinated to the general interest of the human family.' (Proposal defeated.)

1804 —Haitian independence from France declared along with the creation of a Haitian state 60 years before the American Emancipation Proclamation. Haiti becomes the first nation of free people in the Americas and the only successful slave rebellion in history.

1807 —The United States Congress outlaws the importation of African slaves into the U.S. Nevertheless, some 250,000 slaves are illegally imported between 1808 and 1860.

1815 —The Congress of Vienna is held by states that defeated Napoleon. International concern for human rights is demonstrated for the first time in modern history. Freedom of religion is proclaimed, civil and political rights discussed, slave trade condemned.

1830 —Congress passes the Indian Removal Act in order to free land for settlement, forcing 70,000 Native Americans to relocate. In 1838, in what came to be known as the 'Trail of Tears,' the U.S. government forcibly removed more than 16,000 Cherokee Indian people from their homelands in Tennessee, Alabama, North Carolina, and Georgia, and sent them to Indian Territory (today known as Oklahoma). Many (approximately 4,000) Cherokees died on the long treks westward.

1833 —Great Britain passes Abolition Act, ending slavery in the British Empire.

1841 —Russia, France, Prussia, Austria and Great Britain sign the Treaty of London abolishing slavery.

1848 —Some 200 women and men meet in Seneca Falls, New York, to draft a 'bill of rights' outlining the social, civil and religious rights of women.

1857 —In the Dred Scott case, the Supreme Court ruled that African-Americans could not be free nor could they be citizens. The case was later overturned in the Civil Rights Act of 1866.

1863 —On January 1, U.S. President Abraham Lincoln issues the Emancipation Proclamation, declaring that 'all persons held as slaves within any State, or designated part of a State, the people whereof shall then be in rebellion against the United States' are 'forever free.'

1865 —The Thirteenth Amendment to the United States Constitution, abolishing slavery in the United States, takes effect on December 18.

1868 —The Fourteenth Amendment to the United States Constitution is ratified on July 28. The amendment prohibits abridgment of citizenship rights and reaffirms the principles of due process and equal protection of the law for persons born or naturalized in the United States and subject to the laws thereof.

1870 —The Fifteenth Amendment to the Constitution, which states that 'the right of citizens of the United States to vote shall not be denied or abridged by the United States or by any State on account of race, color, or previous condition of servitude,' goes into effect on March 30.

1871 —José Martí, Cuban literary and political figure and revolutionary leader of Cuba's fight for independence from Spain, after six months of forced labor in the San Lázaro quarries near Havana (the result of trumped- up charges), publishes *Political Prison in Cuba*. The tract denounces Spanish cruelty to Cuban political prisoners, many of whom were youth. Martí is 18 years old when he publishes the account, which famously recounts the story of Lino Figueredo, a 12-year-old boy whom Martí knew and who died in prison as a result of torture and ill-treatment.

1880s into the 1960s —A majority of American states enforce segregation through 'Jim Crow' laws; many states and cities could impose legal punishments on people for consorting with members of another race. The most common types of laws forbid intermarriage and order business owners and public institutions to keep their black and white clientele separated. These laws put into question the social significance of the Thirteenth, Fourteenth, and Fifteenth Amendments to the U.S. Constitution listed above.

1885 —Berlin Conference on Africa passes anti-slavery act.

1890 —Brussels Conference passes anti-slavery act.

1893 —Women in Aotearoa/New Zealand are given the vote—the first in the world.

1902 —The Commonwealth of Australia established. Women are entitled to vote and stand for election in the first federal election in 1902.

1907 —Central American Peace Conference provides for the right of aliens to appeal to courts where they reside. The Canadian government passes discriminatory laws against Indian, Japanese, and Chinese.

1908 —The Federal government of Canada passes into law the Continuous Passage Act, blatantly discriminatory against Indians for whom it is impossible to come to Canada via direct passage from India.

1915 —Genocide of Armenians perpetrated by Turks. Viscount James Bryce and Arnold Toynbee are commissioned to write what becomes a 700-page report entitled *The Treatment of Armenians in the Ottoman Empire 1915-16*, the 'first serious attempt to deal with crimes against humanity' (Fisk *The Great War* 325). The report contains detailed eyewitness accounts of the genocide.

1919 —At the end of World War I, the Treaty of Versailles requires that Kaiser Wilhelm II be placed on trial for a 'supreme offense against international morality and the sanctity of treaties.' He escapes, but for the first time in history, nations seriously consider imposing criminal penalties on heads of state for violations of fundamental human rights. At Versailles, other treaties stress minorities' rights, including right to life, liberty, freedom of religion, right to nationality of the state of residence, complete equality with other nationals of the same state, and exercise of civil and political rights. The International Labor Organization (ILO) is established to advocate human rights represented in labor law, encompassing concerns such as employment discrimination, forced labor, and worker safety.

1920 —League of Nations Covenant requires members to 'endeavor to secure and maintain fair and humane conditions of labor for men, women and children,' 'secure just treatment of the native inhabitants of territories under their control,' and 'take measures for the prevention and control of disease.' The Nineteenth Amendment to the United States Constitution, granting women the right to vote, is ratified on August 26.

1923 —The Chinese Immigration Act 1923, better known in the Chinese-Canadian community as the Chinese Exclusion Act, is passed by the Federal Government of Canada, virtually banning all forms of Chinese immigration to Canada. Due to the contribution of the Chinese communities in Canada during World War II, the act is revoked in 1947. However, independent Chinese immigration to Canada (like the immigration of all people of color) only comes after the liberalization of Canadian immigration policy in 1967.

1924 —The United States Congress approves the Snyder Act, admitting all Native Americans born in the United States to full U.S. citizenship.

1926 —Geneva Conference passes Slavery Convention.

1930 —Convention Concerning Forced or Compulsory Labor (ILO) is adopted.

1933–1939 —A series of discriminatory laws are passed in Germany (the 'Laws of April' and the 'Nuremberg Laws') which progressively exclude people of Jewish ancestry from employment, education, housing, health care, marriages of their choice, pension entitlements, professions such as law and medicine, and public places such as theatres, cinemas and vacation resorts. Physically and mentally disabled people are murdered by gas, lethal injection, and forced starvation.

1939–1945 —During World War II, 6 million European Jews are exterminated by Hitler's Nazi regime. Millions of other civilians (gypsies, communists, Soviet POWs, Poles, Ukrainians, people with disabilities, labor unionists, 'habitual' criminals, socialists, Jehovah's Witnesses, homosexuals, Free Masons, vagrants and beggars) are forced into concentration camps, subjected to 'medical' experiments, starved, brutalized, and murdered.

1941 —United States President Franklin D. Roosevelt, in a speech before the United States Congress, identifies 'Four Freedoms' as essential for all people: freedom of speech and religion, freedom from want and fear. President Roosevelt and British Prime Minister Winston Churchill adopt the Atlantic Charter, in which they state their hope, among other things, 'that all men in all the lands may live out their lives in freedom from want and fear.'

1942 —Following the attack on the United States by Japan on 7 December 1941, the U.S. government forcibly moves some 120,000 Japanese-Americans from the western United States to detention camps, while the Canadian government inters 22,000 people of Japanese descent (three- quarters of them were naturalized or native-born Canadians); their detention lasts from three to four years.

Some 40 years later, the U.S. and Canadian governments acknowledge the injustice of their actions with payments to Japanese-Americans and Japanese-Canadians of that era still living. Jurist René Cassin of France urges that an international court be created to punish those guilty of war crimes.

1945 —The United Nations (UN) is established. Its Charter states that one of its main purposes is the promotion and encouragement of 'respect for human rights and for fundamental freedoms for all without distinction as to race, sex, language or religion.' Unlike the League of Nations Covenant, the Charter underscores the principle of individual human rights.

1946 —Commission on Human Rights established by the UN Economic and Social Council (ECOSOC). Commission on the Status of Women is established by ECOSOC (where it was originally a sub-commission of the Commission on Human Rights).

1947 —India achieves independence, thanks in large part to non-violent protests by Mahatma Gandhi.

1948 —On 10 December the UN General Assembly adopts the Universal Declaration of Human Rights, the primary international articulation of the fundamental and inalienable rights of all members of the human family and the first comprehensive statement of nations as to the specific rights and freedoms of all human beings.

1949 —Convention on the Right to Organize and Collective Bargaining (ILO) is adopted. Geneva Conventions provide standards for more humane treatment for prisoners of war, the wounded and civilians. The Statute of Council of Europe asserts that human rights and fundamental freedoms are the basis of the emerging European system.

1950 —European Convention on Human Rights and Convention for Suppression of Traffic in Persons and Exploitation of Prostitution of Others (UN) are adopted. United States Senator Joseph McCarthy launches a vigorous anti-communist campaign, charging, but not substantiating, treachery among the top ranks of the U.S. government. The United States Senate eventually condemns McCarthy for his conduct.

1951 —Convention on the Status of Refugees (UN) is adopted.

1953 —European Commission on Human Rights and Court of Human Rights are created; Convention on Political Rights of Women (UN) is adopted.

1954 —The United States Supreme Court rules in Brown v. Board of Education that racial segregation in public schools is unconstitutional.

1957 —Convention on Nationality of Married Women (UN); Convention Concerning Abolition of Forced Labor (ILO) and Convention Concerning Indigenous and Tribal Populations (ILO) are adopted. The United States Congress approves a civil rights bill to protect voting rights for African-Americans. It is the first civil rights bill since the Reconstruction period, which immediately followed the Civil War.

1958 —Convention Concerning Discrimination in Employment and Occupation (ILO) is adopted.

1959 —UN Declaration on the Rights of the Child is adopted.

1961 —European Social Charter defines economic and social rights for member States of the Council of Europe. Amnesty International established in Great Britain.

1962 —In Australia, the Commonwealth Electoral Act was amended to grant all Aborigines the right to vote in federal elections. Enrollment was voluntary but, once enrolled, voting was compulsory. Despite this amendment it was illegal under Commonwealth legislation to encourage Aborigines to enroll to vote. The National Farm Workers (later known as the United Farm Workers of America) is organized by Cesar Chavez to protect migrant American farm workers, most of who were of Mexican origin.

1964 —The 1964 U.S. Civil Rights Act makes racial discrimination in public places illegal and requires employers provide equal employment opportunities for African-Americans. The legislation attempts to address African-Americans, being denied the vote in the South and states that uniform standards must prevail for establishing the right to vote.

1965 —International Convention on the Elimination of All Forms of Racial Discrimination (UN) is adopted. A new Voting Rights Act authorizes the U.S. government to appoint examiners to register voters where local officials have made African-American registration difficult.

1966 —International Covenant on Civil and Political Rights and the International Covenant on Economic, Social and Cultural Rights (UN) are adopted and opened for signature. Together these documents further developed rights outlined in the Universal Declaration of Human Rights.

1967 —Over 90 percent of Australians vote for constitutional changes to ensure full participation and equal treatment for Indigenous Australians. The referendum gives the Commonwealth Parliament the power to make special laws for Aboriginal Australians. Convention on Non-Applicability of Statutory Limitations to War Crimes and Crimes Against Humanity (UN) is adopted.

1968 —First World Conference on Human Rights is held in Tehran. The United Nations convened member states to evaluate the failures and successes of human rights promotion since the adoption of the Universal Declaration of Human Rights and to work toward the elimination of racial discrimination and apartheid. René Cassin wins the Nobel Peace Prize.

1969 —The Organization of American States (OAS) adopts the American Convention on Human Rights.

1972 —The United States Senate approves a constitutional amendment, the Equal Rights Amendment, banning discrimination against women because of their sex. The amendment is later defeated for lack of sufficient ratification among the states.

1973 —International Convention on Suppression and Punishment of the Crime of Apartheid (UN) is adopted.

1975 —In Australia, the *Racial Discrimination Act 1975* is enacted. Declaration on Rights of Disabled Persons (UN) is adopted.

1976 —International Covenant on Civil and Political Rights and the International Covenant on Economic, Social and Cultural Rights enter into force after sufficient ratification among UN member states.

1977 —United States signs the International Covenant on Civil and Political Rights and the International Covenant on Economic, Social and Cultural Rights. A human rights bureau is created within the United States Department of State. Its first reports on human rights are issued that year. Amnesty International wins the Nobel Peace Prize.

1979 —The Code of Conduct for Law Enforcement Officials (UN) and Convention on the Elimination of All Forms of Discrimination Against Women (UN) are adopted.

1980 —The United States Supreme Court orders the federal government to pay some $120 million to eight tribes of Sioux Indians in reparation for Native American land seized illegally by the government in 1877. United States signs the Convention on the Elimination of All Forms of Discrimination Against Women.

1981 —In Australia, the *Human Rights Commission Act 1981* is enacted, which establishes the national Human Rights Commission. African Charter on Human and Peoples' Rights is adopted by the Organization for African Unity (OAU). Declaration on the Elimination of All Forms of Intolerance Based on Religion or Belief was adopted after nearly 20 years of drafting (UN).

1982 —Principles of Medical Ethics (UN) are adopted.

1984 —Convention Against Torture and Other Cruel, Inhuman or Degrading Treatment or Punishment (UN) is adopted. In Australia, the Sex Discrimination Act 1984 is enacted.

1985 —Committee on Economic, Social and Cultural Rights established (UN). International Convention against Apartheid in Sports (UN) is adopted.

The United States Senate votes to impose economic sanctions on South Africa in protest against the government's apartheid policy.

1986 —Declaration on the Right to Development (UN) is adopted.

1988 —After 40 years of lobbying by NGOs, the U.S. ratifies the Convention on the Prevention and Punishment of the Crime of Genocide (the 'Genocide Convention').

1989 —Convention on the Rights of the Child (UN) and the Second Optional Protocol to the International Covenant on Civil and Political Rights, aiming at the abolition of the death penalty, are adopted. In Tiananmen Square, Chinese authorities massacre student demonstrators struggling for democracy.

1990 —International Convention on the Protection of the Rights of All Migrant Workers and Members of Their Families (UN) is adopted.

1991 —Aung San Suu Kyi, leader of the non-violent movement for human rights and democracy in Burma/Myanmar, wins the Nobel Peace Prize.

1992 —In Australia, the *Disability Discrimination Act 1992* is enacted. The United States ratifies the International Covenant on Civil and Political Rights. A Security Council resolution to deploy the United Nations Protection Force in the former Yugoslavia (UN) is adopted. A Security Council resolution condemns 'ethnic cleansing' in Bosnia and Herzegovina (UN). Security Council resolution demands that all detention camps in Bosnia and Herzegovina be closed (UN). Rigoberta Menchú Tum is awarded the Nobel Peace Prize for her work on behalf of the Mayan peoples in Guatemala, site of persistent abuses of rights and a long civil war sponsored by the U.S. in which over 150,000 people perished or were disappeared. In her acceptance speech she explicitly links the cause of indigenous peoples with wider struggles for rights: 'This Nobel Prize represents a standard bearer that encourages U.S. to continue denouncing the violation of Human Rights, committed against the people in Guatemala, in America and in the world, and to perform a positive role in respect of the pressing task in my country, which is to achieve peace with social justice.'

1993 —Criminal Tribunal on the Former Yugoslavia is established in The Hague to prosecute persons responsible for crimes against humanity and war crimes since 1991, the first international war crimes tribunal since the Nuremberg Trials following WWII. Vienna Declaration and Program of Action adopted by

185 nations present at the Second World Conference on Human Rights. The UN General Assembly creates the post of High Commissioner for Human Rights. Australia creates the Office of the Aboriginal and Torres Strait Islander Social Justice Commissioner to monitor the human rights of Indigenous Australians.

1994–2005 —UN Decade for Human Rights Education declared.

1994 —Emergency session of the Commission on Human Rights convenes to respond to genocide in Rwanda. The first UN High Commissioner for Human Rights, Jose Ayala Laso, takes his post. United States ratifies the International Convention on the Elimination of All Forms of Racial Discrimination and the Convention Against Torture and Other Cruel, Inhuman, or Degrading Treatment or Punishment. United States signs the Convention on the Rights of the Child.

1995 —Beijing Declaration at the World Conference on Women declares 'women's rights are human rights.' The Platform for Action adopted at the conference contains dozens of references to human rights pertaining to women.

1997 —Mary Robinson, former President of the Republic of Ireland, becomes the second UN High Commissioner for Human Rights.

1998 —Establishment of the International Criminal Court, the first ever permanent, treaty-based, international criminal court established to promote the rule of law and ensure that the gravest international crimes do not go unpunished. Fiftieth anniversary of the Universal Declaration of Human Rights. Adoption on 9 December by the UN of the Declaration on the Right and Responsibility of Individuals, Groups and Organs of Society to Promote and Protect Universally Recognized Human Rights and Fundamental Freedoms known generally as the Declaration on Human Rights Defenders: 'The Declaration rests on a basic premise: that when the rights of human rights defenders are violated, all our rights are put in jeopardy and all of us are made less safe' (Kofi Annan UN Secretary General).

2005 —Convention on the Protection and Promotion of Diversity of Cultural Contents and Artistic Expressions (CCD) adopted by UNESCO General Assembly; approved by 148 votes with only U.S. and Israel opposing. This consensus recognizes that cultural goods are rich expressions of the mosaic of cultures by the human species along its history. Therefore, cultural goods cannot be treated like commodities or services and ruled by the 'free market' and negotiated under the framework of the WTO. Critics say that CCD doesn't go far enough to protect and promote indigenous cultures within countries especially from transnational copyrights and patent industries.

Works Cited

'Africa Alive Postcards.' *Africa Alive.* 15 June 2005 <http://africaalive.org/postcards/>.

Agamben, Giorgio. 'Beyond Human Rights.' *Means Without End: Notes on Politics.* Trans. Vincenzo Binetti and Cesare Casarino. Minneapolis: University of Minnesota Press, 2000: 15-28.

Agosin, Marjorie, ed. *A Map of Hope: Women's Writing on Human Rights—An International Literary Anthology.* New Brunswick: Rutgers University Press, 1999.

The Agronomist. Dir. Jonathan Demme. Think Film; HBO/Cinemax, 2004.

'Aids in Africa Facts.' *African American Self Help Foundation* 14 June 2005 <http://www.Aashf.org/pages/aids/aidsFacts.htm>.

'AIDS Orphans—The Facts.' *Avert.Org.* 15 June 2005 <http://www.avert.org/aidsorphans.htm>.

Ainger, Katherine. 'To Open a Crack in History: Movements for Global Justice in the 21st Century.' Bigelow, Bill and Bob Peterson, eds. *Rethinking Globalization: Teaching for Justice in an Unjust World.* Milwaukee: Rethinking Schools Press, 2002: 342-5.

'Alberta's ailing homes.' Editorial. *The Globe and Mail* 25 May 2005: A18.

Alimov, Rashid and Igor Kudrik. 'Duma adopts NGO bill in final reading.' *Bellona* 23 December 2005, <http://www.bellona.no/en/international/russia/envirorights/info_access/41364.html>.

All Africa Rights Initiative. *The Johannesburg Statement on Sexual Orientation, Gender Identity, and Human Rights.* 12 February 2004. <http://www.hrw.org/lgbt/pdf/joburg_statement021304.htm>.

Amnesty International. '2000 United Nations Commission on Human Rights—Time to defend the defenders.' *Amnesty International.* 20 March 2005 <http://www.amnesty.org.uk/news/press/12637.shtml>.

—. 'Administrative Detention.' <http://web.amnesty.org/pages/isr-action-detention>.

—. 'Afghanistan children devastated by war: Afghanistan's lost generations.' 1 November 1999. *Amnesty International Canada.* 10 January 2006 <http://www.amnesty.ca/child/asa1113.php>.

—. 'Americas: Human Rights Defenders: Persecution reaches emergency proportions.' 11 October 2003. *Amnesty International.* 10 June 2005. <http://news.amnesty.org/mavp/news.nsf/print/ENGAMR010112003>.

—. *Amnesty International Handbook.* Seventh Ed. 1 March 2006 <http://www.amnesty-volunteer.org/aihandbook/preface.html>.

—. *Amnesty International Report 2003.* New York: Amnesty International, 2002.

—. *Amnesty International Report 2004.* London: Amnesty International, 2004.

—. *Amnesty International Report 2005.* London: Amnesty International, 2005.

—. 'Amnesty International Americas. Regional Overview 2004.' *Amnesty International.* 10 June 2005 <http://web.amnesty.org/report2005/2am-index-eng>.

—. 'Brazil: Espírito Santo state under siege—authorities cannot afford to make mistakes.' 27 September 2002. *Amnesty International.* 25 March 2005 <http://web.amnesty.org/library/Index/ENGAMR190262002?open&of=ENG-2M3>.

—. *Casualties of War: Women's Bodies, Women's Lives.* London: Amnesty International, 2004.

—. *Childhood Stolen: Grave Human Rights Violations Against Children.* London: Amnesty International, 1995.

—. 'Children—10 Steps for Implementing Children's Rights.' *Children: The Rights of Every Child.* Amnesty International Canada. 3 January 2005 <http://www.hrw.org/children/>.

—. *Clouds of Injustice: Bhopal Disaster 20 Years On.* London: Amnesty International, 2004.

—. *Crimes of Hate, Conspiracy of Silence: Torture and Ill-Treatment based on Sexual Identity.* London: Amnesty International, 2001.

—. 'Cuba "Essential measures"? Human rights crackdown in the name of security.' *Amnesty International.* 23 March 2005 <http://web.amnesty.org/library/Index/ENGAMR250172003?open&of=ENG-CUB>.

—. 'Cuba: 71 prisoners of conscience continue to be imprisoned for expressing their ideas.' *Amnesty International.* 18 March 2005 <http://news.amnesty.org/index/ENGAMR250052005>.

—. *In the Firing Line: War and Children's Rights.* London: Amnesty International, 1999.

—. 'Killing the Future: Children in the Line of Fire.' 30 December 2002. *Amnesty International.* 20 January 2006 <http://web.amnesty.org/library/Index/engMDE020052002?OpenDocument&of=COUNTRIES%5CISRAEL/OCCUPIED+TERRITORIES>.

—. *Kosovo: The Evidence.* London: Amnesty International, 1998.

—. *Lives Blown Apart: Crimes Against Women in Times of Conflict.* London: Amnesty International, 2004.

—. *Made in Britain: How the UK Makes Torture and Death its Business.* London: Amnesty International, 1997.

—. 'More protection, less persecution: Human rights defenders in Latin America.' 4 June 1999. *Amnesty International.* 25 March 2005 <http://web.amnesty.org/library/Index/ENGAMR010021999?open&of=ENG-2M2>.

—. *Political Violence in Colombia: Myth and Reality.* New York: Amnesty International, 1994.

—. 'Restrictions on Tunisian Human Rights Defenders.' 22 December 2005 <http://web.amnesty.org/pages/tun-201205-news-eng>.

—. (with Oxfam International). *Shattered Lives: The Case for Tough International Arms Control*. London: Amnesty International and Oxfam International, 2003.

—. *Stolen Sisters: A Human Rights Response to Discrimination and Violence Against Indigenous Women in Canada*. Ottawa: Amnesty International, 2004.

—. 'Stop the Killing.' (Pamphlet). Amnesty International Canada Action Appeal (October 2003).

—. *Undermining Global Security: The European Union's Arms Exports*. London: Amnesty International, 2004.

—. 'UN Global Compact: the Nine Principles.' *Amnesty International*. 5 January 2005 <http://web.amnesty.org/pages/ec-globalcompact9principles-eng>.

—. 'United States of America: Human dignity denied: Torture and accountability in the "war on terror." ' 26 January 2006. <Http://web.amnesty.org/library/Index /ENGAMR511452004>.

—. 'World Social Forum: A Symbol of Hope.' *Amnesty International*. 24 January 2005 <http://news.amnesty.org/index/ENGASA20170120042004>.

Anderson, Tim. 'Imperial 'Transition' and Human Rights.' 21 April 2005. *Znet* 25 April 2005<http://www.zmag.org/conent/showarticle.cfm?SectionID=60&ItemID=7699>.

Annual Report of the Indian National Human Rights Commission (NHRC). New Delhi, 2003-04. 15 May 2006 <http://nhrc.nic.in/>.

Arslan, Zühtü. 'Taking Rights Seriously: Postmodernism and Human Rights.' *Res Publica* 5 (1999): 195-215.

ATD Fourth World, *How Poverty Separates Parents and Children: A Challenge to Human Rights*. Méry-sur-Oise, France: Fourth World Publications, 2004.

Babic, Jovan. 'Foreign Armed Intervention: Between Justified Aid and Illegal Violence.' *Humanitarian Intervention: Moral and Philosophical Issues*. Aleksandar Jokic, ed. Peterborough: Broadview Press, 2003: 45-70.

Baird, Vanessa. *Sex, Love and Homophobia: Lesbian, Gay, Bisexual and Transgender Lives*. London: Amnesty International, 2004.

Bakan, Joel. *The Corporation: The Pathological Pursuit of Profit and Power*. Toronto: Penguin, 2004.

Barlow, Maude. 'Who's in Charge of the Global Economy?' 20 January 2006 <http://www.canadians.org/browse_categories.htm?COC_token=&ste...>.

Barratt Brown, Michael. 'War And Human Rights, Terrorism And Debt.' *The Bertrand Russell Peace Foundation*. 21 February 2005 <http://www.russfound.org/consult1 /papers1/mbb.htm>.

Bautista, Maria Cynthia Rose Banzon. 'Migrant Workers and their Environments: Insights from the Filipino Diaspora.' *United Nations University*. 10 February 2005 <http://www.unu.edu/hq/japanese/gs-j/gs2002j/shonan18/Bautista4abstE.pdf>.

Baxi, Upendra. *The Future of Human Rights*. New Delhi: Oxford UP, 2002; rpt 2005.

BBC News. ' "War on Terror" Curbing Human Rights.' *BBC News* 15 January 2005 <http://news.bbc.co.uk/1/hi/world/americas/1763641.stm>.

—. 'Azerbaijan probes child-organ traffickers.' *BBC News World Edition* 21 February 2005 <http://news.bbc.co.uk/2/hi/europe/3513439.stm>.

—. 'India tops weapons purchase table.' *BBC News World Edition* 31 August 2005 <http://news.bbc.co.uk/1/hi/world/south_asia/4200812.stm>.

Bellis, Mary. 'ARPAnet–The First Internet.' *About.* 19 January 2005 <http://inventors.about.com/library/weekly/aa091598.htm>.

Belton, Neil. *The Good Listener: Helen Bamber A Life Against Cruelty.* New York: Pantheon Books, 1998.

Biel, Eric R. 'Denying Justice to Victims of Human Rights Abuse.' *Center For American Progress.* 17 January 2005 <http://www.americanprogress.org/site/pp.asp?c=bi JRJ8OVF&b=40728>.

'The Big Ideas 2005.' *Adbusters* 13.1 (2005): n.p.

Bigelow, Bill and Bob Peterson, eds. *Rethinking Globalization: Teaching for Justice in an Unjust World.* Milwaukee: Rethinking Schools Press, 2002.

Black, Robert E., Saul S. Morris, and Jennifer Bryce. 'Where and why are 10 million children dying every year?' *The Lancet* 361 (28 June 2003): 2226-2234.

Blore, Shawn. 'A nonchalant killer defends Rio-style justice.' *The Globe and Mail* 31 May 2005: A14.

Bode, Nicole. 'Prostitution Horror for Young Women.' 2 April 2005. *New York Daily News* 18 January 2006 <http://www.nydailynews.com/front/v-pfriendly/story /296058p-25346...>.

Boelens, Rutgerd and Hugo de Vos. 'Water Law and Indigenous Rights in the Andes.' *Cultural Survival Quarterly* 28.4 (Winter 2006): 19-21.

Booker, Salih and William Minter. 'Global Apartheid.' 9 July 2001. *The Nation* 25 March 2005 <http://www.thenation.com/doc.mhtml?i=20010709&s=booker>.

Brazier, Chris. 'Running for Rights: A New Internationalist Olympics.' *New Internationalist* 179 (January 1988). 10 February 2005 <http://www.newint.org/issue179/keynote.htm>.

Brooks, Daniel and Guillermo Verdecchia. *The Noam Chomsky Lectures: A Play.* Vancouver: Talonbooks, 1998.

Buncombe, Andrew. 'U.S. Supreme Court Clears Way for Relatives to Sue Shell over Saro-Wiwa's Death.' *Common Dreams News Center.* 21 January 2005 <http://www.commondreams.org/headlines01/0327-02.htm>.

Burrows, Gideon. *The No-Nonsense Guide to the Arms Trade.* Toronto: New Internationalist, 2002.

Campaign Against Depleted Uranium. 'Introduction.' *Campaign Against Depleted Uranium.* 17 January 2005 <http://www.cadu.org.uk/intro.htm>.

'Can There Be Labor Rights without Labor Unions?' *Thai Labour Campaign.* 16 January 2006 <http://www.thailabour.org/docs/CodesReport/LaborRightsLaborunio...>.

CBC News. 'Documents suggest Canadian involvement in Arar interrogation.' 22 April 2005. *CBC News.* 26 January 2006 <http://www.cbc.ca/story/canada/national/2005/04/21/arar050421.html>.

—. 'Fight Against Terrorism Threatens Human Rights: UN.' 10 December 2004. *CBC News*. 14 January 2005 <http://www.cbc.ca/story/world/national/2004/12/10 /arbour-un041210.html>.

—. 'War leading cause of hunger, says agency.' *CBC News*. 23 May 2005 <http://www.cbc.ca/story/world/national/2005/05/23/hunger-050523.html>.

—. 'Sharp rebuke for ambassador over Arar comments.' 17 June 2005. *CBC News* 26 January 2006 <http://www.cbc.ca/story/canada/naional/2005/06/16/arar050616 .html>.

CBS. 'Human Rights Watchdog Slams U.S.' *CBSNEWS.com*. 17 January 2005 <http://www.cbsnews.com/stories/2005/01/13/world/main666676.shtml>.

Chatterjee, Pratap. 'Meet the New Interrogators: Lockheed Martin.' 9 November 2005. *CorpWatch*. 26 January 2006 <http://www.corpwatch.org/article.php?id=12757>.

Chelala, César. 'How China can show its human-rights face.' *The Globe and Mail* 24 October 2005: A17.

Chomsky, Noam. *The Umbrella of U.S. Power: The Universal Declaration of Human Rights and the Contradictions of U.S. Policy*. New York: Seven Stories Press, 1999.

—. 'Amsterdam Forum Program Transcript, 21-30 May 2003, Interview with Andy Clark.' 21 January 2005 <http://www2.rnw.nl/rnw/en/features/amsterdamforum/ 030517ch_trans.html>.

Clapp, Jennifer. 'Piles of Poisons in Mexico.' 22 March 2002. *Global Policy Forum*. 21 January 2006 <http://www.globalpolicy.org/globaliz/special/2002/0510poison.htm>.

Clark, Roger. 'Principles of Human Rights Monitoring, June 23, 2003.' 10 January 2005 <http://www.chrf.ca/english/programs/downloads/ihrtpproceedings/24th /Monitoring.pdf>.

Claude, Richard Pierre, and Burns H. Weston. *Human Rights in the World Community: Issues and Action*. 2nd ed. Philadelphia: University of Pennsylvania Press, 1992.

Coalition to Oppose the Arms Trade (COAT). *Coalition to Oppose the Arms Trade*. 23 January 2005 <http://coat.ncf.ca/>.

Cockburn, Alexander. 'Refusing Reebok's Human Rights Award.' 7 February 2002. *Working for Change*. 16 January 2006 <http://www.workingforchange.com/print item.cfm?itemid=12779>.

Cockrell, Cathy. 'Beauty in the Aftermath of Bloodshed: Argentine Artist Explores Human Rights Terrain.' *Berkeleyan* 17 January 2005 <http://www.berkeley.edu /news/berkeleyan/2000/03/15/aftermath.html>.

Cohen, Stanley. *States of Denial: Knowing about Atrocities and Suffering*. Cambridge: Polity, 2001.

Cognitive Science Laboratory, Princeton University. *Wordnet: A Lexical Database for the English Language*. 15 June 2005 <http://www.cogsci.princeton.edu/cgi-bin /webwn>.

Commission on Human Security. *Human Security Now*. New York, 2003. 26 January 2006 <http://www.humansecurity-chs.org/finalreport/index.html>.

Conetta, Carl. 'Disappearing the Dead: Iraq, Afghanistan, and the Idea of a "New Warfare."' Research Monograph #9. 18 February 2004. *Project on Defense Alternatives*. 22 February 2005 <http://www.comw.org/pda/0402rm9.html#7>.

Convergence of Movements of the Peoples of the Americas. 'First Hemispheric Forum against Militarization.' *Sitiocompa*. 31 January 2005 <http://www.sitiocompa.org /desmilitarizacion/engmain.htm>.

Cooper, Joshua. 'Indigenous Peoples, Governments Continue to Lack Consensus as Draft Declaration Deadline Approaches.' *Cultural Survival Quarterly* 28.4 (Winter 2005): 7.

Cullen, Shay. 'Killing Children For Their Organs.' 7 February 2002. *Reflections—Philippine Daily Inquirer* 17 February 2005 <http://www.preda.org/archives/1993-94-95-96/r9503011.htm>.

Daly, Frances. 'The Non-Citizen and the Concept of "Human Rights." ' *Borderlands* 3.1 (2004). 5 January 2005 <http://www.borderlandsejournal.adelaide.edu.au/>.

Danaher, Kevin. *10 Reasons to Abolish the IMF and World Bank*. 2nd ed. New York: Seven Stories Press, 2004.

Deen, Thalif. 'U.N. Committee Silent on Anti-Terrorism Abuse.' *Human Rights First: Human Rights Defenders*. 25 March 2005 <http://www.humanrightsfirst.org/defenders/hrd_global/hrd_global_02.htm>.

'Democracy and Human Rights at WHINSEC.' *Western Hemisphere Institute for Security Cooperation*. 14 June 2005 <http://www.benning.army.mil/whinsec/democracy. Asp?id=95>.

Diebel, Linda. 'They just killed Digna.' *The Toronto Star* 18 September 2005: A10-11.

DiMauro, Peter. 'Reporter Sued for Libel—U.S. Website Threatened.' 30 June 2001. Hague-jur-commercial-law. 23 January 2006 <http://lists.essential.org/pipermail /hague-jur-commercial-law/2001-June/000144.html>.

Dobriansky, Paula. 'Dobriansky Says U.S. Leading Advocate for Human Rights.' *Embassy of the United States: Japan*. 24 January 2005 <http://japan.usembassy.gov/e/p /tp-gl0052.html>.

Donnelly, Jack. *Universal Human Rights in Theory and Practice*. 2nd ed. Ithaca: Cornell University Press, 2003.
—. 'Human Rights, Globalizing Flows, and State Power.' *Globalization and Human Rights*. Ed. Alison Brysk. Berkeley and Los Angeles: University of California Press, 2002: 226-41.

Donoghue, Andrew. 'Microsoft staff defend blog censorship.' *ZDNet*. UK 5 January 2006 <http://news.zdnet.co.uk/business/0,39020645,39245872,00.htm>.

'Duma Approves NGO Bill.' *Gulfnews.com*. 24 December 2005 <http://archive.gulfnews.com/articles/05/12/24/10006954.html>.

Dussel, Enrique. *Ethics and Community*. Maryknoll, NY: Orbis Books, 1988.
—. *The Invention of the Americas: Eclipse of 'the Other' and the Myth of Modernity*. Trans. Michael D. Barber. New York: Continuum, 1995.

Ebadi, Shirin. 'Nobel Lecture, Oslo 2003.' 10 December 2003. *Nobelprize.org*. 14 June 2005 <http://nobelprize.org/peace/laureates/2003/ebadi-lecture-e.html>.

'Education targeted in WTO talks.' *CAUT/ACPPU Bulletin* 53.1 January 2006: A1, A5.

Elkins, Caroline. 'Massacre in the Kenyan Gulag: The True Horror of British Colonial Rule.' *Indymedia@UK*. 25 January 2005 <http://www4.indymedia.org.uk/en/2005/01/304043.html>.

Ellis, Deborah. *Three Wishes: Palestinian and Israeli Children Speak*. Toronto: Groundwood Books, 2004.

'Emerging Ideas.' *Utne* (Jan.-Feb. 2006): 21.

Engler, Yves. 'Haiti Debt.' 12 January 2005. *ZNet* 21 January 2006 <http://www.zmag.org/content/showarticle.cfm?ItemID=7006>.

Engler, Yves and Anthony Fenton. *Canada in Haiti: Waging War on the Poor Majority*. Vancouver and Black Point: Red and Fernwood Publishing, 2005.

Etcheson, Craig. ' "The Number"—Quantifying Crimes Against Humanity in Cambodia.' Documentation Center of Cambodia. Phnom Penh, Cambodia, Mapping Project, 1999. 25 January 2006 <http://www.mekong.net/cambodia/toll.htm>.

'Ethyl Corp. sues Canada under NAFTA, illustrating what could happen later under OECD-MAI rules.' 16-30 June 1997. *Third World Network*. 22 January 2006 <http://www.twnside.org.sg/title/eth-cn.htm>.

Eviatar, Daphne. 'A Big Win for Human Rights.' 9 May 2005. *The Nation* 10 June 2005 <http://www.thenation.com/docprint.mhtml?i=20050509&s=eviatar>.

Fahrenheit 9/11. Dir. Michael Moore. Alliance Atlantis, 2004.

Farmer, Paul. *Pathologies of Power: Health, Human Rights, and the New War on the Poor*. Berkeley: University of California Press, 2003.

'Fields of Shame: Sex Slavery Exposed.' 21 May 2003. *NBC 4* 18 January 2006 <http://www.nbc4.tv/print/2220869/detail.html>.

Fischlin, Daniel and Ajay Heble, eds. *Rebel Musics: Human Rights, Resistant Sounds, and the Politics of Music Making*. Montreal: Black Rose Books, 2003.

Fisher, William F. and Thomas Ponniah. *Another World is Possible: Popular Alternatives to Globalization at the World Social Forum*. Nova Scotia: Fernwood, 2003.

Fisk, Robert. 'Margaret Hassan's Suspected Execution Will Be Seen As "Proof" of Evil.' *The Star* (South Africa) 17 November 2000. *Common Dreams News Center*. 25 March 2005 <http://www.commondreams.org/views04/1117-29.htm>.
—. *The Great War for Civilisation: The Conquest of the Middle East*. New York: Knopf, 2005.

Foster, Cecil. *Where Race Does Not Matter: The New Spirit of Modernity*. Toronto: Penguin, 2005.

'Fourth World Movement/USA.' *Volunteer Solutions*. 1 February 2005 <http://www.volunteersolutions.org/vcgno/org/2632373.html>.

'The Fourth World War: An Unembedded View of Global Resistance.' 26 August 2004. *Democracy Now!* 1 February 2005 <http://www.democracynow.org/article.pl?sid=04/08/26/1421221>.

Freeman, Alan. 'Righting the civil wrongs of a racist past.' *The Globe and Mail* 14 June 2005: A3.
—. 'Won't Pay Columnists to Promote Policies, Bush Vows.' *The Globe and Mail* 27 January 2005: A20.

Free the Children. 16 January 2006. <http://www.freethechildren.com/index.php>.

Free the Children. 'UN Convention on the Rights of the Child in Depth.' *Free the Children*. 15 January 2005 <http://www.freethechildren.org/peace/childrenandwar /uncrcindepth.html>.

Friesen, Joe. 'Bombings still echo in London's diverse core.' *The Globe and Mail* 8 August 2005: A10.

Galeano, Eduardo. 'Cuba Hurts.' *The Progressive* 4 January 2005 <http://www.progres-sive.org/june03/gal0503.html>.

—. 'Los Derechos de los Trabajadores ¿Un Tema para Arqueólogos?' *Patria Grande* 3 January 2005 <http://www.patriagrande.net/uruguay/eduardo.galeano/escritos /un.tema.para.arqueologos.htm>.

—. 'Ni Derechos Ni Humanos.' *Nadir* 3 January 2005 <http://www.nadir.org/na-dir/initiativ/agp/free/9-11/derechoshumanos.htm>.

—. 'Nothingland—or Venezuela?' 29 September-October 2004. *New Left Review* 24 April 2005 <http://www.newleftreview.net/NLR26302.shtml>.

—. 'To Be Like Them.' *Juárez: The Laboratory of Our Future.* Charles Bowden. New York: Aperture, 1998: 121-29.

Gardner, Gary. 'First, Do No Harm.' *Worldwatch* 19.1 Jan.-Feb. 2006: 30-31.

GPI Atlantic. *Genuine Progress Index for Atlantic Canada.* 22 January 2005 <http://www. gpiatlantic.org/>.

George, Susan. *Another World is Possible If...* London: Verso, 2004.

Gill, Leslie. *The School of the Americas: Military Training and Political Violence in the Americas.* Durham: Duke University Press, 2004.

Giordano, Al. 'Welcome to the Narcosphere.' 16 February 2004. *Narcosphere.* 25 February 2006 <http://narcosphere.narconews.com/story/2004/2/16/175416/747>.

—. 'State Dept. works "through" HRW.' 26 June 2004. *Narcosphere.* 24 February 2006 <http://narcosphere.narconews.com/comments/2004/6/17/15422/6410/5?>.

—. 'Vivanco Attacks Telesur: "The Airwaves are Falling!" ' 17 July 2005. *Narcosphere.* 24 February 2006 <http://narcosphere.narconews.com/story/2005/7/17/9548/56987>.

Gitlin, Todd. 'The Heart of Being Human.' *New Internationalist* 298 (January/February 1998). 10 February 2005 <http://www.newint.org/issue298/human.html>.

Goodman, Amy. 'The Haiti Coup One Year Later: A Look Back at the U.S. Role in the Overthrow of Aristide.' 28 February 2005. *Democracy Now!* 22 January 2006 <http://www.democracynow.org/article.pl?sid=05/02/28/145624>.

Gómez-Peña, Guillermo. *The New World Border: Prophecies, Poems & Loqueras for the End of the Century.* San Francisco: City Light Books, 1996.

Gordon, Joy. 'Cool War: Economic sanctions as a weapon of mass destruction.' November 2002. *Harper's Magazine* 26 January 2006 <http://www.scn.org/ccpi /HarpersJoyGordonNov02.html>.

Green Belt Movement. *Green Belt Movement.* 16 February 2005 <http://www. greenbeltmovement.org/index.php>.

Greenberg, Karen J., and Joshua L. Dratel, eds. *The Torture Papers: The Road to Abu Ghraib.* Cambridge: Cambridge University Press, 2005.

Greenfield, Gerard. 'Metalclad vs. Mexico: The Toxicity of NAFTA's Ruling.' 2001 *Against the Current*. 21 January 2006 <http://www:solidarityus.org/atc/90Greenfield.html>.

'Guatemala: State Publicly Acknowledges Responsibility for Mack Murder.' 21 April 2004. *Human Rights First*. 18 January 2006 <http://www.humanrightsfirst.org/media/2004_alerts/0421.htm>.

Harper, Tim. 'Evo taps Bolivian pride.' *Toronto Star* 23 January 2006: A10

Hartley, Aidan. 'What would a despot drive?' *The Gazette* 6 July 2005: A21.

Hattotuwa, Sanjana. 'From Violence to Peace: Terrorism and Human Rights in Sri Lanka.' *OJPCR: The Online Journal of Peace and Conflict Resolution* 5.1 (2003): 9-14. <http://www.trinstitute.org/ojpcr/5_1hattotuwa.htm>.

Hayner, P. B. *Unspeakable Truths: Confronting State Terror and Atrocity.* New York: Routledge, 2001.

The Heartland Alliance for Human Needs and Human Rights. 'Statement, 18 December 2001.' *National Network for Immigrant and Refugee Rights*. 15 January 2005 <http://www.nnirr.org/dec18/sample_org.html>.

Henríquez, Hugo Azcuy. *Derechos Humanos: Una Aproximación a la Política*. Havana: Editorial de Ciencias Sociales, 1997.

Herman, Edward S. 'Freedom of Expression in the West: Myth and Reality.' *Human Wrongs: Reflections on Western Global Dominance and its Impact Upon Human Rights*. Just World Trust. Mudra: Other India Press, 1996: 171-80.
—. *The Myth of the Liberal Media: An Edward Herman Reader*. New York: Peter Lang, 1999.
—. and Noam Chomsky, *Manufacturing Consent: The Political Economy of the Mass Media*. New York: Pantheon, 2002.

Herrera, Carlos. 'The true facts about U.S. interventionism in Venezuela and its mechanisms.' 25 March 2005 <http://www.vheadline.com/readnews.asp?id=27831>.

'Hina Jilani, UN Special Representative on Human Rights Defenders.' *Frontline: Defenders of Human Rights Defenders*. 20 December 2005 <http://www.frontline defenders.org/platform/1302>.

'HIV & AIDS in Africa.' *Avert.Org*. 15 June 2005 <http://www.avert.org/africa.htm>.

Hodge, James, and Linda Cooper. *Disturbing the Peace*. Maryknoll: Orbis Books, 2004.

Holmes, Signy. 'What your Mama never told you about NAFTA.' *The Manitoban Online*. 20 January 2006 <http://umanitoba.ca/manitoban/2005-2006/1123/1417>.

House, Christie R. 'The Rights of Human Beings.' *General Board of Global Ministries*. 17 January 2005 <http://gbgm-umc.org/nwo/99so/hbeings.html>.

'Human Rights Defenders in Guatemala: The Case of Myrna Mack Chang.' *Human Rights First*. 22 December 2005 <http://www.humanrightsfirst.org/defenders/hrd_guatemala/hrd_mack/...>.

'Human Rights Explained.' *JHR (Journalists for Human Rights)*. 25 March 2005 <http://www.jhr.ca/publicationsdifferentrightsexplained.htm#aged>.

'Human Rights in the Middle East are Deteriorating.' *ArabicNews* 15 January 2005 <http://www.arabicnews.com/ansub/Daily/Day/050115/2005011506.html>.

'The Human Rights of Aged Persons: The People's Movement for Human Rights Education.' *The People's Movement for Human Rights Education.* 25 March 2005 <http://www.pdhre.org/rights/aged.html>.

'The Human Rights of Indigenous People: In the Red.' 10 December 2003. *Isla: Information Services Latin America.* 14 June 2005 <http://isla.igc.org/Features/Colombia/SR5HemeraResumen.html>.

'Human Rights Research and Education.' *Human Rights Interactive Network.* 23 January 2005 <http://www.webcom.com/hrin/research.html>.

Human Rights Watch. 'Anti-Racism Summit Needs Concrete Results.' *Human Rights Watch.* 25 April 2005 <http://www.hrw.org/press/2001/08/durban0827.htm>.

—. 'Anti-Terror Campaign Cloaking Human Rights Abuse: New Survey Finds Crackdown on Civil Liberties.' *Human Rights Watch.* 14 January 2005 <http://www.hrw.org/press/2002/01/wr2002.htm>.

—. 'Caste: Asia's Hidden Apartheid.' *Human Rights Watch.* 25 April 2005 <http://www.hrw.org/campaigns/caste/presskit.htm>.

—. 'Children's Rights.' *Human Rights Watch.* 9 February 2005 <http://www.hrw.org/children/>.

—. 'Crypto Controls Threaten Human Rights.' *Human Rights Watch.* 26 January 2005 <http://www.hrw.org/press98/sept/crypto.htm>.

—. 'Cuba: Beating and Incarceration of Human Rights Activists Condemned.' *Human Rights Watch.* 5 January 2005 <http://www.hrw.org/press/2002/04/cuba0425.htm>.

—. 'Cuba: Human Rights and U.S. Policy.' *Human Rights Watch.* 5 January 2005 <http://www.hrw.org/press/2003/09/cuba090403-tst.htm>.

—. 'Disappointment as U.S. Bolts Race Conference.' *Human Rights Watch.* 25 April 2005 <http://www.hrw.org/press/2001/09/usbolt0903.htm>.

—. 'End Global Caste Discrimination.' *Human Rights Watch.* 25 April 2005 <http://www.hrw.org/press/2001/03/caste0321.htm>.

—. 'HIV/AIDS & Human Rights.' *Human Rights Watch.* 15 June 2005 <http://www.hrw.org/doc/?t=hivaids&document_limit=0,2>.

—. Human Rights Overview 'India 2005.' 15 May 2006. <Http://hrw.org/english/docs/2005/01/13/india9824.htm>.

—. *Human Rights Watch World Report 2004: Human Rights and Armed Conflict.* New York: Human Rights Watch, 2004.

—. *Human Rights Watch World Report 2006: U.S. Policy of Abuse Undermines Rights Worldwide.* New York: Human Rights Watch, 2006. 26 January 2006 <http://www.hrw.org/english/docs/2006/01/13/global12428.htm>.

—. 'Human Rights Watch and the World Conference Against Racism, Racial Discrimination, Xenophobia and Related Intolerance.' *Human Rights Watch.* 25 April 2005 <http://www.hrw.org/campaigns/race/submission.htm>.

—. 'India Human Rights Press Backgrounder: Anti-Terrorism Legislation.' *Human Rights Watch.* 14 January 2005 <http://www.hrw.org/backgrounder/asia/india-bck1121.htm>.

—. *The Internet in the Mideast and North Africa: Free Expression and Censorship.* New York: Human Rights Watch, 1999.

—. 'The Johannesburg Statement on Sexual Orientation, Gender Identity, and Human Rights, 2004.' *Human Rights Watch.* 15 June 2005 <http://wwwhrw.org /lgbt/pdf/joburg_statement021304.htm>.

—. 'Letter Urging Jamaican Government to Protect Rights Defenders and Address Violence and Abuse Based on Sexual Orientation and HIV Status.' 30 November 2004. *Human Rights Watch.* 15 June 2005 <http://hrw.org/english/docs/2004/11/30 /jamaic9750.htm>.

—. 'The Mine Ban Treaty and the Americas.' January 1999. *Human Rights Watch.* 25 January 2005 <http://hrw.org/landmines/mbt-americas.htm>.

—. 'Opportunism in the Face of Tragedy: Repression in the Name of Anti-Terrorism.' *Human Rights Watch.* 14 January 2005 <http://www.hrw.org/campaigns/september11 /opportunismwatch.htm>.

—. 'Racial Discrimination and Related Intolerance.' *Human Rights Watch.* 25 April 2005 <http://www.hrw.org/wr2k1/special/racism.html>.

—. 'Restrictions on AIDS Activists in China.' *Human Rights Watch.* 20 June 2005 <http://www.hrw.org/reports/2005/china0605/>.

—. 'Time to End the U.S. Embargo on Cuba.' *Human Rights Watch.* 5 January 2005 <http://www.hrw.org/press/2002/05/cuba0517.htm>.

—. 'U.K.: New Anti-Terror Law Rolls Back Rights.' *Human Rights Watch.* 14 January 2005 <http://www.hrw.org/press/2001/12/UKbill1214.htm>.

—. 'U.S.: Congress tries to Undermine War Crimes Court.' *Human Rights Watch.* 3 January 2005 <http://www.hrw.org/english/docs/2004/12/08/usint9794.htm>.

—. 'U.S.: Makeshift Process of Military Commissions Imperils Justice.' *Human Rights Watch.* 5 January 2005 <http://www.hrw.org/english/docs/2004/08/27 /usdom9274_txt.htm>.

—. 'Women's Rights.' *Human Rights Watch.* 9 February 2005 <http://www.hrw.org /women/>.

Hunter, Anna. 'The Violence that Indigenous Women Face.' *Canadian Dimension.* 29 April 2005 <http://www.canadiandimension.mb.ca/v39/v39_2ah.htm>.

Huntington, Samuel P. 'The Clash of Civilizations.' *Alamut: Bastion of Peace and Information.* 19 January 2005 <http://www.alamut.com/subj/economics/misc/clash.html>.

Ignatieff, Michael. *The Rights Revolution.* Toronto: Anansi, 2000.

—. *The Lesser Evil: Political Ethics in An Age of Terror.* Toronto: Penguin, 2004.

Inter-American Commission on Human Rights. *Report on Terrorism and Human Rights.* 14 January 2005 <http://www.cidh.org/terrorism/eng/toc.htm>.

International Criminal Court. 'International Criminal Court: Historical Introduction.' *International Criminal Court.* 4 January 2005 <http://www.icc-cpi.int/about /ataglance/history>.

—. *Rome Statute of the International Criminal Court.* The Hague: Public Information and Documentation Section of the ICC, 2002.

International Federation for Human Rights and the World Organisation Against Torture. *Human Rights Defenders on the Front Line Annual Report 2004.* 25 April 2005 <http://www.fidh.org/>.

International Gay and Lesbian Human Rights Commission. 16 February 2005 <http://www.iglhrc.org/site/iglhrc/>.

International PEN. *Anti-Terrorism, Writers and Freedom of Expression*. London: International PEN, 2003.

Ishay, Micheline R. *The History of Human Rights: From Ancient Times to the Globalization Era*. Berkeley: University of California Press, 2004.
—. *The Human Rights Reader: Major Political Writings, Essays, Speeches, and Documents from the Bible to the Present*. New York: Routledge, 1997.

Ivins, Molly. 'Media Concentration is a Totalitarian Tool.' *Common Dreams News Center*. 2 February 2005 <http://www.commondreams.org/views03/0131-09.htm>.

Jackson, Cliff. 'Casualties in the Third World.' *Double Standards*. 26 January 2005 <http://www.doublestandards.org/ded.html>.

Jain, Tarun. 'Defying Labels, Defining Themselves.' *India Together*. 5 February 2005 <www.indiatogether.org/2004/sep/adv-dntlabel.htm>.

' "Jim Crow" Laws.' Martin Luther King, Jr., National Historic Site Interpretive Staff. *National Parks Service*. 4 January 2005 <http://www.nps.gov/malu/documents /jim_crow_laws.htm>.

Joffe-Walt, Benjamin. 'Women Tell of Brutal Rapes in Secret Camp.' 27 May 2004. *San Francisco Chronicle*. 18 January 2006 <http:www.sfgate.com/cgi-bin/article.cgi?file=/chronicle/archive/200…>.

Johnson, Larry. 'Iraqi Cancers, Birth Defects Blamed on U.S. Depleted Uranium.' *Seattle Post-Intelligencer* 17 January 2005 <http://seattlepi.nwsource.com/national /95178_du12.shtml>.

Just World Trust. *Human Wrongs: Reflections on Western Global Dominance and its Impact Upon Human Rights*. Mudra: Other India Press, 1996.

Kant, Immanuel. *The Metaphysics of Morals*. Trans. Mary Gregor. Cambridge: Cambridge University Press, 1995.

Kapadia, Nisha. 'India's Greatest Planned Environmental Disaster: The Narmada Valley Dam Projects.' *Environmental Justice Case Studies*. 10 January 2005 <http://www. umich.edu/~snre492/Jones/narmada.html>.

Keefer, Michael. 'George Galloway Speaking Truth to Power.' *ColdType*. 10 May 2005 <http://www.coldtype.net>.
—. 'Footprints of Electoral Fraud: The November 2 Exit Poll Scam.' 5 November 2004. *Centre for Research on Globalization*. 26 January 2005 <http://globalresearch.ca/articles/KEE411A.html>.

The Kerr Center. 'The Ogallala Aquifer.' 30 January 2006 <http://www.kerrcenter. com/publications/ogallala_aquifer.pdf.>.

Khan, Irene. 'Foreword.' *Amnesty International Report 2005*. 10 May 2005 <http://web. amnesty.org/report2005/message-eng>.

Kick, Russ. *50 Things You're Not Supposed to Know*. New York: The Disinformation Company, 2003.

King, Martin Luther. 'A Revolution of Values.' *Rethinking Globalization: Teaching for Justice in an Unjust World*. Eds. Bill Bigelow and Bob Peterson. Milwaukee: Rethinking Schools Press, 2002: 327-8.

King, Thomas. *The Truth About Stories*. Toronto: Anansi, 2003.

Klassen, Nicholas. 'U.S. Foreign Military Interventions.' *Adbusters* 13.3 (May/June 2005): n.p.

Knight, Danielle. 'NAFTA ruling undermines environmental accords.' 21 November 2000. *Third World Network*. 22 January 2006 <http://www/twnside.org.sg/title/accords.htm>.

Koufa, Kalliopi K. 'Human Rights and Terrorism: Extracts from the Second Progress Report Prepared by Ms. Kalliopi K. Koufa, United Nations Special Rapporteur on Terrorism and Human Rights.' *UNESCO.org*. 13 January 2005 <http://portal.unesco.org/shs/en/file_download.php/c4ccc0392f9d89d7bfd846aef62285a3exp_koufa_en.pdf>.

'Koyaanisqatsi, a state of life that calls for another way of living.' *Ratical.org*. 12 January 2005 <http://www.ratical.org/koya.html>.

Kurunganthi, Kavitha. 'Persistent and Tenacious Struggle.' *India Together*. 5 February 2005 <http://www.indiatogether.org/2004/dec/hrt-bhopal04.htm>.

Landless Workers Movement. 'Human Rights.' *Landless Workers Movement*. 12 January 2005 <http://www.mstbrazil.org/humanRights.html>.

Lasn, Kalle. 'Bioeconomics.' *Adbusters* 13.1 (2005): n.p.

—. and Tim Walker. 'Let's Fight for a New Human Right.' *Adbusters* 13.1 (2005): n.p.

Lawrence, Felicity. 'Gangmaster Culture Is out of Control.' *Guardian Weekly* 14-20 January 2005: 14.

Lawson, Edward. 'Human Rights and HIV/AIDS.' *Encyclopedia of Human Rights*. 2nd ed. Washington: Taylor and Francis, 1996.

Lazare, Daniel. *The Velvet Coup: The Constitution, the Supreme Court, and the Decline of American Democracy*. London: Verso, 2001.

León-Portilla, Miguel, and Earl Shorris et al. eds. *In the Language of Kings: An Anthology of Mesoamerican Literature—Pre-Columbian to the Present*. New York: Norton, 2001.

Lerner-Lam, Arthur, Leonardo Seeber, and Robert Chen. 'Virtual Technology as a Human Right.' *Christian Science Monitor* 26 January 2005 <http://www.christianscience monitor.com/2005/0103/p09s01-comv.htm>.

Lewis, Stephen. 'Politics, Resources and the Environment: A Witches Brew.' *The Kenneth Hammond Lectures on Environment, Energy and Resources 2000 Series, Malthus and the Third Millennium*. Chesworth, Ward, Michael R. Moss, and Vernon G. Thomas, eds. Guelph: Faculty of Environmental Sciences, University of Guelph, 2001: 1-19.

—. *Race Against Time*. Toronto: Anansi, 2005.

Liberty. 'Terrorism.' *Liberty: Protecting Civil Liberties, Promoting Human Rights*. 14 January 2005 <http://www.liberty-human-rights.org.uk/index.html>.

—. *Suspect Community—The Impact of Anti-Terrorism Powers on the British Muslim Population*. 22 January 2005 June 2004 <http://www.liberty-human-rights.org.uk/resources/policy-papers/2004/anti-terror-impact-brit-muslim.PDF>.

Lindenbaum, Stephanie. 'The Reebok Human Rights Award for Young Activists.' 16 January 2006 <http:fletcher.tufts.edu/news/2005/07/reebok.shtml>.

Lippman, Matthew. 'Multinational Corporations and Human Rights.' *Human Rights in the World Community: Issues and Action*. 2nd Ed. Claude, Richard Pierre and H. Burns, eds. Philadelphia: University of Pennsylvania Press, 1992: 392-99.

Llewelyn Leach, Susan. 'A young activist calls attention to a cause.' 11 May 2005. *The Christian Science Monitor* 16 January 2006 <http://www.csmonitor.com/2005/0511/p17s01-wosc.htm>.

Lorde, Audre. 'The Master's Tools Can Never Dismantle the Master's House.' *Feminism and 'Race.'* Bhavnani, Kum-Kum, ed. N.Y.: Oxford University Press, 2001: 89-92.

Lutz, Ellen. 'Indigenous Peoples and Water Rights.' *Cultural Survival Quarterly* 29.4 (Winter 2006): 11-13.

—. 'Indigenous Women's Voices Deserve Our Attention.' *Cultural Survival Quarterly* 28.4 (Winter 2005): 5-6.

Maathai, Wangari. 'Nobel Lecture.' *Nobelprize.org*. 20 January 2005 <http://nobelprize.org/peace/laureates/2004/maathai-lecture-text.html>.

Manila, Wilhelmina Paras. 'Sarah's Reel Life: The Screen Version of the Sarah Balabagan Story Has the Manila Government in a Fix.' *AsiaWeek.com*. 26 January 2005 <http://www.asiaweek.com/asiaweek/97/0328/feat1.htm>.

'Manitoba introduces nursing-home bill of rights.' *The Globe and Mail* 11 March 2005: A8.

Mann, Howard. 'The Final Decision in Methanex v. United States: Some New Wine in Some New Bottles.' August 2005. *International Institute for Sustainable Development*. 22 January 2006 <www.iisd.org/investment/itn/archive.asp>.

Marcos, Subcomandante Insurgente. *The Story of Colors / La historia de los colores: A Folktale from the Jungles of Chiapas*. Illus. Domitila Domínguez. Trans. Anne Bar Din. El Paso, TX: Cinco Puntos, 1999.

'Marilyn Waring.' *Wikipedia*. 15 January 2005 <http://en.wikipedia.org/wiki/Marilyn_Waring>.

Marks, Stephen. 'The Glass is Half Full: Human Rights Fifty Years after the UDHR.' *SIPAnews Faculty Forum* 16 January 2005 <http://www.sipa.columbia.edu/PUBS/SIPA_NEWS/FALL98/facultyforum.html>.

Marmon Silko, Leslie. *Ceremony*. New York: Penguin, 1986.

Marshall, Andrew. 'Charm Tong: Educating Burma.' 3 October 2005. *Time Asia* 16 January 2006 <http://www.time.com/time/asia/magazine/printout/0,13675,5010510...>.

Mathiason, Nick. 'Microsoft in Human Rights Row.' 1 February 2004. *Guardian Unlimited* 26 January 2005 <http://observer.guardian.co.uk/business/story/0,6903,1136045,00.html>.

McCarthy, Shawn. 'U.S. Moral Authority Hurt by Prison Abuses, Rights Group Says.' *The Globe and Mail* 14 January 2005: A11.

McGregor, Karen. 'Shell to Face U.S. Lawsuit for Saro-Wiwa Execution.' 19 September 2000 *Independent*. *Ratical.org*. 21 January 2005 <http://www.ratical.org/corporations/ShellNigeria.html>.

McMurtry, John. *The Cancer Stage of Capitalism*. London: Pluto, 1999.

Meek, James. 'Silent screams: Our self-righteous prime minister is complicit in the endless atrocities in Chechnya.' 14 December 2002. *The Guardian*. 22 February 2006 <http://www.hrvc.net/articles/meek.htm>.

Mehrotra, Deepti Priya. 'The Right Fight.' *India Together*. 5 February 2005 <http://www.indiatogether.org/2004/nov/rti-natlmeet.htm>.

Mekay, Emad. 'WTO Special: Developing Nations Push Back.' *Inter Press Service News Agency*. 22 December 2005 <http://www.ipsnews.net/newsasp?idnews=31434>.
—. 'WTO Special: Subsidies Concession Largely Symbolic, Groups Say.' *Inter Press Service News Agency*. 22 December 2005 <http://www.ipsnews.net/newsasp?idnews=31478>.

Mental Disability Rights International. 'Grave Abuses Continue in Paraguayan Psychiatric Institution.' *MDRI: Mental Disability Rights International*. 28 January 2005 <http://www.mdri.org/>.

Millennium Ecosystem Assessment. 'Living Beyond Our Means: Natural Assets and Human Well-Being.' 3 April 2005 <http://www.millenniumassessment.org/en/index.aspx>.

'Missing the Mark: A School Report on rich countries' contribution to Universal Primary Education by 2015.' April 2005. *Oxfam*. 25 April 2005 <http://www.oxfam.org.uk/what_we_do/issues/education/gce_missing.htm>.

Mission, Gina. 'The Breadwinners: Female Migrant Workers.' *Winmagazine* 26 January 2005 <http://www.geocities.com/wellesley/3321/win15a.htm>.

Mitchell, Parker, and George Roter. 'Africa's Weekly Silent Tsunami.' *The Globe and Mail* 11 January 2005: A17.

Modern Heroes Modern Slaves. Dir. Marie Boti. Montreal: Productions Multi-Monde, 1997.

'Mom Says: Clean Your Room.' *Utne* (Nov.-Dec. 2005): 71.

Monbiot, George. 'Publish and Be Damned.' *Guardian Weekly* 29 April 1996. *Monbiot.com*. 23 January 2006 <http://www.monbiot.com/archives/1999/04/29/publish-and-be-damned/>.
—. 'A Televisual Fairyland.' *Guardian Weekly* 28 January–3 February 2005: 6.

Montague, Peter. 'The Precautionary Principle.' *Rachel's Environment and Health Weekly* 19 February 1998. *Ratical.org*. 18 January 2005 <http://www.ratical.org/co-globalize/REHW586.html>.

Mossallanejed, Ezat. *Torture in the Age of Fear*. Hamilton: Seraphim Editions, 2005.

'Mukhtaran Bibi: Rape Survivor Who Transformed Tragedy Into Hope.' *Beliefnet*. 16 June 2005 <http://www.beliefnet.com/story/157/story_15720.html?rnd=65>.

Murphy, Terry. 'Who, Exactly, Are 'The Cuban Five'?' *Canadian Dimension*. 5 January 2005 <http://www.canadiandimension.mb.ca/v37/v37_4tm.htm>.

Muzadi, K. H. Hasyim, and H. Choesnoer Rhoviq. 'Human Rights and Democracy in Islamic Teachings: Indonesian Experiences.' *Documentation for Action Groups in Asia*. 20 January 2005 <http://www.daga.org/press/ia/chrislim/chrislim06.htm>.

Muzaffar, Chandra. *Rights, Religion and Reform: Enhancing Dignity through Spiritual and Moral Transformation*. London: RoutledgeCurzon, 2002.

—. 'Introductory Remarks.' *Human Wrongs: Reflections on Western Global Dominance and its Impact Upon Human Rights*. Just World Trust. Mudra: Other India Press, 1996.

Nardi, Jason. 'WTO Special: The TRIPs Traps for Health and Knowledge.' *Inter Press Service News Agency*. 22 December 2005 <http://www.ipsnews.net/newsasp?idnews=31487>.

Nash, June C. *Mayan Visions: The Quest for Autonomy in an Age of Globalization*. New York: Routledge, 2001.

Nelson, Joyce. 'Introduction.' *The Noam Chomsky Lectures: A Play*. By Daniel Brooks and Guillermo Verdecchia. Vancouver: Talonbooks, 1998: 7-9.

New Internationalist World Guide 2001/2002. Oxford: New Internationalist Publications, 2001.

'No Future.' *Adbusters* 12.5 (2004): n.p.

Nolen, Stephanie. 'Federal tsunami aid hits $425-million...as cash woes hurt African AIDS fight.' *Globe and Mail* 11 January 2005: A1.

—. 'Face to Face with the Lord's Resistance.' *The Globe and Mail* 27 April 2005: A18.

Nomai, A.J. 'Food disparagement laws: A threat to us all.' 23 January 2006 <http://www.geocities.com/CapitolHill/Lobby/1818/3_2VeggieLibel.htm>.

Okri, Ben, et al. 'The Case of Ken Saro-Wiwa.' *New York Review of Books* 21 January 2005 <http://www.nybooks.com/articles/1913>.

Olcott, Martha Brill. 'Democracy, Human Rights and the War on Terrorism in Central Asia.' *The September 11 Digital Archive*. 16 January 2005 <http://911digitalarchive.org/objects/16.html>.

Olujic, Maria B. 'Women, Rape, and War: The Continued Trauma of Refugees and Displaced Persons in Croatia.' *Anthropology of East Europe Review* 13: 1 Spring 1995. 18 January 2006 <http://condor.depaul.edu/~rrotenbe/aeer/aeer13_1/Olujic.html>.

'188 anti-WTO protesters released.' *China View* 22 December 2005 <http:// news.xinhuanet.com/english/2005-12/18/content_3939066.htm>.

Ontario Human Rights Commission. 'Statement on Racial Profiling.' *Ontario Human Rights Commission*. 25 April 2005 <http://www.ohrc.on.ca/english/consultations/racial-profiling-statement.shtml>.

—. 'The Effects of Racial Profiling.' *Ontario Human Rights Commission*. 25 April 2005 <http://www.ohrc.on.ca/english/consultations/racial-profiling-report_6.shtml>.

Palast, Greg. 'The Truth Buried Alive.' April 2003. *Utne* 23 January 2006 <http://www.utne.com/cgi-bin/udt/im.display.printable?client.id=utn...>.

—. 'Columns: Theft of Presidency.' 26 January 2006 <http://www.Gregpalast.com/columns.cfm?subject_id=1&subject_name=Theft%20of%20Presidency>.

Pangalangan, Raul C. 'Sweatshops and International Labor Standards: Globalizing Markets, Localizing Norms.' *Globalization and Human Rights*. Alison Brysk, ed. Berkeley: University of California Press, 2002: 98-112.

Parmly, Michael E. 'Sale of Human Organs in China.' *Hearing Before the Subcommittee on International Operations and Human Rights, House International Relations, Washington DC*

June 27, 2001. U.S. Department of State. 22 February 2005 <http://www.state.gov /g/drl/rls/rm/2001/3792.htm>.

Patriquin, Martin. 'Quebec farm segregated black workers.' *The Globe and Mail* 30 April 2005: A1.

Pearlstein, Deborah. *Ending Secret Detentions.* New York: Human Rights First, 2004.

PEN America. 'Anti-Terrorism, Writers and Freedom of Expression: A PEN Report.' *PEN American Center.* 14 January 2005 <http://www.pen.org/freedom/antiterror 2003.htm>.

'Pioneer and Patriot Bev Harris TVNL Woman of the Year.' 22 December 2004. *Bella Ciao.* 3 January 2005 <http://bellaciao.org/en/article.php3?id_article=4848>.

Pocha, Jehangir S. 'China's Other Great Wall.' *Utne* (July-August 2005): 13-14.

'Poems from Africa.' *Africa Alive.* 15 June 2005 <http://www.africaalive.org/poems /poems01.htm>.

Pollis, Adamantia. 'A New Universalism.' *Human Rights: New Perspectives, New Realities.* Pollis, Adamantia and Peter Schwab, eds. Boulder: Lynne Rienner Publishers, 2000: 9-30.

Pollis, Adamantia and Peter Schwab. 'Human Rights: A Western Construct With Limited Applicability.' *Human Rights: Cultural and Ideological Perspectives.* Pollis, Adamantia and Peter Schwab, eds. New York: Praeger Publishers, 1979: 1-18.
—. 'Globalization's Impact on Human Rights.' *Human Rights: New Perspectives, New Realities.* Pollis, Adamantia and Peter Schwab, eds. Boulder: Lynne Rienner Publishers, 2000: 209-223.
—. 'Introduction.' *Human Rights: New Perspectives, New Realities.* Pollis, Adamantia and Peter Schwab, eds. Boulder: Lynne Rienner Publishers, 2000: 1-8.

Poniatowska, Elena. *Massacre in Mexico.* Trans. Helen R. Lane. New York: Viking Press, 1975.

Power, Jonathan. *Like Water on Stone: The Story of Amnesty International.* London: Allen Lane, 2001.

'Professor McCoy Exposes the History of CIA Interrogation, From the Cold War to the War on Terror.' Interview with Amy Goodman. 17 February 2006. *Democracy Now!* 18 February 2006 <http://www.democracynow.org/article.pl?sid=06/02/17/152222>.

'Protests Continue at WTO Conference as Talks Stall Over Agricultural Trade.' 14 December 2005. *Democracy Now!* 22 December 2005 <http://www.democracynow.org /article.pl?sid=05/12/14/154256>.

PBS. 'The Issue: Children's Rights.' *PBS: Speak Truth to Power.* 5 January 2005 <http:// www.pbs.org/speaktruthtopower/issue_child.html>.

de Queiroz, Mario. 'World Social Forum: Original Venue, New and Improved Methodology for Giant Meet.' *Common Dreams News Center.* 30 January 2005 <http://www. commondreams.org/headlines05/0127-10.htm>.

Rabossi, Eduardo. *La Carta Internacional de Derechos Humanos.* Buenos Aires: Editorial Universitaria de Buenos Aires, 1987.

Rawal, Baharat. 'The Second Freedom Struggle.' *India Together.* 5 February 2005 <http://www.indiatogether.org/2005/fcb/rti-hazare.htm>.

'Report from the Commission of Human Rights of the Universidad Autónoma, Mexico City, Oaxaca de Juárez, March 23 2005.' 29 April 2005 <http://boston porciporfm @yahoo.com>email.

'Rich countries pilloried by OECD over international aid.' *Guardian Weekly* January 28-February 03 2005: 29.

Rickard, Stephen. 'Bricks Without Straw: Taking Action on the Annual Country Reports on Human Rights Practices.' *Robert F. Kennedy Memorial Center for Human Rights.* 16 January 2005 <http://www.rfkmemorial.org/CENTER/Rickard _Testimory.htm>.

'Rights Activists Suffer in War on Terror.' 18 April 2005. *Daily Times* (Pakistan). 25 April 2005 <http://www.dailytimes.com.pk/default.asp?page=story_15-4-2005_pg4_9>.

'Rights group leader says U.S. has secret jails.' 6 June 2005. *CNN.COM.* 26 January 2006 <http://www.cnn.com/2005/US/06/05/amnesty.detainee/>.

Ron, James. 'Finding bias in rights reporting.' *The Globe and Mail* 31 May 2005: A17.

Rose, David. *Guantánamo: The War on Human Rights.* New York: New Press, 2004.

Rosenthal, Eric, and Clarence J. Sundram. 'Recognizing Existing Rights and Crafting New Ones: Tools for Drafting Human Rights Instruments for People with Mental Disabilities.' 12 February 2005 <http://www.mdri.org/pdf/oxford-article.pdf>.

Rosset, Peter. 'U.S. Opposes Right to Food at World Summit.' *People's Food Sovereignty.* 15 January 2005 <http://www.peoplesfoodsovereignty.org/docs/070902.htm>.

Roy, Arundhati. *An Ordinary Person's Guide to Empire.* Cambridge: South End Press, 2004.
—. *Power Politics.* 2nd Ed. Cambridge: South End Press, 2001.
—. 'What We Call Peace Is Little Better than Capitulation to a Corporate Coup.' *Common Dreams News Center.* 16 January 2005 <http://www.commondreams.org /views04/1103-20.htm>.

Ruiz, Albor. 'Documented Terrorist Activities against Cuba (and Other Countries).' *Free the Cuban Five.* 5 January 2005 <http://www.canadiannetworkoncuba.ca/FTF /documentedanti-ter.html>.

Rusk, James. 'Conditions on reserve "atrocious," doctor says.' *The Globe and Mail* 24 October 2005: A5.

Safo, Amos. 'Ghana; Commentary: Where old age is not welcome.' *Africanews* 69 (Nov. 2001): 3. 15 May 2005 <http://web.peacelink.it/afrinews/69_issue/p3.html>.

Saldamando, Alberto. 'Contamination of American Rivers Triggers International Complaint.' *Cultural Survival Quarterly* 28.4 (Winter 2006): 26-28.

Salman, Ali. 'Human Rights and Islam: Some Points of Convergence and Divergence.' 3 January 2005 <http://www.renaissance.com.pk/octvipo2y1.html>.

Saloojee, Riad. 'Rights and Security: We Must Have Both.' *Canadian Council on American-Islamic Relations.* 19 January 2005 <www.caircan.ca/oped_more.php?id =1318_0_10_0_C>.

Sanders, Richard. 'Canada Pension Plan Investments in America's Big Four "Missile Defence" Contractors and other Top U.S. War Industries.' *Conversion!* 55 (Dec 2004). 13 April 2005 <http://coat.ncf.ca/ourmagazine/links/55/55.htm>.

Sari, Dita. 'Why I Rejected the Reebok Human Rights Award.' 4 February 2002. *Counterpunch*. 16 January 2006 <http://www.counterpunch.org/ditasari.html>.

Saunders, Doug. 'Britain passes new anti-terrorism law.' *The Globe and Mail* 12 March 2005: A16.

Scheper-Hughes, Nancy. 'The Global Traffic in Human Organs.' *Current Anthropology* 41.2 (2000): 191-224.

—. 'Organ Trade: The New Cannibalism.' *New Internationalist* 300 (April 1998): 14-17. *Organs Watch*. 21 February 2005 <http://sunsite3.berkeley.edu/biotech /organswatch/pages/cannibalism.html>.

Schlosser, Eric. *Fast Food Nation: The Dark Side of the All-American Meal*. New York: Perennial, 2002.

'School of the Americas Closes.' *Washington Post* 17 December 2000: 11.

Schmidt, Janet C., Patrick A. Manson, and Tricia A. Windschitl, eds. *Our World, Our Rights: Teaching About Rights and Responsibilities in the Elementary School*. New York: Amnesty International USA, 2000.

Schultz, Jim. 'Bolivia's War Over Water.' *The Democracy Center*. 6 June 2005 <http:// www.democracyctr.org/waterwar/>.

Schulz, William F. *Tainted Legacy: 9/11 and the Ruin of Human Rights*. New York: Thunder's Mouth Press, 2003.

'Scientific Facts on Ecosystem Change.' *Green Facts.org*. 3 April 2005 <http://www. greenfacts.org/ecosystems/>.

Seager, Ashley. 'Britain criticised for accepting Nigerian debt repayments.' 5 December 2005. *The Guardian* 21 January 2006 <http://www.guardian.co.uk/g8/story /0,13365,1657909,00.html>.

Searls, Helen and Daniel Lloyd. 'Censorship for Hire.' 5 December 2005. *Living Marxism*. 23 January 2006 <http://www.mcpotlight.org/media/press/livmarx_may97.html>.

Sen, Amartya. *Development as Freedom*. New York: Anchor, 2000.

Señorita Extraviada/Missing Young Woman. Dir. Lourdes Portillo. New York: Women Make Movies, 2001.

Sforza, Michelle and Mark Valliantos. 'NAFTA & Environmental Laws: Ethyl Corp. v. Government of Canada.' 18 April 2005. *Global Policy Forum*. 20 January 2006 <http://www.globalpolicy.org/socecon/envronmt/ethly.htm>.

Shah, Anup. 'Kurds and Human Rights.' *Human Rights Watch*. 21 February 2005 <http://www.globalissues.org/HumanRights/Abuses/Kurds.asp>.

—. 'Media Conglomerates, Mergers, Concentration of Ownership.' 15 April 2004. Corporate Influence in the Media. 22 February 2005 <http://www.globalissues.org /HumanRights/Media/Corporations/Owners.asp>.

—. 'The Scale of the Debt Crisis.' 2 July 2005. *Global Issues* 21 January 2006 <http:// www.globalissues.org/TradeRelated/Debt/Scale.asp>.

Shiva, Vandana. *Earth Democracy: Justice, Sustainability, and Peace*. Cambridge: South End Press, 2005.

—. 'Relocalization, Not Globalization.' *Rethinking Globalization: Teaching for Justice in an Unjust World*. Bigelow, Bill and Bob Peterson, eds. Milwaukee: Rethinking Schools Press, 2002: 248-9.

—. 'The Living Democracy Movement: Alternatives to the Bankruptcy of Globalization.' *Another World is Possible: Popular Alternatives to Globalization at the World Social Forum*. Fisher, William F. and Thomas Ponniah, eds. Nova Scotia: Fernwood, 2003: 115-24.

'Short History of the Internet.' *FortuneCity*. 19 January 2005 <http://www.fortunecity.com/marina/reach/435/inhist.htm>.

Singer, Peter. 'Famine, Affluence and Morality.' *Philosophy and Public Affairs* 1.1 (Spring 1972): 229-243 [rev. ed.]. 16 January 2006 <http://www.utilitarian.net/singer/by/1972——.htm>.

'Situation of detainees at Guantánamo Bay.' United Nations Commission on Human Rights. 15 February 2006.

Smyth, Julie Carr. 'Voting Machine Controversy.' *Cleveland Plain Dealer* 28 August 2003. *Common Dreams Newscenter*. 26 January 2006 <http://www.commondreams.org/headlines03/0828-08.htm>.

'Social Movements' Manifesto.' *Another World is Possible: Popular Alternatives to Globalization at the World Social Forum*. Fisher, William F. and Thomas Ponniah, eds. Nova Scotia: Fernwood, 2003: 346-53.

Solomon, Alisa. 'Another World Turns.' 27 January 2005. *The Nation* 28 January 2005. <http://www.thenation.com/doc.mhtml%3Fi=20050214&s=solomon>.

Stanford, Jim. 'Sex, hurricanes, New Orleans and Cuba.' *The Globe and Mail* 12 September 2005: A15.

'State of Fear: The Global Attack On Rights.' *New Internationalist* 376 (March 2005): 3 September 2005 <http://www.newint.org/issue376/be-very-afraid.htm>.

Steele, Jonathan. 'A Global Gulag to Hide the War on Terror's Dirty Secrets.' *The Guardian* 15 January 2005 <http://www.guardian.co.uk/usa/story/0,12271,1390317,00.html>.

Steger, Manfred B. *Globalization: A Very Short Introduction*. Oxford: Oxford University Press, 2003.

'Sudan arrests aid worker over reporting of rapes.' *The Globe and Mail* 31 May 2005: A12.

Tamang, Stella. 'Peace Teachers: The History of Tamang Women as Conflict Mediators.' *Cultural Survival Quarterly* 28.4 (Winter 2005): 14-15.

—. 'Stella Tamang Discusses the Growth of the Indigenous Women's Movement in South Asia.' *Cultural Survival Quarterly* 28.4 (Winter 2005): 16-17.

Tamimi, Azzam. 'Islam and Human Rights.' *Institute of Islamic Political Thought*. 3 January 2005 <http://www.ii-pt.com/web/papers/islam&h.htm>.

Tembo, Benedict, and Newton Sibanda. 'Zambia's aged struggle.' *Africanews* 10 May 2005 <http://web.peacelink.it/afrinews/69_issue/p4.html>.

Tharoor, Shashi. 'Are human rights universal?' *New Internationalist* 332 (March 2001): 3 September 2005 <http://www.newint.org/issue332/essay2.htm>.

'Third World Debt.' 21 January 2006 <http://www.worldcentric.org/stateworld/debt.htm>.

Thompson, Ian. 'Seeking Justice for the Cuban Five: Interview with Leonard Weinglass.' *National Committee to Free the Cuban Five.* 5 January 2005 <http://www.freethefive.org/legalfront.htm>.

Toope, Stephen J. 'Report' for the Canadian Commission of Inquiry into the Actions of Canadian Officials in Relation to Maher Arar. 14 October 2005. 10 January 2006 <http://www.ararcommission.ca/eng/17.htm>.

'Trade Case Study: Ethyl Corp and MMT.' *Friends of the Earth International.* 20 January 2006 <http://www.foei.org/trade/activistguide/ethly.htm>.

Trinh, Minh-ha T. *Woman, Native, Other.* Bloomington: Indiana University Press, 1989.

Turner, Ted. 'My Beef with Big Media: How Government Protects Big Media—and Shuts out Upstarts Like Me.' July/August 2004. *Washington Monthly* 2 February 2005 <http://www.washingtonmonthly.com/features/2004/0407.turner.html>.

United Nations. *Annual Report 2003: Implementation of Activities and Use of Funds.* Geneva: Office of the High Commissioner for Human Rights, 2004.
—.'Ad Hoc Committee on a Comprehensive and Integral International Convention on the Protection and Promotion of the Rights and Dignity of Persons with Disabilities.' *UN Enable.* 28 January 2005 <http://www.un.org/esa/socdev/enable/rights/adhoccom.htm>.
—. UNAIDS. *UNAIDS: Joint United Nations Programme on HIV/AIDS.* 15 June 2005 <http://www.unaids.org/en/default.asp>.
—. *Convention on the Rights of the Child.* Geneva: Office of the High Commissioner for Human Rights, 2003.
—. 'A United Nations Priority: Human Rights in Action.' *Human Rights.* 8 February 2005 <http://www.un.org/rights/HRToday/action.htm>.
—. 'The World of Children at a Glance.' United Nations High Commission on Refugees. *UNHCR: The UN Refugee Agency.* 19 January 2005 <http://www.unhcr.ch/children/glance.html>.

UNIFEM. *United Nations Development Fund for Women (UNIFEM).* 15 June 2005 <http://www.unifem.org/>.

United Nations Development Programme. *Human Development Report 2000: Human Rights and Human Development.* New York: Oxford University Press, 2000.
—. *Human Development Report 2001: Making New Technologies Work for Human Development.* New York: Oxford University Press, 2001.
—. *Human Development Report 2002: Deepening Democracy in a Fragmented World.* New York: Oxford University Press, 2002.
—. *Human Development Report 2003: Millennium Development Goals: A Compact among Nations to End Human Poverty.* New York: Oxford University Press, 2003.
—. *Human Development Report 2005: International Cooperation at a Crossroads: Aid, Trade and Security in an Unequal World.* New York: Oxford University Press, 2005.

'The USA Patriot Act.' *Electronic Frontier Foundation: Defending Freedom in the Digital World.* 14 January 2005 <http://www.eff.org/issues/usapa/>.

'U.S. rights panel rejects Guántanamo probe.' *The Globe and Mail* 21 April 2005 <http://www.theglobeandmail.com/servlet/story/RTGAM.20050421.w2guan0421/BNStory/International>.

'Uzbek police detain dozens of activists.' *The Globe and Mail* 31 May 2005: A12.

Valdes, Nelson. 'Banning Cuban Academics and Writers: Habana Night vs. Latin Scholars in Vegas.' *Counterpunch.* 17 October 2004 <http://www.counterpunch.org/valdes10022004.html>.

'Venezuela's Chavez says he'll share oil wealth.' *The Globe and Mail* 30 September 2005: B9.

The Via Campesina. 'Tlaxcala Declaration of the Via Campesina.' *Via Campesina Information.* 2 January 2005 <http://www.virtualsask.com/via/lavia.deceng.html>.

Ward, Olivia. 'Canadian builds seat for war criminals.' *The Toronto Star* 3 December 2005: A16.

—. 'U.N. summit threatened.' *The Toronto Star* 3 September 2005: A19.

'Water for health enshrined as a human right.' 27 November 2002 *World Health Organization.* 1 March 2006 <http://www.who.int/mediacentre/news/releases/pr91/en/>.

Watt, Patrick. *Social Investment and Economic Growth: A Strategy to Eradicate Poverty.* Oxford: Oxfam Great Britain, 2000.

'Welcome to Lannan.' Lannan Foundation. *Lannan.org.* 2 March 2006 <http://ee.lannan.org/lf/about/>.

Whitfield, Teresa. *Paying the Price: Ignacio Ellacuría and the Murdered Jesuits of El Salvador.* Philadelphia: Temple University Press, 1995.

' "The War on Terrorism" and Human Rights: Aid to Abusers.' *Federation of American Scientists.* 14 January 2005 <http://www.fas.org/terrorism/at/docs/Aid&Humanrights.html>.

Who's Counting? Marilyn Waring on Sex, Lies & Global Economies. Dir. Terre Nash. Ottawa: NFB, 1995.

'Women's Global Charter for Humanity.' *World March of Women.* 21 January 2005 <http://www.marchemondiale.org/en/charter3.html>.

The Worldwatch Institute. *State of the World 2005: Redefining Global Security.* New York: W.W. Norton, 2005.

'Workers kick back at Reebok.' 8-14 August 2002. *Asheville Global Report* 16 January 2006 <http://www.agrnews.org>.

Wright, Ronald. *A Short History of Progress.* Toronto: Anansi, 2004.

Yates, Michael D. 'The Road We've Taken.' *Utne* (July-August 2005): 62-67.

Yeatman, Anna. 'Is Australia a model for Canada?' *Toronto Star* 23 January 2006: A19.

York, Geoffrey. 'Chinese ban on Wikipedia prevents research, users say.' *The Globe and Mail* 10 January 2006: A2.

'The 0.7-per-cent Solution.' Editorial. *The Globe and Mail* 18 January 2005: A18.

Index

on education, 215-16; enforceability of, 61, 146; on freedom, 11-12, 46-47, 83; gaps in, 8-9, 35n1, 91, 173, 188; on justice, 7, 153; purpose of, xiii, xiv, xv, 183, 187, 222n8; on security, 3, 139, 140, 195; on torture, 141, 15

Universal Human Rights in Theory and Practice (Donnelly), 200n5

Unocal Corporation, 44-45

Uruguay, 176

USAID, 98

Uzbekistan, 14, 84, 133, 141

Vatican, 91, 98

Venezuela, 41, 171, 176-77, 178

Via Campesina, 212-13

Vietnam, 85, 145

Vivanco, José Miguel, 28, 176

Walker, Tim, 9

Walzer, Michael, 149

war, 132, 145; casualties, 135, 144-48, 155nn7-11, 196, 221n3, 221n6; and children, 109, 145, 215; crimes, xvi, 84-85, 140-41, 145, 149-51, 195; and economics, 140, 151; and hunger, 60, 202; resolution of, 127-28, 133-34

Waring, Marilyn, 58

water, ix, 77n3; access to, xv, 27, 51, 61-63, 77n4; commodification of, 59, 152; contaminated, 34, 61, 62-63, 65, 122

Water Law and Indigenous Rights Program (WALIR), 63

Waweru, David Ndung'u, 99

wealth, xvii, 6-7, 33-34, 51

weapons, 134-35, 221n3; manufacture of, 72, 130n9; trade in, 10, 35n2, 36n5, 132, 204, 209, 222n7

Welsh, Christine, 88

Western Hemisphere Institute for Security Cooperation (WHISC), 156n13

Whifield, Emily, 160

Winfrey, Oprah, 167

Witness (human rights organization), 206, 220n3

women, 19, 31, 196, 198-99; as caretakers, 75, 103, 183; disempowerment of, 3, 78-79, 81-87, 215; elderly, 107-108; and Female Genital Mutilation (FGM), 2-3, 84, 86-87, 196; in government, 27, 102, 129n2; indigenous, 87, 88-90, 127-28; and labor, 67, 77n7, 84, 102; as peacemakers, 126-28; and prostitution, 84-85, 97, 112; and resistance, 62-63, 70, 82-83, 87-88, 196, 213; violence against, 82-90, 97, 221n3

Women's Global Charter for Humanity, 88

World Bank (WB), 37, 43, 50, 54, 56, 61, 88, 97, 211; projects funded by, 53, 62, 152-53

World Conference on Human Rights, 183

World Food Summit, 61

World Health Organization (WHO), 86

World March of Women, 87-88

World Organisation Against Torture, 14-15

World Social Forum (WSF), 75, 212, 213

World Trade Organization (WTO), 37, 40-43, 62, 170, 211, 213, 216, 222n8

World War I, 146

World War II, xiii, 91, 145, 146, 190

Worldwatch Institute, 153, 206

Wright, Ronald, 70, 188-89, 191

Wu, Harry, 71

Yahoo, 207

Yakovenko, Igor, 182

Yale Declaration, 105

Yemen, 91

Zambia, 87, 106

Zappa, Frank, 195

Zhao Jing (a.k.a. Michael Anti), 207

Zimbabwe, 100

ALSO from BLACK ROSE BOOKS

EDUARDO GALEANO: Through the Looking Glass
Daniel Fischlin, Martha Nandorfy

Part political biography, part cultural theory—especially in relation to the telling of history and the relations between literature and human rights—this book is the first full-length, critical study of the life and work of Eduardo Galeano.

> "Traces a magnificent path through the immense and difficult work of Galeano. Especially insightful is the exploration of how the great journalist is transformed into a poet, how the militant activist in search of justice transmutes into an artist."
> —Enrique Dussel, *The Invention of the Americas*

> "Fischlin and Nandorfy skillfully guides us into the cultural world of one of the finest and most daring writers of our time, known equally for artistic brilliance, intellectual rigour, and a sharp wisdom forged in the fires of history."
> —Ronald Wright, *Time Among the Maya*

"Neither straightforward biography nor ordinary literary criticism, this book is a provocative study of rights, story, and memory."
> —Barbara Harlow, *Resistance Literature and After Lives*

450 pages ✳ paper 1-55164-178-X $24.99 ✳ cloth 1-55164-179-8 $53.99

REBEL MUSICS: Human Rights, Resistant Sounds, and the Politics of Music Making
Daniel Fischlin, Ajay Heble, editors

A fascinating journey into a rich, complex world, where music and politics unite, where rebel musicians are mobilizing movements for political change and social justice.

> "Casts a wide net with respect to musicians, span of years and nationalities."
> —*Small Press Review*

"A rich collection that inspires, delights, and educates."
> —Howard Zinn, *A People's History of the United States*

"Diverse and challenging, celebratory but refreshingly realistic, I strongly recommend *Rebel Musics* to all those interested in music and its political possibilities."
> —Chris Gibson, University of New South Wales

Apart from the editors, contributors include: cabaret artist, author and musician Norman Nawrocki; film makers Marie Boti and Malcolm Guy; musician Jesse Stewart; poet George Elliott Clarke; author Timothy Brennan; author Martha Nandorfy; radio host Ray Pratt; and editor, author, and music reviewer Ron Sakolsky.

264 pages ✳ paper 1-55164-230-1 $24.99 ✳ cloth 1-55164-231-X $53.99

OF RELATED INTEREST

PARTICIPATORY DEMOCRACY: Prospects for Democratizing Democracy
Dimitrios Roussopoulos, C.George Benello, editors

This wide-ranging collection probes the historical roots of participatory democracy in our political culture, analyzes its application to the problems of modern society, and explores the possible forms it might take on every level of society.

Apart from the editors, contributors include: George Woodcock, Murray Bookchin, Don Calhoun, Stewart Perry, Rosabeth Moss Kanter, James Gillespie, Gerry Hunnius, John McEwan, Arthur Chickering, Christian Bay, Martin Oppenheimer, Colin Ward, Sergio Baierle, Anne Latendresse, Bartha Rodin, and C.L.R. James.

DIMITRIOS ROUSSOPOULOS is an author, activist and political economist. C.GEORGE BENELLO taught at Goddard College until his untimely death.

380 pages ✳ paper 1-55164-224-7 $24.99 ✳ cloth 1-55164-225-5 $53.99

YEAR 501:The Conquest Continues
Noam Chomsky

From the brutality of Christopher Columbus upon his arrival in the Americas to the persecution of Indonesians in the 1960s, Chomsky appeals to the reader to review the evidence amassed over the last 500 years.

"Offers a savage critique of the new world order." —*MacLean's Magazine*

"Tough, didactic, [Chomsky] skins back the lies of those who make decisions." —*Globe and Mail*

A world renowned author, linguist, radical philosopher, and outspoken critic of the mass media and U.S. foreign policy, NOAM CHOMSKY is Institute Professor of the Department of Linguistics and Philosophy at MIT.

331 pages ✳ paper 1-895431-62-X $19.99 ✳ cloth 1-895431-63-8 $48.99

---

send for a free catalogue of all our titles

C.P. 1258, Succ. Place du Parc
Montréal, Québec
H2X 4A7 Canada
or visit our website at http://www.blackrosebooks.net

to order books

In Canada: (phone) 1-800-565-9523 (fax) 1-800-221-9985
email: utpbooks@utpress.utoronto.ca

In United States: (phone) 1-800-283-3572 (fax) 1-651-917-6406

In UK & Europe: (phone) London 44 (0)20 8986-4854 (fax) 44 (0)20 8533-5821
email: order@centralbooks.com

Printed by the workers of

for Black Rose Books